Also by Charles Mosley

Lichfield in Retrospect
American Presidential Families
Debrett's Handbook: 1981 Edition (editor)
Burke's Peerage and Baronetage: 1996 (editor)
Debrett's Guide to Entertaining

DEBRETT'S GUIDE TO BEREAVEMENT

Practical Guidance for Coping with the Loss of a Loved One

Charles Mosley

HEADLINE

To my late parents,
without whom I would know
much less of bereavement

First published in 1995
by HEADLINE BOOK PUBLISHING

Reprinted in this edition in 1995
by HEADLINE BOOK PUBLISHING

10 9 8 7 6 5 4 3 2 1

British Library Cataloguing in Publication Data

Mosley, Charles
    Debrett's Guide to Bereavement
    I. Title
    306.88
    ISBN 0-7472-1258-9

Typeset by
Letterpart Limited, Reigate, Surrey

Printed and bound in Great Britain by
Mackays of Chatham PLC, Chatham, Kent

HEADLINE BOOK PUBLISHING
A division of Hodder Headline PLC
338 Euston Road
London NW1 3BH

Contents

PART III: PRACTICAL MATTERS

Acknowledgements

Among other things, I have tried in this book to cover attitudes to bereavement and a short account of funeral rites as held or practised by all the major religious movements in the UK. In case readers wish to find out more about a religious movement, I have listed below useful names, addresses and telephone/fax numbers, along with those of other, non-religious organisations.

I would like to express my thanks for information and guidance to the following:

David Adams, Registrar of the Cemeteries and Crematorium Department, Southend-on-Sea; Beth Allen, General Secretary Quaker Home Service (for address see Anne Hosking below); Dr Baljit Singh Bagga, General Secretary of the European Institute of Sikh Studies, 116 Station Road, Harpenden, Hertfordshire AL5 4RH, tel./fax 01582 766447; Mary Banks, musicologist; The Rt Rev. G. E. Birtill, BA, BD, The Moravian Church in Great Britain and Ireland, Moravian Church House, 5 Muswell Hill, London N10 3TH, tel. 0181–883 3409/1912, fax 0181–442 0112; Leslie Bona, Volunteer Resources Officer, National Association of Bereavement Services, 20 Norton Folgate, London E1 6DB, tel. 0171–247 1080 (referrals) or 0171–247 0617 (administration), fax 0171–247 0617; The British Humanist Association, 47 Theobalds Road, London WC1X 8SP, tel. 0171–430 0908; The British Tourist Authority, Thames Tower, Blacks Road, London W6 9EL,

1

tel. 0181–846 9000; John Brooke-Little, Norroy and Ulster King of Arms, of the College of Arms, Queen Victoria Street, London EC4V 4BT; Raymond F. Caddy, Major and Literary Secretary, The Salvation Army (United Kingdom Territory with the Republic of Ireland), Territorial Headquarters, 101 Queen Victoria Street, London EC4P 4EP, tel. 0171–236 5222, fax 0171–236 6272; S. F. Captain, President, The World Zoroastrian Organisation, 135 Tennison Road, South Norwood, London SE25 5NF; Paul Cavendish, of West Brompton, London, to whom I am particularly indebted for information on modern developments in Roman Catholic funeral rites; Hubert Chesshyre, Chester Herald, of the College of Arms; The Inquiry Centre, The General Synod of the Church of England, Church House, Great Smith Street, London SW1P 3NZ, tel. 0171–222 9011, fax 0171–799 2714; Mrs Jane Cox, of The Benefits Agency, 2a Yew Tree Road, Slough, Berkshire SL1 2AQ; Mrs Marjorie J. Crossley, Hon. Secretary, The Trustees of the Countess of Huntingdon's Connexion, 69 Jubilee Road, Middleton, Manchester M24 2LT, tel. 0161–643 4108; CRUSE – Bereavement Care, Main Office, 126 Sheen Road, Richmond, Surrey TW9 1UR, tel. 0181–940 4818 – they also run a Bereavement Helpline for people suffering from the loss of a friend or relative, 0181–332 7227; Clarence Dover, Fellowship Secretary, The Fellowship of Churches of Christ, 1 Wheatley Drive, Carlton, Nottingham NG4 1FE, tel. 0115 9874676; The Archivist, Dulwich College, London SE21 7LD.

Martin Foster, of the Liturgy Office of the (Roman Catholic) Bishops' Conference, usually at 39 Eccleston Square, London SW1V 1PL, tel. 0171–821 0553, but temporarily situated at Allington House (First Floor), 136–142 Victoria Street, London SW1E 5LD; The Rev. John O. Fulton, BSc, BD, General Secretary of the United Free Church of Scotland, 11 Newton Place, Glasgow G3 7PR, tel. 0141–332 3435; Tony Gardiner, The Pagan Federation, BM Box 7097, London WC1N 3XX, tel. 01691 671066; Alan Grayson, District Manager, Christian Science Committees on Publication for Great Britain and Ireland, 2 Elysium Gate, 126 New Kings Road, London SW6 4LZ, tel. 0171–371 0600, fax 0171–371 9204; A. Haviland-Nye, Dhammācariya (roughly the Buddhist equivalent of MA), FCA, Director, The British Buddhist Association, 11 Biddulph Road, London W9 1JA, tel. 0171–286 5575; Carmen Henry, Bahá'í Information Officer, Bahá'í Community of the United Kingdom, 27 Rutland Gate, London SW7 1PD, tel. 0171–584 2566, fax 0171–584 9402; Anne Hosking, Administrative Secretary, Religious Society of Friends (Quakers), Friends House, Euston Road, London NW1 2BJ, tel. 0171–387 3601, fax 0171–388 1977.

INFORM (Information Network Focus on Religious Movements, a non-sectarian charity set up in 1988 to research new religious movements, including what some would call cults, though INFORM itself is scrupulously objective and fair), Houghton Street, London WC2A 2AE, tel. 0171–955 7654, fax 0171–242 0392 – make it clear that the fax is specifically intended for INFORM; The Jehovah's Witnesses of IBSA House, The Ridgeway, London NW7 1RP; The Rev. Dr Peter Jupp, the United Reformed Church representative to the Funerals and Crematoria Committee and Director of the National Funerals College Project at the Institute of Community Studies (the United Reformed Church is at 86 Tavistock Place, London WC1H 9RT, tel. 0171–916 2020, fax 0171–916 2021); Audrey King, of Age Concern England, Astral House, 1268 London Road, London SW16 4ER, tel. 0181–679 8000, fax 0181–679 6069; Lesbian & Gay Bereavement Project, Vaughan M. Williams Centre, Colindale Hospital, London NW9 5HG, tel. 0181–200 0511 (office), 0181–455 8894 (helpline); Dr Emmanuel Lewis, of The Tavistock Clinic, 120 Belsize Lane, London NW3 5BA, tel. 0171–435 7111; John Luby, of The City of London Crematorium, Aldersbrook Road, Manor Park, London E12 5DQ, tel. 0181–530 2151/4.

The Rev. Abey T. Mammen, BA, BD, Vicar and President Mar Thoma Church UK, Diocese of North America and Europe of Mar Thoma Syrian Church of Malabar, Mar Thoma Centre, 22 Altmore Avenue, London E3 2BY, tel. 0181–471 2446; The Marine & Environmental Protection Division of The Ministry of Agriculture Food and Fisheries (from whom you must get permission to dispose of a corpse at sea), Nobel House, 17 Smith Square, London SW1P 3JR, tel. 0171–238 5873; Deacon Meliton, of The Ecumenical Patriarchate (Greek Orthodox Church) under the direction of Gregorios, Archbishop of Thyateira and Great Britain, of 5 Craven Hill, London W2 3EN, tel. 0171–723 4787, fax 0171–224 9301; The Public Affairs Administration Offices of the Church of Jesus Christ of Latter Day Saints (Mormons), 751 Warwick Road, Solihull, West Midlands B91 3DQ, tel. 0121–711 2244, fax 0121–711 2249, telex 336235; Moyses Stevens Ltd, Floral Arts, 157 Sloane Street, London SW1X 9BT, tel. 0171–259 9303/493 8171, fax 0171–730 3002; David Murphy, General Secretary of The Catholic Truth Society, 192 Vauxhall Bridge Road, London SW1V 1PD, tel. 0171–834 4392, fax 0171–630 1124; Margaret Benger and Mrs Theresa Quinn, both of The National Association of Memorial Masons, Crown Buildings, High Street, Aylesbury, Buckinghamshire HP20 1SL, tel. 01296 434750, fax 01296 431332; The Natural Death Centre, 20 Heber Road, London NW2 6AA, tel. 0181–208 2853, fax 0181–452 6434; Linda Nicholson, musicologist and fortepianist, of Archway House, 21 Clapham Common North Side, London SW4 0RQ, tel. 0171–720 8443.

The Very Rev. Robert J. Patkai, MTh, Chairman of the Lutheran Council of Great Britain, Lutheran Church House, 8 Collingham Gardens, London SW5 0HW, tel. 0171–373 1141; C. R. Perry, President of the Seventh-Day Adventist Church (British Isles Headquarters), Stanborough Park, Watford, Hertfordshire WD2 6JP, tel. 01923 672251, fax 01923 893212; Nima Poovaya-Smith, Keeper of Arts, Cartwright Hall, Lister

Park, Bradford, West Yorkshire BD9 4NS, tel. 01274 493313; The Department of Social Security, Public Inquiries, London SW1A 2LN, tel. 0171–210 5983; Mrs Susan Sperber, of The Burial Society of the United Synagogue, Woburn House, Tavistock Square, London WC1H 0EZ, tel. 0171–387 7891, fax 0171–383 2582, who was sufficiently interested by my draft section on Jewish funeral rites and bereavement practices to order a copy of my last book, which deals with neither – thank you, Susan, thank you; The Terrence Higgins Trust, 52 Gray's Inn Road, London WC1X 8JU, tel. 0171–831 0330 (administration), 0171–242 1010 (helpline), 0171–405 2381 (legal line); Malcolm Thomas, Librarian of the Religious Society of Friends (for address see Anne Hosking above); Robert Towler, of INFORM; Simon Truelove, tel. 0181–642 8211, spokesman for the National Association of Funeral Directors, 618 Warwick Road, Solihull, West Midlands B91 1AA, tel. 0121–711 1343.

Farrokh Vajifdar, writer and lecturer on Zoroastrianism, 27 Cleveland Road, Barnes, London SW13 0AA, tel. 0181–878 4810; Hugo Vickers, for sharing reminiscences of the many times he has acted as an executor and for information on ceremonial at funerals of Knights of the Garter; Denise Watson (tel. 0117 9628132), of The Compassionate Friends, an organisation devoted to helping parents who have lost a child, of whatever age, 53 North Street, Bristol BS3 1EN, tel. 0117 9539639; Ken West, of Carlisle Bereavement Services, Cemetery Office, Richardson Road, Carlisle, Cumbria CA2 6AL, tel. 01228 25022; Tim Whittaker, of The National Trust, for information on the whereabouts of mausolea and burial vaults attached to the family seats of some of this country's greater landed dynasties; David Williamson, co-editor of *Debrett's Peerage*; Jean M. Woodman, Administrator of the British Humanist Association, 47 Theobald's Road, London WC1X 8SP, tel. 0171–430 0908, fax 0171–430 1271; Craig Young, of Chosen

Heritage Ltd, who organise pre-paid funeral arrangements for people still in the prime of life (or indeed at any stage of life), and who may be contacted at East Grinstead, West Sussex, tel. Freefone 0800 525555.

I am grateful to the QHS (Quaker Home Service) Literature Section for permission to quote from Diana Lampen, *Facing Death* (Quaker Home Service, 1979).

Introduction

'Oh death, where is thy sting-a-ling-a-ling?' chants the drunken surgeon in *Decline and Fall*. All over the place, most of us would retort; pretty near ubiquitous, in fact. The aim of this book is to act as a kind of first-aid kit to help you draw the pain of that sting. I hope, in other words, that it contains not just a salve designed to soothe the smart of the sting, but a compendium of actions to be prescribed, rather as a good first-aid kit might contain a leaflet advising you to change the dressing every twenty-four hours after a sting as well as to apply the original salve for the sting itself.

It is predominantly a useful book with a strong infusion of historical background to set the practical advice in context. It is not one of the fairly numerous publications that tell you what you ought to be feeling or how you ought to be expressing yourself according to the latest fashion in psychobabble. There are hordes of these, together with pamphlets on the subject prepared by charities and booklets put out by state-run organisations, to say nothing of anthologies of comforting thoughts run up by religious bodies.

The parrot cry that death is the great modern taboo is largely nonsense. Over the year and a half I spent preparing this book I built up a pile of press cuttings discussing every aspect of death and ways of coping with it. They included numerous major feature articles in broadsheet and tabloid newspapers and mass-circulation magazines. These examined both personal case histories of bereavement and bereavement as psychological phenomenon. Every type was covered: loss of a child, loss of a parent, loss of a pet. Euthanasia, living wills, funeral practices, religious differences, green burial, parliamentary debates and lobbying, business developments among the big undertaking combines – all got a look in. The reporting of the facts was generous; mostly accurate, occasionally inaccurate.

The thoughtfulness of the comment is another matter. Indeed, I wouldn't be writing this book if it had seemed to me to be adequate. Never mind the quality, feel the bulk. The pile of cuttings eventually swelled to over a foot thick – and I was monitoring only three newspapers regularly. My collection of books on the subject, either borrowed or bought, currently fills a couple of good-sized shelves in my library. I can confidently state that over the last few years there has not been so much public discussion of the matter in all its aspects since the Etruscans (see the section on Historical Background) – and they lacked our modern eclecticism as well as a national newspaper network.

In many cases the practical advice I offer is bound up with activity that the law insists on anyway if one is next of kin or an executor. Activity can be a balm, helping to soothe the emotions as well as to tidy up the administrative loose ends of another person's now finished life. It isn't always a balm, though. One person's grief-banishing round of practical tasks, to be tackled efficiently, briskly and sensibly, each one ticked off against a list as it gets accomplished, thus diminishing the sense of loss a little more each time, is another's obstacle race-cum-assault course of tiresome, stress-inducing chores which simply add extra items of baggage to the burden of grief. I do not believe that when one is bereaved one's emotions can be channelled anyway. In my experience – and it is not inconsiderable, as you will see – one's reactions to a death are spontaneous to the point of being uncontrollable, like a twitch, a tic or a spasm. I would strongly contest the assertion by the author of the *Which* consumer guide *What to Do When Someone Dies* (see the Bibliography for further details) that getting personally involved in organising a funeral 'assists' the process of grieving and speeds up a 'healthy recovery' and that this is 'established fact'. Nothing about the human psyche is established fact. Personal involvement may help some people, but not others.

What qualifications do I have for writing a book about bereavement? You shall judge for yourself. I lost my mother at fourteen, the same age as Tchaikovsky was when his mother died. This was famously for him, as much less famously for me, a grievously traumatic experience, one of the most devastating to which anyone could ever be exposed. I have spoken to psychiatric specialists who suggest that there are even worse losses, namely that of the father in very early infancy, both for a male child and a female one, so I am not laying any claim to exclusively painful loss. And I am no sort of Tchaikovsky in either talent or sexual tastes. But I can better him in bereavement. My father committed suicide last year, after talking of doing so for eighteen months before that. I have known another six suicides quite well. Two of them were at one time among my best friends. At least two women who are now ex-lovers have attempted suicide.

Many others draw well ahead of me in the bereavement stakes. I have never lost a child, having had no child to lose. Anyone who has is exposed to what is surely the most shattering type of bereavement of all in our present age. Perhaps the saddest thing about losing a child is that it can lead to the break-up of the parents' marriage. As they say, the four greatest traumas are bereavement, divorce, losing your job and moving house. What they don't much mention is how one of these can lead to some or all of the others. In particular, bereavement is often the precursor to moving house, either because the current one is now too large for the surviving spouse or partner or because there isn't enough money to keep it up, particularly where inheritance tax bites hard.

At least my bereavements were staggered in time. Let me cite Case History A, in which an unmarried man in early middle age was hit hard by a triple bereavement within the space of a few months, on average one death of a close relative roughly every ninety days. Timothy M. was of upper-middle-class Catholic stock. He was exceptionally devoted to his mother, an artistic and comely woman of great sensitivity who had had a moderately successful career as an actress in provincial straight theatre. She, his father and a favourite grandmother all died within the short time of each other specified above. He had trained as an accountant and was the member of the family chiefly engaged in winding up the deceased persons' estates. Cumulatively, these were subject to grave depredations from the Inland Revenue because so many senior members of the family had died within such a brief space of time. It is therefore possible that he faced a Herculean task in trying to salvage any wealth his own generation of the family inherited, but it was nevertheless alleged that he procrastinated in discharging various administrative tasks to do with the winding-up process. This delay was said to have had grave financial consequences.

Some years later he took early retirement from his very well-paid and responsible job in the City with a sizeable nest-egg of savings. Within a few years he had lost it all in disastrous investments. He even lost the roof over his head and for over a year stayed with various friends, a few weeks at a time here, a month or more there. He managed to land temporary jobs in his professional field but never for very long. One Christmas things got too much. He had been babbling for several days about religious matters, in particular the Devil and exorcism. Now he rearranged all the pictures and ornaments in the house where he was staying, burned several pieces of furniture on the open drawing-room fire and smashed an obsolete radiogram. Shortly afterwards he entered the psychiatric wing of the local hospital, where he subsequently spent about six weeks. It is impossible to prove that his bereavement brought on this illness, but it seems highly likely and most of his circle of friends certainly thought so.

Even the most rigorous clinical tests and research could not establish a direct, exclusive and necessary causal link between bereavement and illness, whether of the mind or of the body. But I imagine that in Case B common sense would infer a pretty straightforward link. Anthea N. was the pampered wife of a husband she adored and who adored her. He not only provided every possible material luxury for her but even bought her clothes and shoes for her, choosing them himself. She did not have to do any housework, for he insisted on her having servants and could afford to employ them. He died suddenly and unexpectedly and she was shattered. She took to cleaning the chandeliers in the washing machine and had to be put under round-the-clock supervision in the family home, something that, luckily, the family could afford.

The truth is that bereavement takes people in probably as many different ways as there are types of human personality. Many writers have spoken of a cycle of bereavement encompassing shock, denial, anger, bargaining, depression and acceptance. Such a list may have a superficial and partial validity, but it hardly scratches the surface of the ways in which people react to bereavement. Some lose a great deal of weight; others react by overeating and consequently putting it on. Some do first one then the other, shedding, say, 20lb or so over six months then replacing them in the next six. Some take to drink, others to sex. Still others give up sex. Some socialise intensively; others withdraw into a solipsistic little shell and refuse all social contact.

The withdrawal from social life is a particularly fascinating instance. It may not arise in the directly bereaved person but in someone else in their social behaviour towards her. Mary Jones, in her book *Secret Flowers* (see Bibliography), gives an example. When her husband Stanley was taken ill, a relative on his side of the family, with whom relations had always been on a perfectly friendly footing, not only never phoned after Stanley had gone into hospital but never got in touch with her after his death. In addition this relative stayed away from the funeral. In fact, he never spoke to Mary again.

In the worst position of all are the bereaved people, usually family but sometimes colleagues or 'nominal' friends, who actually disliked the deceased. Here the post-death reaction can best be described as 'liberation'. The trouble is that, first, the bereaved may find it horrendously difficult to admit to themselves that they disliked the dead person. If they don't admit it to themselves fairly soon after the death they could suffer more painfully than if they had been 'ordinary' bereaved. Secondly, even if they admit the dislike they may suffer guilt later on. Some psychiatric practitioners argue that the bereaved who disliked the dead relative or other acquaintance most are precisely those who feel the most guilt.

Bereavement can also bring about a rapprochement of sorts in a damaged relationship. In Case C Edith H., of upper-middle-class dissenter Protestant stock (she was formerly a churchgoer but had in later years stopped attending services), was in her second marriage. Both partnerships had been childless. The current marriage had broken down after six years. Edith took a lover and early in the sixth year of this second marriage stopped having sexual relations with her husband. Four months later he lost his job and three weeks afterwards she moved out of the family home and set up residence with her lover in a flat about a mile away, returning to the marital home once or twice a week for an hour or so at a time to collect her post or sort out other small administrative details. She remained on reasonably friendly terms with her husband, although both of them gave way to tears on occasion, which suggests that they were suffering considerable distress. But she never again passed a night in the marital home till the day she heard the news that her father, who lived abroad, had died. Then, and only then, she spent a single night in the same bedroom she had once shared with her husband, though chastely curled up on a sofa rather than in the marriage bed. She talked throughout the night with her husband about whether her father had gone to heaven.

Some bereaved people even take on the personality traits of their dead relative, friend or spouse. In the course of research for this book I came across a case history in a book by a psychiatric worker. Here a widow who had been positively dull in company while her sparkling conversationalist of a husband was alive adopted more and more of his verve and wit in the months after his death. Another widow took up her dead husband's leisure occupation of gardening, even though she had never cared for it when he was alive.

There are differences in the way bereavement hits you depending on your sex. The Compassionate Friends organisation (see the chapter on children in Part III) was specifically set up to help people cope with the loss of a child. The person at The Compassionate Friends I spoke to when researching this book is definitely of the opinion, based on considerable experience, that men and women react to bereavement in very different ways. Men, at least those attuned to traditional British culture, keep a stiff upper lip; women express themselves with more overt concern.

I try to remain objective about this. I deliberately do not say women react more 'naturally' – I am not at all sure that reacting with tears and sobbing is more natural. For instance, in classical vase depictions mourners are often shown tearing their hair and beating their breasts. Today, in most circles in Britain, such behaviour would be thought ludicrously histrionic. Was it any more 'natural' in classical times, then? Conversely, are modern mourners who do not tear their hair or beat their breasts but confine themselves to sobs and tears – an overwhelming majority in this country – more unfeeling than those of the past, together with perhaps some recent immigrants to Britain from the Mediterranean countries, who express sorrow in more dramatic gestures? I certainly question the glib judgement that the British specifically, or 'Western culture' generally, are bad at grieving. We may grieve too introvertedly now, but arguably we grieved too extrovertedly a century ago, in the high old Victorian times. Which is better?

For every person who finds it easier to grieve loudly and dramatically there is someone else who prefers to nurture a sense of loss discreetly and subtly. It does people an injustice if you assume that they can cut a period of mourning short by 'letting it all hang out'. Not only is the very phraseology banal, but an eloquent Freudian argument runs that mourning is itself a mechanism for coming to terms with loss. Mourning is a withdrawal by the bereaved of feelings of devotion and affection, in the sense of non-sexual love as well as the sexual kind, from a person who now no longer exists physically.

Accordingly, I would have thought that the mourning period could not really be twisted into a different shape, or prolonged or abbreviated artificially. Lily Pincus, much the wisest of the recent writers on the subject of all those I researched, suggests that there is a cycle of mourning which is roughly commensurate with that of the seasons, or about a full year. Yet many books on bereavement behave as if mourning is something that can be manipulated, played down or talked out of existence, as if you could make it summertime by putting the clocks forward at the end of March.

The charity Help the Aged, for instance, publishes quite a useful little pamphlet called *Bereavement* (see Bibliography). But some of its advice, particularly the injunction not to turn to alcohol, drugs or excessive smoking, or to try to hurry the healing process, is a counsel of perfection. If a grieving widower is going to hit the bottle, no amount of pi advice in a pamphlet is going to stop him. And if he's elderly, is it really the end of the world if he does hit the bottle? What is one trying to keep alive for if one is in one's eighties and one's wife of fifty years has just died? If a widow has to go out to work to keep a roof over her head and those of her five children, she can't afford not to hurry the healing process – assuming that such a thing is possible. Beware of simplistic nostrums.

Beware, too, of woolliness in writings on bereavement. Most authors' thoughts on the subject are mush. The clerics tend to be the worst. Easily the best are the series of leaflets put out by Chosen Heritage Limited (FREEPOST, East Grinstead, RH19 1ZA). Perhaps because they are a business offering pre-paid funeral plans, they also provide much the most sensible and concrete advice in a condensed form on how to cope with bereavement. This is not an example of 'product placement'; indeed, their pre-paid funeral plan itself, though I think it is genuinely the best on the market at present, as they claim, still leaves one or two questions unanswered. (The service in this field offered by competing companies, together with the specialised market, is changing so rapidly that it is more a subject for one of the personal finance journalists who write in the daily or weekly press than for a book like this.) For a full list of Chosen Heritage's pamphlet titles, see the Bibliography.

It is often said that over the last two centuries the suppression of emotions became too much of a habit for British people. And yet the Victorians, who influenced so much of the British people's social behaviour for so much of this century – well into the 1960s, I would argue – and usually in the direction of repression rather than self-expression, indulged in orgies of grief for their dead. Nevertheless, for much of this century grief seems to have been as throttled back as any other emotion. Some writers, notably David Cannadine, have seen the First World War as a much more potent influence than Victorianism on late twentieth-century bereavement patterns. What is certain is that it is only in recent years that the majority of books on death and dying have recommended the bereaved to have a good emotional wallow in the way the Italians and other people who live around the Mediterranean basin are popularly supposed to do.

But for some types of personality, a tight-lipped approach still works, or perhaps one should say is more congenial. Some writers of the 'let-it-all-hang-out', 'crying's-good-for-you' school talk as if they were up against an opposition, an anti-life bunch of pro-repression emotion-inhibitors more concerned with shoring up society than the emotional health of the individual. I wonder. Surely many of us who remain impassive on being told of the death of a close friend or near relative are not following specific precepts, merely a sense of privacy. This may be a very fundamental part of our character and to monkey around with a person's character is at best impertinent, at worst plain dangerous. Also, a person's decision to keep a stiff upper lip may be bound up with notions, however vague, of what is good form, particularly as in British culture good form tends to be expressed in understatement.

One argument for following a traditional set of behaviour patterns following a death is that it reduces the loss to manageable proportions. I was faintly amused to read in the British Humanist Association guide to non-sectarian funerals (see the entry for Humanists in Part II and the Bibliography) that humanists who officiate at a funeral (implicitly a cremation rather than burial) for other humanists are advised not to allow the coffin to remain in view of the mourners for the duration of the ceremony.

Among other reasons, the author explained that it could be more distressing for mourners that way than if the coffin were hidden by curtains or subject to 'symbolic removal' (surely she means literal removal if the coffin is not to be in full view). She went on to say that this could help the bereaved accept the

16

finality of death. I would want to take issue with all these statements. First, they are purely personal projections of the author's own point of view. Many mourners, whether humanists or believers, would prefer to keep the coffin in view. Second, distress can't be conjured away like a rabbit in a magic show any more than the coffin at a cremation can be 'symbolically' removed rather than materially removed. Distress is what bereavement, death, dying and funerals are all about. Most people tend to be worried by lack of distress in a mourner rather than its presence.

Let me introduce a personal note to illustrate this last point. I never wept for my mother. I developed psoriasis instead, a complaint which many dermatologists believe can be triggered by shock or stress. Other diseases which can be triggered by stress, and which are often categorised under the label 'auto-immune', are varieties of thyroid conditions, rheumatoid arthritis, systemic lupus, pernicious anaemia and possibly also some sorts of diabetes. It has been suggested that Aristotle Onassis developed the myasthenia gravis which reduced him to a half-blind burbler as a result of the death of his dearly loved only son. Too much grief can make a cardio-vascular condition that already existed very much worse. You can die of a broken heart, in other words.

I never wept for my father or four grandparents, either. Indeed, I broke into laughter shortly after being told the news of my mother's death. The laughter shocked my father at the time, he later told me. I believe he thought it heartless. Clearly he hadn't read his Byron:

> I am very lonely, and should think myself miserable, were it not for a kind of hysterical merriment, which I can neither account for, or conquer, but, strange as it is, I do laugh and heartily, wondering at myself while I sustain it.

Byron wrote this in a letter to John Cam Hobhouse after the

deaths within a single month of Charles Skinner Matthews, one of Byron's own friends; J. Wingfield, a friend of both his and Hobhouse's; and Mrs Byron, the poet's mother.

When, early last year, my Dalmatian bitch was hit by a car, her leg was broken and they told me she would probably die, I did weep. I also wept on being told of the death of the headmaster of my preparatory school – and this was many years after I had left the place, though his character was so extraordinary that the thought of it departing this world gave the news unusual impact. Possibly this indicates some coldness in me towards relatives rather than dogs and dominies. And I don't at all recommend my own outlook as a model for others. I would only say that that is the way bereavement catches me. I know it catches others that way, too. Not many others, probably, but a few. So learn that tears are not the invariable accompaniment to bereavement, and do not judge from lack of them in another that you are dealing with a psychopath. And, above all, avoid making shallow and rigid judgements about what is the best way to (a) break the news of a death, (b) react to it yourself, (c) react to the reaction in others.

This book is one of a series on how to conduct your life according to a set of patterns. At the same time the patterns are just that, patterns, not rigid schemata. What *Debrett's Guide to Bereavement* aims specifically to do is advise you in certain forms of loss in the light of historical evolution, together with providing information on the practical steps to take when experiencing loss. The historical evolution I believe to be particularly important since one cannot understand why certain patterns in coffin-use versus shroud-use, or cremation versus burial, developed in this country unless one goes back to classical civilisation and even further.

In my trawl through the huge number of books that tell you what to feel or how to express feelings I have seldom found one that rises much above the sort of bromide homily churned out by radio and television 'personalities' and the more superficial breed of agony aunt. I am not criticising the help that agony aunts and 'personalities' give – concern is no more genuine or effective because it is expressed in good, literate, effective English rather than clichés and journalese. Nonetheless, literature does have more power than triteness to move people. And even soothing people's emotions, so that they learn to accept what has happened to them in a state of calmness, is to move them after a fashion.

Writers on death are similar to science-fiction writers telling us about other planets. However vivid their description of that distant location, however ingenious their imagined account of its landscape, customs, language and system of government, they haven't actually been there. Is death an 'it' at all anyway? Death, rather than bereavement, is usually portrayed as male, at least in Western culture, though in languages with genders for their nouns such as French and Latin the word for death (*la mort*; *mors*, *mortis* respectively) is feminine.

Feminine in gender is not at all the same as female in sex, though to read the nonsense written by ignorant hack journalists sucking up modishly to debased versions of feminism (nothing wrong with feminism, merely with debased versions of it), you might be forgiven for thinking it was. In fact, even our most distinguished writers seem to think of this particular 'it' – death – as a 'him'. So far the only author I have come across who sees death as female is St Francis of Assisi. He refers to what he calls 'the death of the body' as 'our sister'. And there is an oil on canvas by an otherwise extremely obscure painter, Thomas Cooper Gotch (1884–1931), called 'Death the Bride', which is reproduced in black and white in John Morley's *Death, Heaven and the Victorians* (see Bibliography). Even that is only a study, however.

I introduce the above point at this stage because, as with my earlier book in this series, *Debrett's Guide to Entertaining*, I have used the pronouns 'he', 'him' and 'his' or 'she', 'her' and 'her' in something like alternate paragraphs rather than follow the clumsy 'he/she'-'his/her' formula within a single sentence. Unlike entertaining, where tradition dictates that men look after things like wine while women concentrate on arranging the flowers and writing out the invitations, bereavement is fairly sex-neutral, though the funerary customs themselves are a good deal less so.

Similarly I refer throughout to 'undertaker' rather than the more fashionable and mealy-mouthed title 'funeral director' when discussing a member of those commercial firms who carry out funerals. Despite certain occupational skills, they are in the end tradesmen rather than members of a profession. The term 'funeral director' might have been apt in the last century. In those days he dictated the degree of elaboration with which a funeral was conducted by playing on the snobbish fears of the bereaved. Yet even so he tended to be called an undertaker. But now, at a moment when the consumer increasingly questions the old rituals and use of materials such as rare hardwoods to make coffins which will soon rot away or be burned, what one might call the 'auteur' theory of under-taking as 'funeral direction' – akin to directing a film – is obsolete. As in film-making, it is ultimately the producer (i.e., the bereaved) who calls the tune, if only because he puts up the money.

There is a more solid difficulty about writings on death. Many books on the subject seem to me not to make sufficient distinction between three quite separate states: (a) bereave-ment, or something which is a highly personal experience; (b) the slipping away of someone close to you, that is to say 'pre-bereavement', something which necessarily happens to other people only, even though it may be the precursor of your own bereavement proper; and (c) one's own death, which is purely theoretical, like the anticipation of one's first sexual encounter – until it actually happens, by which time it is too late.

Bereavement is a different thing from death and I want to stress that I am writing a guide to bereavement, not to dealing with the dying. Accordingly, I shall try to give advice on what to do after the death has occurred of another person, not on what to do when contemplating either his death or your own. At the same time, I quite accept that the death of another, particularly, it is said, one's surviving parent, makes one uncomfortably aware of one's own mortality.

But you may find it some comfort to reflect that more than half of all the human beings who have ever existed are generally reckoned to be now alive. Moreover, the proportion of living to dead is forecast to strengthen in favour of the living in the immediate future. It is the 'upside' if you like (or whatever the opposite of a downside is) to the world over-population crisis, and a comfort to those of us who live by the printed word since our potential readership is growing all the time. There is little point in writing for a readership of the dead, though posterity, which is equally non-existent physically as yet, is a different matter. I take still more comfort from the thought that bereavement is supremely of life, for only those who are left behind can be called bereaved.

PART I

Historical Background

Ancient Greece

Our civilisation has its earliest origins chiefly among the ancient Greeks and Romans. Much of that civilisation is still with us, especially as regards bereavement. It is only fairly recently that the majority of the better class of epitaphs stopped being written in Latin. The very word 'epitaph' comes from the Greek word for 'upon' and 'a tomb', meaning something written on a gravestone. The word 'cemetery' comes from the Greek *koimētērion*, 'sleeping place', as in sleep of death. The archivist at Dulwich College in south-east London has confirmed my guess that Raymond Chandler had a fine classical education there and probably bore the etymology in mind when calling the first of his Philip Marlowe novels *The Big Sleep*. The word 'sarcophagus' comes from the Greek, too; in that language it means 'flesh-eater', though it doesn't crop up in classical Greece. Apparently, sarcophagus was first used in later centuries of a sort of limestone coffin in which corpses decomposed sooner than usual. More quicklime, by the sound of it. 'Obituary' comes from the Latin verb for to die. I could go on and on, but surely I have made my case.

Where attitudes to bereavement are concerned there is undoubtedly a native British tradition, too. This has begun to reassert itself after centuries of neglect, as is shown by the increasing popularity of New Age cults, among them Druidism. Accordingly, I shall sketch not just the funeral rites and attitudes to bereavement of the ancient Greeks and ancient

25

Romans but some of those existing in these islands independent of the classical tradition.

In the Greece of the Bronze Age the dead could be
cremated or buried, though on the whole cremation was rarer.
It looks as if the dead were thought of as leading some kind of
existence similar to that of the living. For instance,
Mycenaean tombs (high Mycenaean civilisation had come to
an end by about 1100 BC) were furnished with food and drink,
arms and armour, ornaments and domestic utensils. But one
of the most recent writers on ancient attitudes to death
stresses how rash it is to leap to conclusions about how people
thought from purely circumstantial material evidence. Fair
enough. No Mycenaean texts survive that say 'Dear Posterity,
We believe in an afterlife. Yours sincerely, Agamemnon'. So
just because the Mycenaeans put what archaeologists call
'grave goods' with their dead, it doesn't necessarily follow that
they believed in an afterlife.

One can be a little more confident in stating that the
Mycenaeans lacked that awe of the dead to which the Etruscans in Italy were so notably subject several centuries later,
and to which I shall come presently. If the tomb had initially
been prepared for several occupants who were to be laid to
rest there simultaneously, more dead might be added from
time to time. The Mycenaeans had no inhibitions about
making room for the latest arrival by shifting a senior
occupant to one side. So the Mycenaeans by and large did
not subscribe to what archaeologists like to call a cult of the
dead. For instance, they used fire more for sanitary purposes,
or at most for ritual purification, than for grand pyres and
sacrifices.

The later Greeks sometimes recycled Bronze Age tombs,
notably at Knossos in Crete, but in general there was a fairly
sharp move away from mass burials towards individual ones at
about the end of the twelfth century BC. Nevertheless, there
are cases in Crete where a tomb originally intended by its

Bronze Age 'designers' as home for an inhumation (burial without burning first) was later used by Iron Age 'interlopers' to store a person's ashes.

Grieving for the departed changes less down the centuries than methods of disposal. Judging from pictorial representations on vases – our chief illustrative source for knowledge of Greek civilisation – mourners expressed their sense of loss by clutching at their heads or perhaps tearing at their hair – behaviour which is common enough today. There can be interesting sex demarcations, however. In later depictions women tend to do their lamenting with both hands, men with only one. Moreover, women tend to be shown seated and men as standing. Mourners of both sexes may also have moved in some kind of procession, possibly while accompanying the corpse to the grave.

Athens is not only the modern capital of Greece but was for much of the classical period the leading Greek city. It has thrown up a particularly plentiful variety of archaeological finds, including pottery and tombs. This makes it perhaps our chief source of information about certain ancient Greek attitudes to bereavement as well as funerary practices. Nevertheless, from around 800 BC it is not at all representative of the rest of Greece in this regard; rather the reverse if anything.

It seems that Athens had its own cemetery from before the end of Mycenaean civilisation in the late twelfth century BC. For some reason – probably the belief of certain literary figures, notably Homer, that the eternal resting place of the dead was in the west (a belief continued to a certain extent in Rome, which we will look at in a moment) – towns at this period tended to develop their cemeteries to the west of the other buildings, and Athens was no exception. In Athens the dead were often buried with their feet pointing west, whereas in the city of Megara, itself a near neighbour of Athens to the west, the late seventh-century Athenian legislator Solon is recorded as maintaining that the dead were buried facing east. Even in Athens there was no hard and fast rule on this point, however, and it has proved impossible so far to check whether or not Solon was giving an accurate account.

In the post-Mycenaean era cremation became more popular in Athens, though in the Peloponnese further south-west ordinary burial was the custom. Quite why there should have been these divergences is hard to say. Certainly one cannot point to material reality as influencing culture, in the way the glibber sort of Marxist would want to do. On the southern Aegean island of Thera, for example, there was virtually no woodland to provide fuel, yet the inhabitants obstinately went on cremating their dead. In contrast, the Therans' northern neighbours, the islanders of Tenos and Naxos, seem to have preferred burial at this period.

In Athens, as indeed often elsewhere, the distinction between cremating someone and burying him uncremated was not a hard and fast one. After the deceased had been burned on the funeral pyre his ashes were placed in containers which were buried. So whether he was buried intact or cremated he still ended up underground. (Modern students of comparative religion divide such methods of disposing of the dead into 'burial', 'cremation' and 'cremation-burial'.) Objects placed in graves consisted of simple vessels for the storage of liquids – olive-oil containers as well as jars to drink from – and jewellery, the latter mostly fashioned of bronze. Weapons had sometimes been put in graves at an earlier date and were to feature again in them later on, but not in this intermediate period.

Subsequent generations of Athenians seem to have begun to dispose of their dead in different ways, based as far as anyone can see on the age of the deceased: cremation was for adults only, burial for infants. Similar differences existed elsewhere in Greece more or less throughout antiquity. There also appear to have been subtle differences in the way the sexes were treated, though experts are not absolutely confident about this. Yet on the face of it the shape of the pots used to hold the ashes of cremated people varied between men and women: those with handles on the neck were for men, those with handles on the swelling contours for women. Later in this intermediate period, the pots originally used for men's ashes only (if that was indeed their purpose) seem to have taken over exclusively and been used for the cremated remains of both sexes.

By the ninth and eighth centuries BC many Athenian graves were sited beside roads. This was something which was to be a regular feature in Roman civilisation too, and roadside graves had existed in the Mycenaean period long before. The old option of cremation or burial was more equally balanced than ever and the decision to choose one or the other was apparently based purely on an individual family's whim. Other than during the great plague during the Peloponnesian War of the late fifth century or after a particularly bloody battle, when it clearly made sense to have mass cremations, this remained the practice right to the end of the classical era, by which time Rome dominated the Mediterranean world.

Athenian graves might be tagged for future recognition and remembrance either by a mound of earth or a piece of wood, both of which tended to be relatively bad at withstanding the wear and tear of years, or by a vase (sometimes of massive size – in fact, on a scale far above that in everyday use). Vases too tended to be impermanent. They were top-heavy, hence easily knocked over. Moreover, they were made of brittle materials, so once toppled they were prone to being smashed. By far the most permanent sort of memorial device at the grave was the gravestone. This took the form of a slab and was set in the earth pointing upwards with the name of the dead person inscribed near the top, much as is done today in churchyards.

The practice in Sparta was different again. There the only names recorded on monumental slabs or columns erected next to the graves were those of warriors killed in battle and, among women, priestesses, though later on women who died in childbirth also got their names recorded. Sparta was notorious for its small population of citizens, which was greatly outnumbered by the sub-class of enslaved helots, much as white South Africans under apartheid used to be by blacks, so giving birth to as many children as possible was a Spartan citizeness's patriotic duty even if she died in the attempt. The word 'laconic' comes from the Spartans' famous economy with words. They were not a garrulous people. Their epitaphs usually recorded just a person's death 'in battle' or 'in bed'. The latter meant childbirth rather than an excess of passion.

The Athenian gravestone was usually a good deal shorter than its modern equivalent, being seldom as much as 3ft high. And whereas nearly all modern gravestones are plain in colour or, if of a material such as marble, at most slightly streaky in texture (though some have lettering in gold), Athenian ones were often painted in bright colours. (Apparently Victorian ones often were too, but weathering has rubbed out the colouring.) Colouring often went with use of ribbons as a decorative motif. The Athenians used ribbons to signal that an object or feature was sacred, rather as we might use a cross. If the remains had been buried without a cremation, the stone stood at the head of the grave. If the grave contained just ashes, the stone was placed immediately above the urn holding them. Again, as with modern tombstones, the names of additional dead might be added underneath later, for example that of a son dying a few years after his father.

Later still the Athenians put up relatively elaborate tombs over their graves. These might have columns placed on top, surmounted in their turn by sculptures. The sculptures chiefly depicted beasts, both real ones and purely fabulous creatures such as gryphons. Another popular motif was a siren. This forerunner of the genetically engineered hybrid had the body of a bird and the head of a woman. Sirens became almost the standard mythical symbol of mourning. There might also be full-length sculptures of the human form, either standing erect or seated. This relatively elaborate phase had come to an end by about 400 BC and it has been suggested that Athens passed laws forbidding too magnificent a funerary monument as early as this date. Some such restriction was certainly inserted into the Spartan legal code around this time and a similar attempt was made in Athens about a century later.

Funerals in Athens were expensive affairs in themselves. There was not just the cost of monuments and putting goods in graves for use by the dead in the afterlife. The actual rites entailed having to spend money. An afterlife for most people seems to have been taken for granted, whereas belief in reincarnation was apparently rare, though not unknown. But how did the ancient Greeks envisage Elysium (their name for paradise, from the adjective Elysian, meaning happy or delightful)? As with most civilisations, imaginative writers were better at summoning up fantastic visions of the horrors of hell than the delights of heaven. Pindar (circa 522–440 BC), usually considered the principal lyric poet of the age, describes a place where there is plenty of music and games, played amidst gardens.

This view has been caustically described by a couple of distinguished ancient historians of the present day as an English concept. It may well have been a fatal conceit of the Victorians to think of the ancient Greeks as muscular, gentlemanly pagans, an image which was in fact a projection of their own minds, but who am I to quarrel with such an authority as professional ancient historians? So be it, then. You can envisage the way the ancient Greeks thought of their Elysium as somewhere between a country-house party conducted by those smugly self-absorbed patricians the Souls and one run along lines which would have appealed more to the philistine Marlborough House set.

Only the slave seems to have been reckoned wholly unlikely

to enjoy an afterlife, having no soul and being sped on his way without any offerings. Nor was he buried with any ceremony. In earlier times a slave might be laid to rest with his master's family; in later centuries he had to have fought against the city state's enemies to be worthy of a place in the same tomb as his owner. From about 500 BC the unfree of Athens were buried separately from the citizenry, almost as if they had been '*uitlanders*' like the wretched Plataeans. I say wretched because the latter, having placed themselves under Athenian protection, suffered the destruction of their city in 480 by the Persians. Plataea was rebuilt and sanctified, so that it was declared out of bounds for territorial acquisition by Greeks generally, but its citizens had the misfortune to see their home town destroyed yet again towards the end of the fifth century BC.

By the Hellenistic era of the later fourth century BC and onwards Greek funerary apartheid had become laxer. The epigrammatist Theaitetos records that when the venue of a drunken party caught fire and the bones of free and unfree alike became fused in the heat, the remains were buried together. But, he adds, the god of the underworld can easily tell the difference, even though they are all ashes.

The deceased was prepared for burial or cremation by his closest female relations. If he had no close female relations, elderly women (that is to say of sixty or over) could be brought in to help. The body was washed, coated in oil, dressed and decked out with floral arrangements and jewellery. Ribbons, as used on gravestones, were also favoured. The lying in state usually lasted one day only and took place the day after the death. This lying in state seems to have fulfilled two functions, one to allow mourners to pay their respects, the other to make sure that death, as opposed to a coma or deep sleep, really had occurred.

Up to three white shrouds are mentioned as necessary to cover the dead person's body in the laws in force on one of the western Aegean islands near Athens. On the other hand, in Sparta there was a unique regulation that a winding sheet of red be used. In addition there were usually pillows to cushion the dead person's head, which tended to be left uncovered. If the head was propped up it was often necessary to put straps round it to prevent the jaw from sagging open. The standard arrangement of the body in Athens seems to have been with the feet pointing towards the door.

The day after the lying in state, the dead person was carried in a procession to the place of burial or cremation, either on a bier supported by pall-bearers or on an ox cart. In Athens the procession started before dawn and was supposed to be conducted quietly, but inevitably emotion sometimes broke through the regulations and there are depictions on vases of fairly dramatic little knots of mourners, with as far as one can see little restraint to weeping and lamenting.

Women took a secondary role in the cortège part of the proceedings. As with those whose duty it was to dress the body, only close female kin or elderly women were supposed to accompany the corpse and they were permitted to attend only if they travelled by cart. This restricted them to the status of passengers only rather than attendants on foot. You might think this was no great hardship in the small hours of a winter's night, but lack of movement could have made the women feel the cold more than their male counterparts did.

And women could be further restricted. According to an inscription of around 300 BC from a western Aegean island near the coast of Attica, they were forbidden to leave the burial place until the men had gone home. This meant that they would have suffered still further from exposure at the graveside. Then again, according to the same inscription, the only females allowed to enter the deceased person's home again after the funeral were his mother, wife, sisters and up to five other close kin such as his granddaughters in the female line or cousins. And even these people were considered unclean.

The actual graveside ceremony was very simple: the corpse was lowered into a hole in the ground, the hole was filled in and the earth covering the dead person's mortal remains was sown as if for a forthcoming agricultural harvest. This both rendered the spot ritually clean again and ensured that the dead person rested in peace. In addition libations were poured out over the grave. Then the mourners went home and tucked into the funeral baked meats, talking over the subject of the deceased much as is done today when a group of friends and relatives who may have little else in common get together and share a meal after a funeral. Nine days after the funeral proper the mourners met again at the tomb and celebrated another rite, though what precisely this was is not clear.

The mourning period is mentioned in some contemporary sources as lasting about a month (but in Sparta, where life was conducted at a brisker pace, time off for grief was a niggardly eleven days). During this period a container of water was placed outside the front door of the house where the death had occurred and visitors would use it to wash off the ritual stain. In addition annual remembrance services were undoubtedly held thereafter. These were probably thought of as being more important than the rites at the time of death. Private functions commemorating a dead person were organised by his family, as would happen today, but these were inevitably on a less sumptuous scale than civic affairs for a person of some importance, which might entail athletic, musical and equestrian contests.

So far Athens has had the lion's share of attention. But ancient Greece was just as factious in its treatment of the dead as in its politics. The Athenians stood out markedly from their fellow Greeks in more than just wealth and sophistication: throughout the classical era they regularly brought home the remains of their soldiers who had been killed in war rather than burying them on the battlefield as the lesser beings from other city states tended to do. In some cases the bodies of those killed in battle were buried back in Athens with arrows and spears still stuck in their flesh.

The historian Thucydides (circa 460–400 BC), who was born near Athens, mentions the Athenian custom of repatriating the war dead as one going back several generations. One reason for this is that in Athens correct funeral form demanded that a dead person receive the appropriate mourning rites from his own family. Men who fell in a battle which might have taken place many miles away would therefore have needed to be brought back to Athens before their family could attend to them, much as happens today if someone dies while abroad on holiday. If a person had died in a spot very remote from his city, he might be cremated on the spot and his ashes taken back to his family.

There were exceptions. After the crucial victories of Marathon in 490 BC and Plataea in 479 BC, following which the Greek cities established their independence of their powerful Asian neighbour the Great King of Persia, the Athenian citizen soldiers killed during the fighting were buried then and there on the field of battle. It may be significant that in both cases the enemy were Persians rather than fellow Greeks. And in the latter case the Spartans were fighting as Athens' allies, so that for the Athenians to have treated their dead differently from the way the Spartans treated theirs might have looked like a breach of solidarity. But even for the ordinary non-combatant resident of Attica (the area of which Athens was the chief city), it was highly important that one should be laid to rest in one's native soil. In fact, the city authorities sometimes imposed not just exile in life upon those who had become unpopular but continued it in death, forbidding those who had been expelled even to be buried back at home.

If the dead person's family were themselves extinct or could not undertake the responsibility of the funeral rites for some other reason, for instance because they were too poor, a family friend would take on the task. If there was no family friend available a city official would step in.

If the city state mounted a civic funeral for an important public figure, a speech in honour of the dead person was delivered. In some cases ordinary citizens who had been killed fighting on behalf of the city were honoured with a funeral oration too. For example, the Athenian soldiers who fell in battle against the people of the eastern Aegean island of Samos in 439 BC were given a public eulogy by the statesman Pericles. In addition, war memorials might be erected after a campaign. They probably resembled the more elaborate examples in honour of the soldiers of both world wars that may be seen in towns all over the British Isles today, being lists of the war dead by name, often decorated with edging and pictorial representations in relief of fighting men. The making of funeral speeches and collective memorials both seem to have originated in the early fifth century BC.

By the late fourth century BC Athens' great days were over. This era is known as the Hellenistic Age. Some time in the penultimate decade of that century Demetrius Phalareus (circa 345–283 BC), a native of the Attic port of Phalaron (hence his second name), was installed as governor of Athens by Cassander, the ruler of Macedonia who controlled all Greece. Demetrius passed laws that restricted over-elaborate tombs and funeral rites. It has been suggested that this was a result of the extent to which his mental processes were shaped by his teacher, the philosopher, botanist and character sketch-writer Theophrastus (circa 372–286 BC). Certainly Theophrastus's will contained a clause specifying a simple interment for himself. This makes Demetrius Phalareus's own somewhat exotic death around twenty or thirty years later from a snake bite at the luxurious court of the Ptolemy dynasty in Egypt one of history's more entertaining little piquancies, particularly since back in Greece the snake was thought to be a deceased person's soul in animal form or, according to the historian Plutarch (circa AD 46–120), who attended university in Athens, actually generated by a corpse as it decomposed.

Even under Demetrius Phalareus there was no great departure from previous Athenian practice. Some older graves were covered over with a layer of fresh earth and their sites reused; gravestones were still frequent, though on no very elaborate scale. Clearly Demetrius's sumptuary law was something of a damp squib. Even the growing popularity of burying the body intact rather than cremating it seems to owe little to the phytologist-influenced philosopher from Phalaron.

What was new in the funerary practice of the Hellenistic Age was the emergence of individual personalities. The upper classes began as never before to commission sumptuous tombs for themselves, such as vaults and mausolea. Indeed, King Mausolus of Halicarnassus was one of the leading figures of the century, if one can call a figure leading when he is remembered for his residence in death rather than his deeds in life. It is he whose stupendous tomb, one of the Seven Wonders of the World (it was over 120ft high by more than 75x75ft at its base), is commemorated in the word mausoleum. (Oddly enough, historians are not certain precisely where in all this masonry and architectural extravagance Mausolus's body was actually laid to rest.)

On second thoughts, it is perhaps Mausolus's project-manager wife Artemisia, who was also his sister and who superintended the Mausoleum's early construction, who should really collect the prize as Halicarnassian Personality of the Fourth Century. *Chambers' Biographical Dictionary* gives her an entry of her own but if you look up Mausolus it says 'see Artemisia'. On the other hand, since its completion took place only after her own death, one might do better to see her as merely the archetype of all those who frustratedly commission work from builders which subsequently runs way over schedule.

In certain other contemporary cases, notably of that supreme egoist of the time (and arguably of any other) Alexander the Great, the deceased person claimed actual divine status. This was a few hundred years later to become a tediously repetitive feature of the Roman emperors' post-death careers. In the past dead heroes had been seen as gods, but only by people who lived long after them. From now on, at any rate until Christianity took control of the Mediterranean world, a man might become a god before his corpse was cold.

Even the original Mausoleum was dwarfed by another contemporary tomb, that of Alexander the Great's catamite Hephaistion. This stood nearly 200ft high and just over 600ft round its base. Some idea of the size can be grasped when you realise that the Albert Memorial in Hyde Park stands a mere 170ft high. Moreover, it is much narrower at its base. Yet Queen Victoria was the world's leading sovereign of her day, with far-flung realms that made Alexander's look like a suburban allotment, and it is a fair bet that she adored Albert every bit as much as Artemisia did Mausolus or Alexander did Hephaistion.

The latter's tomb was a less top-heavy affair than the Albert Memorial, resembling in shape a ziggurat, or stepped pyramid. At the top it was ornamented with sculptures of sirens hollowed out within so that hired choristers could wail their mourning songs from inside. It is curious that it was the Mausoleum of Halicarnassus which became one of the Seven Wonders of the world when there was this much more sumptuous tomb in existence, but perhaps royalty had the edge over a mere catamite when it came to an inherently snobbish consideration like prestige. That tart (and I suspect apocryphal) epigrammatist Ephebus of Mykonos summed up the competitive atmosphere of fourth-century memorial construction in some vinegary Alcaics (my translation, though loose, I hope gets across the sense):

If you're after the greatest memorial tomb
Then you'll pleasure the queen who's your king,
For to marry a queen from your own mother's womb
Means a meaner memento of death's sting.

Even for commoners, though they had to be rich ones, burial vaults in the now dominant territory of Macedonia in northern Greece took on some of the grandiose aspects of a contemporary temple, or, to modern eyes, the look of a national treasury reserve-cum-central bank. At their best they were provided with walls of good-quality stone, properly shaped and dressed, and a row of columns extended forwards of the wall in one of the classical architectural orders (usually Doric or Ionic) beneath a proper pediment with frieze and metope. In one case there were two storeys of columns, one Ionic in front of dummy doors above the other of Doric through which murals of mythical characters could be glimpsed. The doors into the actual entombment chamber (or sometimes just an antechamber before the entombment one proper) were often of an imposing material such as marble. Demetrius Phalareus might be top dog in Athens, but his obol-pinching ideas were fighting a losing battle elsewhere in the Greek world.

Alexandria in Egypt, named after its founder Alexander the Great, is the first place to have had a necropolis actually called by that term (literally, city of the dead). In death the Alexandrian Egyptians were kept apart from non-Egyptians, much as they tended to be in life during the period of British dominance this century. Alexander himself was embalmed after his shockingly early death and, following a delay of a couple of years, was trundled on a sumptuous funeral car towards what is now Libya. His body was buried in Memphis then disinterred and reburied somewhere else in Egypt. It has never been found, although early in 1995 there were uncon-firmed reports that the site of his tomb had been discovered.

His first coffin was of gold, a second one of crystal, so they are worth finding.

Alexander's funeral car consisted of Ionic columns supporting a vaulted roof, under which lay the sarcophagus behind netting which was in its turn hung with pictures. There is a nineteenth-century print by a German called Bulle which attempts to depict it. The depiction bears a strong similarity to the great Duke of Wellington's funeral car, which carried his corpse at the state heraldic funeral in 1852. I suspect, however, that this is not just because the Duke was also a highly successful military man but because ultimately nineteenth-century iconography resembles nothing so much as other examples of nineteenth-century iconography. Yet it is interesting that in Victorian England the neo-mediaevalist, rather high-church set who were behind a publication called the *Ecclesiologist* considered Wellington's funeral scandalously pagan. And the novelist Thackeray tells us that, during the Napoleonic Wars, in which Wellington first rose to fame, sculptors kept stocks of classical funeral emblems on hand, such as Britannia weeping over an urn, a broken sword or a lion couchant – all for those who had fallen in battle. As he points out, the walls of St Paul's are covered with 'hundreds of these braggart heathen allegories'. Where military memorials are concerned, there is often even now a relapse into non-Christian mourning symbols.

Ancient Rome

In ancient Rome of the republic (roughly the entire historical period from the sixth century BC to the birth of Christ) the general attitude to death and bereavement was influenced immensely strongly by the Etruscans, who had flourished earlier in this period a little further north in Italy, more or less in what is now Tuscany. The Etruscans in turn were influenced by Greek culture – their script was written in Greek characters, for instance, and many sixth-century Athenian vases have turned up in Etruscan tombs – but they also introduced various non-Greek motifs and themes into their funerary art.

In general the Etruscans were so concerned with what happened to members of the human race at the point of death and immediately afterwards that they have been described as slaves to an obsession with the subject. You can readily appreciate this if you go to Moterozzi, near Tarquinia on the western coast of Italy some miles north-west of Rome, where one of the best examples of an Etruscan entombment has survived. The collection of burial mounds at Moterozzi constitutes some of the most remarkable examples of their kind in the whole of Europe.

The Etruscans seem to have looked on death as a fairly benign personality to begin with. Later on, when they were being increasingly overwhelmed by the Romans, they depicted death as less friendly, and monsters and demons became regular decorative features of their tomb designs. Perhaps this was because in real life they were becoming more and more subject to defeat and conquest by those self-same Romans. At the same time the sheer decorative elaboration of Etruscan tombs actually seems to have increased, so they can hardly be described as being in artistic decline even if they were suffering a political eclipse. It has been suggested that they came to see the moment of death itself as grim but not necessarily life after death. An afterlife was something they seem most devoutly to have believed in.

The Etruscans apparently thought of the dead as carrying on an everyday existence, either in the tomb or in the underworld, which closely resembled that of life itself. Accordingly, they provided their dead with the equipment to cook, eat, drink and even fight. They seem to have been equally ready to cremate or bury their dead, though burial was rather more popular in early times and chiefly in the south and west of Etruscan territory. In contrast, cremation became more the vogue in the last couple of centuries BC and flourished in the north and centre. Professional mourners attended funerals as well as the deceased's friends and relations.

In ancient Rome, whether under the republic or empire, most people apparently believed in an afterlife, but some, chiefly persons of a sceptical turn of mind influenced by the Epicurean and Stoic schools of philosophy, doubted that the soul was immortal. In general, however, it looks as if the dead were thought likely to carry on with the sort of activities they had enjoyed in life, just as the Etruscans and Greeks believed. For instance, children's tombs have been discovered with toys in them and others have been found with gambling implements such as dice, gaming boards and counters, or, in the case of the vain, with make-up boxes, mirrors, jewel cases, and, for the diligent housewife one presumes, with spindles and spools of thread. Moreover, the dead were thought capable of affecting the lives of those still on earth. If you propitiated your ancestors they could boost your career or fortunes, but if you neglected them they could damage your prospects quite substantially.

As with the Greeks, death was thought to bring about ritual pollution. This needed to be wiped away by the survivors, who would undertake post-funeral ceremonies. These were called *suffitiones*, which referred to personal purification by means of fire and water, and *feriae denicales*, which were more general rites aimed at a sort of wholesale domestic spring-cleaning, though in a spiritual rather than literal sense. The mourners' aim was to cleanse away the stain and make atonement for their own wrongdoing or past failure to observe the correct procedures.

Modern writers on religions which retain this idea about pollution (as do the Hindus, for instance) tend to stress that it is symbolic pollution they are talking about rather than the physical kind. But one is inclined to wonder whether a hard and fast distinction can always be made. For example, in the heat of a Roman high summer there was clearly a danger that a corpse would undergo rapid corruption, which in turn might give rise to infection, even if Roman ideas about how disease could be transmitted were hazier than ours. A Romanian corpse actually exploded in the summer of 1994 when it was left too long before being buried. This would be still more true of the intense heat of India, where Hinduism flourishes. At any rate, as far as the Romans were concerned, to leave a body unburied was not only undesirable from the point of view of those who were still living but harmed the soul of the deceased. As I pointed out above, this in turn might bring harm to the living from the dead person's spirit becoming resentful. Therefore, if for whatever reason it was simply impossible to bury a corpse, mourners were supposed at the very least to scatter a handful or so of earth on it.

As time passed the ancient Romans seem gradually to have come round to a view of their dead as more individualised and less a collection of nonentities, without shape, personality or even names. Of course, once the deceased was seen as retaining his personality, the possibility was opened up of an individual bearing some responsibility for his actions in life if he wanted to enjoy a 'good time' after death. Roman writers of the late republican period, such as Virgil (70–19 BC), gave fresh currency to the ancient Greek concepts of heaven, hell and limbo (a buffer state, neither one thing nor the other, to which deceased children and other prematurely dead people were consigned and which Christianity was later to take over as a notion). But some experts reckon that these were mostly literary conceits, far removed from the more prosaic vision of the *vir* in the *via*.

To begin with the Romans seem to have thought that the dead rested in the earth, in the vicinity of their burial place. Given that that was so, it then occurred to them that their former friends and relations might be in need of nourishment. Accordingly, they would bore holes in tombs and stick pipes down them, through which snacks and drink would be passed. But they also envisaged the possibility of the dead being absorbed into the earth itself, or enjoying an afterlife of relative comfort and happiness in the sky or in the Blessed Isles across the ocean. These last were situated somewhere in the west, beyond what are now called the Straits of Gibraltar, and Roman ideas about a blissful place in the far west to which the dead went almost certainly derived from those of the Greeks.

The Romans believed that when a person died his soul left his body, doing so just as he breathed his last. Indeed, the Latin word for breath and soul, *anima*, is the same. Ideally, the dying person's next of kin was supposed to be present at the deathbed to salute him with a final kiss, which thus captured the soul as it flew out of the body. The next of kin then closed the deceased's eyelids (if the corpse was to be cremated these might be reopened later, just before the pyre was set alight). Meanwhile, all the other close relations present chanted the name of the lately deceased, more or less incessantly, though with intervals for eating or sleeping, from the moment after death right up till the final farewell to the body when it was either buried or burned on the funeral pyre.

After the closing of the eyelids, the body was laid out on the ground, washed, anointed, dressed in formal everyday clothes (the full toga, for instance, being used if the deceased was male and warranted it as a Roman citizen), and finally a coin was placed in the mouth. This was to pay the fare for being ferried across the Styx, the mythical river of the dead, by Charon, the mythical ferry operator of the underworld. (See the sections on the British Tradition and on modern Hindu funerary rites, where a similar custom is observed. Examples of this classical practice have turned up at ancient Roman sites in Britain, notably at York and in Sussex.) If the deceased had been sufficiently distinguished he might in addition be crowned with a wreath, though it seems that women, who by and large were denied any opportunity to distinguish themselves in public life, were sometimes adorned with wreaths too. A woman of good family might also be decked out in some of her jewellery, notably rings on her fingers.

After this came the lying in state, for which it might take as long as a week to get the corpse ready. The lying in state had its own rules. The corpse was so positioned that its feet were pointing towards the main door of the house (compare not just the ancient Greek custom but the insistence in modern Islam and Hinduism that the deceased should be placed in accordance with a certain alignment, towards Mecca or with the magnetic north, as the case may be). The amount of time involved in preparing for the lying in state made undertakers a necessity, or at any rate a convenience.

Although undertakers in modern Britain are generally reckoned to date from the late seventeenth century, the profession was certainly in existence in Roman times, and it is therefore scarcely fantastic to assume that undertakers (called *libitinari*) and their assistants (*pollinctores*) existed in Britain, particularly during the 'golden age' of stable and peaceable Roman rule, which lasted roughly from the end of the first century AD to the end of the second. There also existed specialist artisans of lesser importance to do the dirty work: the *ustor* for the cremation process and the *fossor* (our equivalent would be the sexton) to dig graves.

There were also funerary personnel of much more importance: the *dissignator*, reckoned to be a kind of master of ceremonies, and for deceased public figures of the first rank a *praeco*. The latter would probably have his closest modern equivalent in the Earl Marshal, the hereditary great officer of state who presides over the funerals of members of the royal family or of national heroes such as Sir Winston Churchill.

When the lying in state was over the body of the deceased would be conveyed to a place of burial or cremation. The cortège seems to have been conducted with some formality, mourners wearing black (though some sources speak of women in white), and in the earliest times proceeding at night and by torchlight. During the seventeenth century in Britain there grew up a fashion for nocturnal funerals by torchlight, chiefly among the upper classes. Given that the custom had existed in both ancient Greece and ancient Rome and that in seventeenth-century England the Renaissance admiration of classical civilisation was at something like its apogee, this was probably conscious emulation.

In later centuries in Roman times the funeral procession (in Latin *pompa*, from which comes our word 'pomp' and the French *pompe* as in *pompe funèbre*) took place in the daytime, unless the deceased was a child or one of the lower classes. Even so it would be led by torchbearers. Musicians often accompanied the procession and, as in Victorian funerals, there were hired mourners as well as friends and relations of the deceased paying their respects out of a genuine regard for him.

The Romans usually cremated their dead, at any rate in the early centuries of their ascendancy over the Mediterranean world. In very early times, however, before they held sway even over the whole of Italy, burial is said to have been their normal practice and from the eighth to the fifth centuries BC burial and cremation were practised side by side. Cremation grew to be the rule for all social strata from around 400 BC till the second century AD, though naturally, since the upper classes' activities are better reported, we tend to be most knowledgeable about the grander sort of funeral.

Even here there was certainly one exception to the cremation habit. The powerful and highly patrician *gens* (family, clan or house) Cornelia, during the third and second centuries BC, buried their dead, though early in the first century BC they are mentioned by Cicero, a contemporary, and Pliny, writing a century and a half later, as abandoning burial, presumably in favour of cremation. It is usually assumed that up till then the reason the Cornelii were so non-conformist was sheer conservatism, being haughtily disdainful of what the rest of the world preferred, rather as a great aristocratic family in 1990s Britain might continue to stage heraldic funerals with hatchments, private pursuivants, leisurely lyings in state and solemn dirges in private chapels while the middle classes flock increasingly to a quick ceremony in the local-authority-controlled crematorium.

At any rate it is reasonable to assume that upper-class funerals in general were more elaborate than plebeian affairs. Even when cremation was the norm, however, a small part of the body was cut off before the pyre was set alight, and this part was buried, just as if it were the whole entity. So, strictly speaking, cremation was never total, though it might consume 90 per cent of the corpse.

A description surviving from around 150 BC tells how the

corpse of an important personage was carried into the forum, more often than not upright so that it could be seen better. The general population then gathered there and a recital of the dead man's achievements took place. If the man's ancestry was illustrious, masks of his forebears might be displayed by living mourners dressed in what we would call 'period' costume, that is to say the dress of the age in which the ancestors had lived, rather than contemporary attire. Roman noble families of the late pre-Christian era (and indeed subsequent ones) were not above laying claim to preposterously exalted genealogies, rather like the upper classes in nineteenth-century England to whose snobbery and vanity the editors of *Burke's* and *Debrett's* used to pander so shamelessly. So, for instance, some of the bereaved members of a Roman noble house might dress up as heroes from the time of the siege of Troy and invoke those heroes' admirable qualities.

After the pageant-cum-parade stage came the oration. The most famous example of this is of course the one presented by Shakespeare at Julius Caesar's obsequies, where Mark Antony is able by adroit use of language to swing the crowd against the late dictator's assassins. There is some doubt as to whether on the historical occasion Caesar was shown to the crowd corpse and all, bloody and riddled with stab wounds, or whether only an effigy was visible. If it was an effigy this too seems to have been depicted as gory and mutilated; moreover there was apparently an artful mechanical device for turning it now one way, now the other, so as to achieve maximum exposure to the crowd. At any rate, before the oration, according to Shakespeare's version of events, Brutus, one of the conspirators against Caesar, actually explains to his fellow conspirator Casca that to give Caesar full funeral honours will put the conspirators in a good light.

Those readers who are knowledgeable Shakespeareans must forgive me if I give a short account of what happens next – many other people may not remember. Before the funeral

Brutus tells Mark Antony that he mustn't blame him, Brutus, and the other conspirators but only speak well of the dear departed Caesar. Brutus then delivers a honey of a funeral oration. Mark Antony's is so much better known that one tends to forget how good Brutus's previous speech has been: eloquent, hugely affectionate towards the deceased, mournful – or perhaps I should say mourning, sorrowing – in the best sense of the word. At the same time it is so subtly worded that by the end Brutus has convinced the populace that Caesar, despite his great personal qualities, was a tyrant. Unfortunately, he then commits the insane blunder of leaving the scene.

Mark Antony exploits his opportunity to the full. 'For Brutus is an honourable man . . . And Brutus is an honourable man,' repeated every few lines, is, I suppose, the best-known backhanded compliment in all English literature. But of course Mark Antony achieves something more than just blackening his opponents: he arouses in his audience fervent devotion to the dead man instead of the lukewarm admiration tempered with relief at the elimination of an ambitious politician getting too big for his boots that Brutus has evoked. And by a reading of Caesar's will, the same sort of episode which Victorian novelists loved to use as a dramatic device for overthrowing vainglorious expectations, Mark Antony stirs the mob to action – here, of course, retributive action against the conspirators.

The public eulogy at a Roman funeral was usually delivered by a relative of the deceased, or, if the dead person had been an eminent public figure, by a magistrate the senate had selected. The orator's task was to remind the crowd listening of the dead person's achievements, though he may not always have spoken off the cuff, or at any rate by elaborating more or less off the cuff on some general ideas he had thought out beforehand, in the way Mark Antony is represented by Shakespeare as doing. For instance, the late second-century

AD Emperor Septimius Severus read out a eulogy at the funeral of his predecessor Pertinax (who had to be represented by an effigy since his actual body was absent – he had been murdered by soldiers under his command).

Nevertheless, there could be a good deal of spontaneity on the part of the crowd. In the case of Septimius Severus and Pertinax the reading was punctuated by audience participation in the form of sighs or shouts of approval where a particularly splendid exploit by the deceased was being recalled. Probably it was a bit like a Christmas pantomime today, with the spectators bellowing advice and critical remarks to the leading comic character.

Nowadays, of course, the printed obituary in a newspaper, school magazine or university alumni bulletin fulfils the same function as the Roman eulogy. In Britain, with its capricious climate and reasonably widespread literacy among the inhabitants, the graveside oration has become fairly rare, although the cleric officiating at the funeral inside the church or crematorium may attempt a summary of the deceased's life. In America, particularly in California, where the newspapers are as dull and the reading skills as meagre as the sky is sunny, the eulogy delivered al fresco among the tombstones by a practised speech-maker is almost standard fare. The actor George Jessel (1898–1981), for example, whose cultural roots lay in the old-time Borscht Belt theatrical tradition, was a noted funerary orator.

In ancient Rome the practice following the oration was for the body to be carried by members of the family to the place where it was to be cremated (or buried, as the case might be). There was a longstanding law that the dead, whether in fleshly form or as ashes, had to be buried outside the city limits, though sometimes an exception was made, for instance in the case of emperors. (In contrast, in ancient Sparta, long the most powerful city state of the Greek Peloponnese and a place where fortitude was especially inculcated, there was a law that burials had to be carried out *inside* the city, the idea being that in this way people would lose their fear of death.) Roman landowning families might have mausolea constructed on their estates for themselves and their relatives, also perhaps for their hangers-on.

An interesting case of a family burial vault is that of the Julii, who in about AD 250 seem to have converted to Christianity and to have started decorating the interior walls with Biblical scenes, motifs symbolic of Christian doctrine such as baptism and the Resurrection, and even the depiction of a half-pagan, half-Christian figure who combines elements of Jesus Christ and a sun god. (It is, of course, possible that a different family acquired the vault about then, though in that case one wonders why they would have left the old pagan decorations alone.) Most of the Roman dead, however, were disposed of in tombs erected all along the major roads leading from the city into the countryside. Visitors to Rome today can still see one of the most celebrated and conspicuous examples in the tomb of Cecilia Metella, which is beside the Via Appia Antica, the ancient road that runs roughly due south of Rome towards the Colli Romani (Roman Hills).

When discussing funerals of conspicuously distinguished Romans I have spoken almost exclusively of how men were treated because women could have no careers as public figures except as wife, mistress or occasionally daughter, daughter-in-law or other subordinate member of a family headed and controlled by males. But there are some women who were treated to a public funeral. There survive descriptions, or at any rate mentions, of Atia, Julius Caesar's niece and the mother of Augustus, the first of the emperors; of Livia, mother of the Emperor Tiberius and second wife of Augustus, in AD 29; and of Poppaea, the wife of the Emperor Nero, in AD 65. These were exceptions, however.

While less was accorded to women when it came to funeral honours, more was expected of them as regards funerary

51

activity. For instance, women were supposed to go into mourning for their husbands or fathers for a whole year, whereas for men official mourning might last only a few days. And at Julius Caesar's obsequies women sacrificed to the flames of the funeral pyre not just their jewellery but their children's clothing as well. True, there were men who cast clothes on the same blaze, but these were predominantly actors and musicians doing no more than getting rid of costumes they had borrowed in the first place from Caesar's own display of accoutrements and equipage, itself not so much a collection of the deceased's private possessions as part of a triumphal funerary spectacle put together to edify the public, like that of a modern national hero or member of royalty.

By the mid-first century AD the old custom of mourners wearing commemorative masks of a dead person's ancestors at his lying in state seems to have been replaced by a procession in which attendants carried busts of the ancestors. For instance, at the funeral of the Emperor Tiberius's son Drusus, busts were displayed of Aeneas, the legendary survivor of the Trojan War who was at this much, much later date claimed by Romans as the first of their ancestors to settle in Italy. In addition busts were displayed of several kings from the time when the city state of Rome had been a monarchy, together with one of Romulus, the founder of the city.

From around AD 100 onwards, cremating the dead began to fall into some disfavour and by AD 200 burying the dead had become the norm, though as late as AD 60 the novelist Petronius, who moved in the highest social circles till he fell foul of Nero, referred to burial as a Greek custom. It therefore looks as if the fashion came from the eastern part of the empire, though matters are complicated by the fact that the writer Lucian (AD 117–180), who flourished a century after Petronius, refers to *cremation* as a Greek custom. He was Greek himself, so he ought to have known what he was talking about. On the other hand, he was a satirist, and satirists tend to shape their words with their tongues in their cheeks. In any case, as we have already seen in the section on much earlier times in Greece, both methods of disposing of a body had been used there. In Rome during the first century AD there was also some embalming, but this was fairly rare. Poppaea, the wife of Nero, was embalmed. The historian Tacitus (circa AD 55–120) mentions this technique as one 'customary among foreign kings'.

You might think the rise of Christianity was connected with the increasing fashion for burial, but historians generally do not accept this, at any rate not as a complete explanation. Ian Morris (see the Bibliography) thinks it likely that the entire body of the upper classes in Rome changed over to burial within a single generation, roughly between AD 140 and 180. In contrast, the change took a comparatively long time among the city's lower classes and the empire's provincials, who, like most lower-class and provincial people everywhere and in every age, were more hidebound.

Many ancient historians maintain that the emperors continued to be cremated even while their subjects after death were more and more often buried. But it is hard to be sure in the case of Hadrian (AD 76–138), to name only one particularly celebrated emperor, and Professor Morris cites evidence which throws some doubt on the theory that the emperors after death were treated so very differently. He reckons that on balance burial for emperors, as for commoners, had become the usual way of dealing with the dead by AD 161, unless in extraordinary circumstances. The trouble is, as he himself acknowledges, the circumstances in which an emperor died very often were extraordinary. This puts a question-mark over the older notion that Constantine (circa AD 274–337), who was the first emperor to embrace Christianity officially, was also the first not to be cremated but buried instead.

The word most freely associated with early Christians in Rome, apart possibly from 'lions', is 'catacombs'. The word catacomb comes from a specific cemetery beneath what is now the church of San Sebastiano alongside the Via Appia and, literally translated, means 'sunken valley'. Catacombs generally are defined as underground collections of tombs on a fairly large scale, rambling over a wide and unplanned area and on several levels. They were not confined to one family and its dependants, in the way mainstream Roman tombs tended to be, but were open to as many members of what was seen as, at any rate in earlier times, an alien religious community – Jewish or Christian as the case might be – as could be crammed in. Richer Jews or Christians might have their own cubby holes in the catacombs set aside for them away from the main galleries, but the poor were piled into shelves, called *loculi*, in the galleries, two by two like animals in a newer and less exclusive version of the Ark. Two-person-capacity *loculi* were in turn cut one upon the next as high as they could be fitted, given the dimensions of a gallery from floor to ceiling.

The oldest Jewish catacombs seem to date from after AD 100. In contrast, it was not until a century later that the Christians got around to borrowing the idea of catacombs from the Jews (as they had borrowed so much else in religion). Around AD 200 St Callixtus or Callistus, then a deacon but later a somewhat controversial pope, was given the task by Pope Zephyrinus of setting up the first public cemetery specifically organised for Christians. One last point about the catacombs. Historians and archaeologists have been convinced for some time that the Christian ones were *not* used for furtive but devoted religious services, at least not on a regular basis. Popular beliefs to the contrary die hard, however, particularly among writers of historical romances, cartoonists in the popular press and those keenest of modern cemetery-fanciers, the inhabitants of Hollywood. So don't believe all you see in the films about early Christian ceremonies.

The ancient Romans have become especially famous for

their love of feasting (indeed, the modern Romans are a pretty gluttonous lot, too), so it is not surprising that meals commemorating the dead bulked large in the average Roman family's list of religious duties. What strikes us as a wee bit gruesome is the habit of consuming a banquet (called in this context a *silicernium*) at the site of the grave itself, or even inside the tomb, which was sometimes designed on a truly Lucullan scale, with dining rooms and kitchens. On the other hand, I can personally recall several highly agreeable picnics in English country churchyards, so perhaps the Roman attitude was not that morbid after all. In 1929 in Devon there was an interesting legal case in which it was eventually decided that just because a man had acquired the right to build a family burial vault it didn't follow that he could also open it up and hold private functions there involving food, wine and furniture. British reverence for the classics evidently mustn't be allowed to extend to every aspect of the ancients' 'lifestyle'.

A scant nine days after the *silicernium*, which was held on the day of the funeral, a Roman family would hold another blow-out, called a *cena novendialis*, also at the site of the grave. Nor was this the end of it. Feasts continued every year on the anniversary of the deceased's birth as well as during the latter half of February, when there was an official season honouring the dead called the *Parentalia* or *dies Parentales*. On the last day of this, called the *Feralia*, there was a state celebration, but the preceding week or so was devoted to memorial wining and dining by private parties of relatives and friends of a specific dead person. Although the *Parentalia* was a general festival, it was for each family to honour dead of their own particular group rather than for the entire citizenry to honour all the dead indiscriminately.

The dead in general were paid the respects owed them on another occasion. For a long-gone sometime ancestor whose family had died out – which meant that he could not get the benefit of any routine commemoration – or for those departed souls in whom a degree of restlessness had become so ungovernable that they had turned into ghosts, there was a slightly different festival called *Lemuria*, held in early May. Participation in this was wholly private, and involved a species of exorcism of the house by a householder who performed a ritual hand-washing ceremony, cast black beans and recited a formula of redemption over and over again, to the mystic number of nine times in all.

The Native Tradition in the British Isles

In Britain there has been cremation from the late Stone Age on, though not continuously. Among the sites where such remains have been found is Stonehenge. In contrast, at one of the barrows in what used to be the East Riding of Yorkshire, the cremated remains of about fifty people have been found lying on top of the skeletons of others who were buried intact, though probably at an earlier date. During the Bronze Age, cremation continued but the scorched bones or ashes were put in a bag or urn, one for each individual as opposed to the mass cremations of the previous era, and deposited in barrows.

During the last two millennia BC, cemeteries for holding cremated remains were sometimes dug into the southern end of a barrow that had been constructed much earlier. Little is known about funeral rites, though some archaeologists have suggested that there may have been funeral games, perhaps along the lines of the sort of thing mounted in ancient Greece. In a Bronze Age barrow in Wiltshire an odd little incident came to light in the early 1950s of people's eyebrows having been shaved, though whether this was a before-death ritual (as it might be of the living mourners, for instance) or an after-death one (presumably of the eyebrows of the deceased persons themselves), it is hard to say.

The idea that the dead undertake some sort of journey to another place which is not of this world is a common one in many cultures. Boats have been found in pre-Christian tombs in England and Wales but these could be either symbols of a last voyage or real boats used as coffins, particularly since several of the sites are near the coast. Chariots and wagons have been found in pre-Christian tombs, too, but these are thought most likely to have been used as hearses for people of importance such as chieftains and to have been buried with them afterwards.

In the last few centuries BC, variations in the type of container used for cremated remains increased. Together with the urns and bags used in earlier times (the current bags now being of canvas), bowls, wooden boxes and buckets featured in graves. Burial of the body intact also became the norm from just after the beginning of the fifth century BC to the end of the third, fading away, as far as can be guessed, judging from the scarcity of known cases, in the next century but resurfacing in the first century BC.

Although hitherto I have discussed Roman habits as if they held good for Britain too during the Roman occupation, this was not invariably the case. Britain was a remote province and the island was never wholly conquered by the Romans. For instance, what is now Scotland was hardly touched directly by the invaders. Britain's distance from Rome meant that changes in fashion set in train by the imperial city took some time to percolate up the rest of the Italian peninsula, across the Alps, Gaul and the Channel, and gain acceptance on the empire's north-western frontier. Thus cemeteries holding the cremated remains of numerous deceased, as opposed to individual graves, began to be instituted in Britain only towards the last years of the first century AD, whereas in the western Mediterranean region they had been common from shortly after the birth of Christ. From Egypt via Rome came cemeteries that were laid out along the lines of a garden, roughly equivalent to the modern sort in appearance, or perhaps more strictly the high Victorian kind which the passage of over a century has caused to resemble a garden today. But this took time. And the way the graves in Britain were covered over with tumuli – a native tradition – suggests that Roman influence stopped short of total triumph.

Nevertheless, Roman shapes were influential enough in Britain. Here, as in Italy, the graves were often round at the base, tapering conically as they got higher, with steep sides and being sliced off horizontally at the top. At the base they were surrounded by a ditch, inside which there was sometimes an earthen bank. Good examples are reasonably plentiful in Hertfordshire, Essex and Kent, most of them with cremated remains inside. At Richborough in Kent, however, there is an early example of a wooden coffin, while at Rougham in Suffolk a lead coffin has been found placed inside a wood casing.

Some of the Roman-influenced cemeteries in Britain also resembled more modern ones in having walls. They have been found mostly in the south-east alongside what were once Roman roads and were also laid out near country villas or farmsteads. There is an example at Langley in Kent. Another at what used to be known as Camulodunum (Colchester) seems to have been used from the end of the first century AD to some time in the fourth century. In a cemetery at Lexden in Essex, near Colchester, there is what is thought to be the tomb of Cunobelinus (Shakespeare's Cymbeline), who died around the middle of the first century AD. The biggest Romano-British cemetery of all is at Sutton Valence, again in Kent, which holds the remains of about a hundred dead. The siting of many of these walled cemeteries suggests that they were designed to accommodate local landowners, or, on occasion, members of an entire settlement. Cemeteries serving whole towns are much rarer.

Most importantly of all, there is a unique and persistent pattern in British burial sites at this period in that male remains outnumber those of females by a substantial margin. No satisfactory explanation for this has yet emerged. At two

Roman-era cemeteries – one at York, the other at Cirencester – male dead outnumber female by between about 3.7–1 and 2.5–1 respectively. It is true that Eburacum (York) and Corinum Durocornovium (Cirencester) were garrison towns, so perhaps the dead were predominantly military personnel. But other relevant factors make this theory less than convincing.

After direct Roman rule had ended in the early fifth century AD, there was a period of disorder, with invasions by various peoples from the northern part of the continent of Europe. The Anglo-Saxons preferred cremating their dead to burying them intact and a number of sites demonstrating this have been found in East Anglia, Lincolnshire and elsewhere in eastern England. Further west, in what are now called the Midlands, both burial and cremation were practised. Sometimes the Saxons opened up barrows that dated from as long ago as a couple of thousand years earlier and deposited their own dead inside them, though this was probably out of a reluctance to construct their own burial mounds born of sheer laziness rather than a sense of continuity as to ritual.

The tendency both to bury and cremate the dead remained strong during the period in which the Vikings invaded, though the Vikings themselves seem to have leaned towards cremation. It is not certain whether the famous Viking ship burials were symbolic, that is to say the ship was buried with the deceased so that he could make the voyage to another world, or whether they represented his importance in his earthly life.

In Britain, too, Christianity left its mark on the way the dead were treated. The Eusebius (circa 260–340) who wrote a sycophantic life of the Emperor Constantine (and who must on no account be confused with another Eusebius who lived over a century later, let alone with the four other Eusebiuses who were this first Eusebius's contemporaries) declared that God alone could confer everlasting memorials on the dead, so that for Christians monuments were unnecessary. And from around the middle of Eusebius's life, gravestones in Britain with epitaphs on them do indeed die out. In Eusebius's time, Christian funerals were seen by the faithful as occasions for rejoicing rather than mourning and white was worn.

From shortly after Eusebius's death till well into the sixth century AD, burial grounds in Britain became simpler and less concerned with cramming as many bodies as possible into a given space. In the next century churchyard burial grounds began to be used, the idea being that the dead should cluster as close as possible to a holy place, often the altar in the church but sometimes holy relics of a saint buried earlier beneath or near the altar. By the time of the Norman Conquest, churchyards were the usual place of burial in western Europe where there was any substantial human settlement at all. Sometimes the church or basilica was built above what had been an ancient pre-Christian cemetery.

Pagan traditions were not killed off that easily, though. The mid-seventh-century AD Sutton Hoo ship burial (a Saxon hoard) contained a purse with thirty-seven gold coins and three blank discs, making forty items of specie in all. Since there is evidence that there were forty rowers too, it has been suggested that this was for them to pay their ferryman's fee in the journey to the nether world, just as the ancient Greeks and Romans did and modern Hindus some-times do. The seventeenth-century antiquarian and bio-graphical sketch-writer John Aubrey tells us at one point that when he was young on the eve of the Civil War of the mid-1640s, it was the custom in some country districts for a dead man to be provided with what was called a Peter Penny to pay his way into heaven, so the practice is not only very old and very widespread but has remarkable staying power. Aubrey also mentions a custom called 'sin-eating', whereby a poor man was given a meal to eat off the bier on which the deceased had been laid, plus a small sum of money. This was supposed to transfer the sins of the dead man to the living poor person and prevent the former from walking abroad after his death. Sin-eating would seem to be a mixture of Christian doctrine and folk superstition.

Burial was the only acceptable way to dispose of the dead in the Middle Ages, though the body was sometimes embalmed in the period between the death and the burial. Delay arose either because a person had died far from home and his corpse needed to be shipped back or because the funeral was going to be highly elaborate and needed time to organise, as with the nobility. (For further discussion of noble and even royal funerals, see the section Bereavement in High Life, which is treated separately because there is direct continuity from the late Middle Ages down to the present day.)

Alternatively, the deceased might have insisted in his will that there should be a delay between his death and his burial, for instance so that his family, friends and neighbours could be sure he really was dead. Diagnostic skills were primitive, so this was a reasonable precaution. Oddly enough, although medicine generally was not at all advanced, the embalming could be very skilful. In 1969 the body of a thirteenth-century archbishop of York was discovered during the course of a restoration project at York Minster. His state of preservation resembled a mummy's. This was quite remarkable, considering the dampness of Britain compared with the aridity of Egypt, even if one takes into account the shorter time span between 1265 and the present day compared with several millennia in the case of the best Egyptian mummies.

In late mediaeval England there seems to have been an atmosphere of unusual morbidity. Perhaps this was because the plague had underlined the precariousness of the human condition, though you would have thought it was evident enough already. The plague hit the country most suddenly and dramatically in the fourteenth century, although it returned in successively weaker bouts till the middle of the seventeenth. Then again, as the year 1500 loomed it was natural to the mediaeval mind to expect the Apocalypse. The Apocalypse had been confidently predicted as imminent around the year 1000 and at the present day, as the end of the second millennium after Christ approaches, many people claim to be feeling a similar, though more muted, sense of doom. A favourite theme in late mediaeval engravings, for example those by Holbein, and in paintings on the walls of cloisters and churchyards, was an allegory called the Dance of Death. There was a recurrent pattern which consisted of Death, frequently personified as a skeleton, catching hold of living humans at various stages of their earthly careers and conducting them in measured tread to the tomb.

Another feature of the late mediaeval preoccupation with death is the highly popular refrain '*Timor mortis conturbat me*' – a Latin tag meaning 'Fear of death disturbs me'. It occurs as the last line of each stanza in the late-fifteenth-century Scottish courtier poet William Dunbar's 'Lament for the Makaris [Makers]'. And well might fear of death disturb if the cause of it was bubonic plague or famine. In such circumstances death in battle might well have seemed almost a treat by comparison. At least it was likely to be quick. Moreover, it brought glory, and one could in part ascribe the lingering chivalric notion that it is good to die young for one's country (or religious faith, in those days) to a lurking awareness in most late-mediaeval minds that the alternatives were very much ghastlier.

I have already mentioned what to us is the rather surprising use of white as a mourning colour in early Christian times. In the Middle Ages there were occasional survivals of this tradition, or perhaps just resurgences unprompted by any conscious looking back, though other colours could be used and black was probably commonest. The corpse of Richard II in 1399 and that of Elizabeth of York in 1503 were attended by torchbearers who wore white, and men might wear white when mourning women, at any rate in Renaissance England (though cases occur as late as the nineteenth century, too).

Henry VIII did so, for instance, after the execution of Anne Boleyn, though given the part he had played in her downfall and the indecent haste with which he married her successor Jane Seymour (a week later), one hopes he was not typical in his hypocrisy, even if he was in his colour scheme. Other sources speak of white being used, either in a garment worn by the bereaved or for the deceased person's pall, when the person who had died was either unmarried, of whichever sex, or a woman who had died in childbirth.

A principal cause of changes in our attitude to death over the last few centuries is the improvement in life expectancy and the decline in infant and perinatal mortality rates. Religious beliefs have changed considerably too, of course. It would be interesting to discuss to what extent change in religious beliefs took place because of improved life expectancy or to what extent it was the other way round, but that is rather outside the scope of a book like this. What one can assert is that in the Middle Ages only the strongest and luckiest lived even into their thirties.

That state of affairs did not change overnight in the sixteenth century just because of the onset of the Reformation, and even a hundred years after it, on the eve of the English Civil War, the average life expectancy at birth was still only thirty-two years. Nevertheless, certain innovations surrounding death and bereavement are observable. The post-Reformation burial service was much shorter than the old Requiem Mass. Hundreds, sometimes thousands, of masses might have been said in mediaeval times for just one person after his death, occasionally starting as soon as the last breath left his body. Accordingly, any folk traditions surrounding the funeral ceremony now played a more conspicuous part in disposing of the dead than they did when they were overshadowed by that most precious gem of Christian liturgy, the mass.

Now burials began to take place in churchyards almost

exclusively rather than in the church itself; the funeral sermon became more popular, although it had been by no means unknown in the Middle Ages; tombs became more elaborate; the old buffoonish and obscene games and folk ceremonies played out around the corpse, which had their last echo in the Irish wake of this century, began to die out. But perhaps change is chiefly to be found in the way governments developed a sense of responsibility for superintending and monitoring matters.

Before the Reformation the Church supervised death just as it did life. When the Church ceased to be dominant, the state took over. Burials have had to be registered since 1538, during Henry VIII's reign, when Thomas Cromwell organised the keeping of parish registers. The current editor of *Davies' Law of Burial* (see Bibliography) disparages this as a mere 'attempt', but it has proved an extremely valuable institution for genealogists. Copies of parish registers were ordered to be sent to the registrar of the local diocese by an act of 1597, and various other laws were passed in succeeding centuries to regularise the keeping of such registers.

Record-keeping was not the only aspect of bereavement with which the government concerned itself. The relief of the poor was another, and this was funded out of the rates, which were levied locally. Paupers who died were often given quite good funerals at public expense, sometimes even better than those of some of their social superiors: for instance, a pauper's corpse might be buried in a coffin, which few other people used, however wealthy, till the late sixteenth century. However, the coffin in question might be a parish or municipal receptacle which was emptied of its contents for the actual burial and subsequently used over and over again.

In pre-Reformation times there had been town guilds of craftsmen engaged in a particular trade or profession which took care of their members in death as well as in life. Some of these gradually developed into straightforward burial clubs rather than continuing to organise masses for the dead, as they had been concerned to do before. This was particularly the case as that system had been in decline for about a century before the Reformation. There appear also to have been specific burial guilds at parish level.

Not that the burial club was a new idea. In ancient Rome there had been such things; they were called *collegia funeratica* if catering for the lower classes (known in this context as *tenuiores*), such as slaves and freedmen. Others, for more prosperous citizens, were called *sodalica* or *sodalitates*. As in the case of mediaeval England many centuries later, members might follow the same calling or trade or be dependants of the same great family. In Rome, where any excuse for a meal has always been greedily seized on, they often dined together or followed the same religious cult as well.

By the eighteenth century in England, however, fear among the poor of a pauper's funeral had become so strong that burial clubs began to flourish in a state of existential neurosis rather than of *gourmandise* or pious professional solidarity. By paying a few pence a week into a fund, the client guaranteed himself a minimum standard of gentility when it came to being buried, however squalid his animate existence had been. The trouble was, even a few pence a week might be a severe drain on a tiny income.

The eighteenth-century burial clubs had a long pedigree then, as well as becoming in their turn ancestors of the 'pre-need planning' schemes run today by the more enterprising undertakers. What became more systematic and pronounced was the element of insurance, for insurance is commercial provision against possible unpleasantness, in this case the loss of face entailed by pauper burial. It is extraordinary that fear of losing face should have been so strong as to impoverish the already poor still further, particularly as any loss of face for the principal person concerned was going to be posthumous. But there can be no doubt that powerful forces of snobbery were at work.

In earlier times the kind of 'insurance' one had taken out was liturgical: funding the saying of masses to induce repose for one's soul and win a reduced sentence in purgatory. Before the Reformation many pious souls had set up chantry bequests, that is to say foundations willed money by dead benefactors for the saying of masses. During the Reformation, particularly in Edward VI's reign, these proved a useful source of funds for a grasping government and were done away with by legislation. In theory, the money from the chantry foundations was to be used to start useful worldly projects like schools, but in many cases they were simply plundered by some of the unscrupulous men on the make who surrounded the boy king. The process might usefully be compared with the selling off of cemeteries for land development by councils in our own time.

The burial clubs, proletarian self-help's response to the rapine of the two preceding centuries, reached their apogee in the nineteenth century and absorbed a huge percentage of the lower classes' earnings. The principle of stinting yourself in life to ensure decent burial in death was given an immense psychological boost by the 1832 Anatomy Act. This decreed that medical students could legally dissect the body of someone given a pauper's funeral. Before that, knowledge of how the body is put together had to be gathered piecemeal and hugger-mugger, with 'resurrection men' (body-snatchers) slaking the thirst for learning among the scientifically minded. It was claimed at the time that 1,000 coffins a year were broken into for this purpose. As so often happens with legislation, whether worthy in aim or not, the Anatomy Act badly overlooked popular psychology. The masses took fright at the thought of being carved up by bloodthirsty and dissolute youths of the order of Bob Sawyer and Ben Allen in *Pickwick Papers* and poured money they could ill afford into 'respectable' funerals. Unwittingly the government gave employment to the undertaking trade.

As well as laws to regulate record-keeping and the poor, sumptuary legislation invaded death's domain. After the Restoration in 1660, a series of acts were passed under which bodies had to be buried in wrappings of wool if in the form of sheets, shifts, shirts or shrouds, although linen proved more popular. As with similar legislation to promote trade in a particular national product, it is not always easy to say how much compliance there was, particularly as in this case one would have to undertake mass exhumations to be sure of finding out.

The year when the first of these laws about using shrouds of wool was passed – 1666 – may be significant. It was the year after the last severe outbreak of plague. During the great onslaughts of mass pestilence, the dead had sometimes been piled carelessly wrapped or even naked on sleds and taken well away from where the living had their homes. In a very badly hit spot, householders might have to lug the bodies of close relatives to a communal plague pit and toss them in unaided. If plague victims were lucky enough to be buried in the churchyard it was with the minimum expenditure of time and ceremonial. Sometimes too many people had died all at once for the churchyard to be able to provide the space. Nevertheless, most people thought it important to observe the customary decencies towards burial. Yet within a generation or two after the last bout of plague in the 1660s, substantial advances in public health and science generally had been made. This meant that death was beginning to strike people at a fractionally less early age and in a fractionally less repulsive form.

An interesting development in the seventeenth century is the growing popularity of family burial vaults, though these were for the well-to-do only. A more universal development is the rise in the late seventeenth century of the undertaker. The first known member of the breed was one William Boyce, who set up shop in the City of London around 1675 – near Newgate, appropriately enough. The 'profession' had ceased to exist long before, in Roman times. Why did it make its reappearance now? One argument goes that since funerals were now more elaborate it was easier to get one person in to organise everything. That does not hold much water: the hugely complex heraldic funerals that were the fashion for great families (see the section on Bereavement in High Life) had flourished a century earlier and were now in comparative decline. Certainly funerals were to become more elaborate again, even when they were not organised under the laws of chivalry and heraldry, but that was chiefly in the nineteenth century. Possibly one should look upon the resurgence of the undertaking trade as just one of several 'modern' institutions which started up in the late seventeenth century, sometimes under growing economic pressure to specialise: insurance companies, banks, the national debt, coffee houses, newspapers, a postal service, Hackney carriages, gentlemen's clubs. The burial clubs and those who catered to them professionally were in a sense part of the insurance industry, too.

It was not till the eighteenth century that there were substantial advances in public health, and these in turn brought a drop in the death rate and a corresponding massive population increase. In 1700 the population of England and Wales stood at something like 5,500,000, whereas a hundred years earlier it had been perhaps 4,000,000. This was an increase of 37.5 per cent. But that increase could not be attributed to any great improvements in public health and longevity between 1600 and the end of the century. In contrast, by 1800 the population had risen to around 9,000,000, an increase of just over 80 per cent on that of 1700. Migration had little to do with the matter since immigration was more or less balanced by emigration. The immediate cause of the population growth in the eighteenth century was a slightly increased birth rate and a greatly reduced death rate, but these in turn were only possible because of advances in medical knowledge. Inoculation against smallpox and other scourges was introduced to Britain from the Ottoman Empire by Lady Mary Wortley Montagu (1689–1762), the eldest daughter of the Duke of Kingston and wife of the British ambassador to the Sublime Porte. At the end of the century, Edward Jenner (1749–1823) introduced the practice of vaccination.

One could make a plausible case for arguing that as soon as humanity began to glimpse the possibility of doing something about its own tendency to die young it became more sensitive, more concerned – more 'caring', as the modern cant term has it. In our own time, as we have improved in turn on the nineteenth and early twentieth centuries in terms of public health, we have even begun to get squeamish. A development parallel to the improvement in medical science in the eighteenth century was philanthropy. Coram's Hospital for Foundlings (that is, abandoned, usually illegitimate, children) was started up in 1745, together with another 153 hospitals proper, such as Guy's, the Westminster, the Middlesex and St George's, between 1700 and 1825. The eighteenth century also witnessed the flourishing of individual philanthropists in Dr Johnson, James Oglethorpe, Jonas Hanway, Robert Nelson and the brothers Charles and John Wesley. Previously there had been a broad tendency to let the living take care of themselves, since with survival so uncertain a man's reward was in heaven, not in this vale of tears we call life. Now it seemed possible to do something about the vale of tears – perhaps not to the extent of being able to drain it of its salt water content altogether, but certainly to ameliorate the dampness – and although religious belief remained strong it underwent a transformation away from passive acceptance of one's lot.

Changes in mourning fashion paralleled changes in vital statistics. In the seventeenth century a bereaved married woman might wear black for years after her husband had died, rather like the war widows in France this century. A hundred years later, the idea of semi-mourning took hold, with the bereaved adopting a costume somewhere between the all-out style of full mourning and ordinary dress.

As the birds were pretty plentiful, and partridge-shooting is, as it were, the duty of an English gentleman of statesmanlike propensities, Sir Pitt Crawley, the first shock of grief over [occasioned by his father's death in mid-September of the same year], went out a little and partook of that diversion in a white hat with a crape round it.

Thackeray, Vanity Fair, *writing of the year 1822*

The partridge season starts on 1 September and the birds aren't likely to remain plentiful for long after that date, so Sir Pitt's period of full mourning was pretty brief. Crape, a dead black material so matt it reflected virtually no light at all, was the nineteenth-century mourning fabric *par excellence*.

The feather tray became a feature of funeral processions. This was a flat sheet of wood on which stood black ostrich feathers, and in the nineteenth century no self-respecting family in mourning would have done without it. Early in the century, those who had carriages started sending them to wait outside the town house of an acquaintance who had recently died. Often, the carriage was empty because the owner was prevented by social usage from calling in person. In *Vanity Fair*, the neighbouring gentry of Hampshire send empty carriages to jog along in the funeral procession of old Sir Pitt to the churchyard at Queen's Crawley, so the custom was not confined to town. A household in mourning might shut its doors to all except the very closest members of the family and in general women stayed away from funerals until fairly late in the nineteenth century.

Yet for all the advances in public health and life expectancy, the outlook for a majority of the population remained extremely grim well into the century. As recently as the 1830s, just before the first set of reasonably accurate vital statistics was compiled following the 1836 Births and Deaths Registration Act, the average working-class person died at twenty-two. The petit bourgeois had a slightly better longevity, dying on average at the age of twenty-five. Even the upper classes could not on average expect to live beyond forty-four. This becomes a particularly gloomy picture when you consider that in Greece during the last few millennia before the birth of Christ a woman lived on average for between twenty-nine and thirty-eight years (the first figure being the norm for the late Stone Age and the second for the last few centuries BC), while a man lived on average to between thirty-three (again late Stone Age) and forty-four (classical era, i.e., sixth and fifth centuries BC). The average age for both sexes at death actually came down by four or five years in Greece during the centuries in which the Roman Empire flourished, though, unlike today, men continued to live longer than women. (Safer medical techniques to help childbirth are responsible for the change.)

Given that the early Victorians were actually worse off in this regard than the very ancient Greeks – just as Greeks during the Roman principate were worse off than when they were independent city states – it is tempting to suppose that empire-building generally, whether undertaken by Italians a couple of thousand years ago or Britons under William IV and Queen Victoria, was a hazardous game, actuarially speaking.

The really stark contrast is not so much between the nineteenth century and preceding ones as between then and our own age in the second half of the twentieth. The atrocious mortality rates of all times before our own meant that few people died in old age, and even when they did they died in the bosom of their families rather than in nursing homes, hospices or sheltered housing, as happens today. This in turn meant that death was far more immediate and could less easily be swept under the carpet.

The Victorians may have been good at sweeping many things under the carpet, but by and large not death. Instead they embraced it. Perhaps they dimly discerned that they had no choice. Never had funeral processions and fancifully designed mausolea in cemeteries been so elaborate; never had the careful distinction between full mourning and half mourning been so nearly theological in its nit-picking concern with minutiae (though one should remember that at sixteenth-century heraldic funerals the distinction between the mourning colours of violet and black for city worthies and livery-company members depended on whether they were personally close to the deceased or just acquaintances in the way of business). Then there were the mutes, the black horses with their nodding plumes, and the black-edged writing paper and envelopes. Perhaps most remarkable of all was the flourishing art, both literary and graphic, of the ghastly, the morbid, the horrific. The Gothic genre had started in the eighteenth century but with few exceptions in a slightly camp, insipid way. Gothic architecture, novels and painting before the Victorian age were insubstantial and picturesque compared with the meaty, pungent, vigorous and acrid products of early to high industrialism.

Mind you, individual Victorians could occasionally hide their heads in the sand as firmly as any modern-day ostrich where death was concerned. President Teddy Roosevelt of the USA, that apostle of bull-necked extroversion and the strenuous life generally, could not bring himself ever again to mention his first wife to his family after her sudden death in 1884. And in 1901, the details of Queen Victoria's funeral had not been properly thought out beforehand, although the old lady was in her eighty-second year when she died. Fritz Ponsonby, her private secretary, tells us in his memoirs that this was because the court feared it would seem morbid.

The lack of preparation was astounding. The Queen had commissioned marble statues of herself and Prince Albert, both in a supine position, from the Italian master Baron Carlo Marochetti forty years earlier. When it came to burying Her Majesty, the one of Victoria was nowhere to be found. The clerk of the works at Windsor claimed never even to have heard of it. Others expressed doubts as to whether the work had ever been carried out. There was some justification for this as the commission was Marochetti's last and, although he did complete it, the two effigies had not been moved from his studio at his death. When the statue of the Queen was at last found it was behind a wall which had been constructed thirty-six years earlier. So it seems that despite the Victorian passion for mourning, there could be just as much reluctance to confront death by making proper preparations as there is today. Yet within a few years a popular writer like Saki could write about a newly bereaved widow declaring only on black suits when playing bridge. Jokes about death had been more heavy-handed in the high Victorian age.

We associate the Victorian age with fogs that blocked out the sun, soot, coal fires and coal-fired steam engines on the railways, dark Satanic mills and grimy heavy industries, to say nothing of the mourning cult which made almost a fetish out of jet beads, inky ostrich feathers and swart bombazine dresses. The finest jet came from around Whitby. Could that be why Bram Stoker has Dracula land there when he arrives in England?

Given this preponderance of black, it comes as a surprise to discover that as late as the nineteenth century white was in relatively common use for mourning. In early Victorian times white was used for the sash and 'weepers' (bands of cloth twisted round the top hat with loose ends falling down behind) worn by a funeral attendant if the deceased was a child or young girl. The stave carried by the funeral attendant would in such cases also be covered in a white cloth. A dead child's pall, though mostly of black, might have a white border. White gloves might be put on too and in some parts of Britain there was a touching little custom at funerals of young girls for another girl about the same age as the deceased to bear a chaplet of flowers or white paper twisted and shaped to look like flowers ahead of the coffin and then hang it up over the place in church where the dead girl had used to sit during divine service. Sometimes a pair of white gloves would be placed inside the chaplet. That arch-devotee of the nineteenth-century mourning cult Queen Victoria ensured that following her own death the satin pall was basically white, though adorned with colours in embroidery. White might also be used for its very contrast with black, for instance to depict a cross on a black pall.

Where the Victorians deserve every credit is in the practical steps they took to limit death's impact. In 1836 the Births and Deaths Registration Act had put the whole business on a national footing but it was not till 1874 that the entire body of legislation for England was consolidated under another Births and Deaths Registration Act. The latter makes it compulsory to register not just every death but also its cause.

The increase in population generally and crowded conditions in cities specifically made legislation dealing with burial grounds necessary. The institution of the cemetery began to catch on as churchyards filled up. Kensal Green, for instance, the first major cemetery in London, was opened in 1832, the year of the Great Reform Bill. Within a few years, cemetery burial came to be regarded as an indication of wealth. Because cemeteries were laid out in virgin territory it was possible to site them well away from ordinary human habitation. Under an act of 1847 a commercially run cemetery was obliged to lie a minimum of 200 yards from the nearest house. This was brought down to 100 yards in 1906. In 1972, all restrictions as to distance were swept away as far as England and Wales were concerned but in Scotland the 100-yards distance is still in force. Unlike cemeteries, crematoria must still be sited 200 yards or more from the nearest private dwelling house unless the owner, lessee and occupier of that dwelling house gives his permission in writing for a nearer position. Moreover, crematoria must not be closer to the public highway than 50 yards, nor must they be built in any part whatsoever of a local council's burial ground if that part is consecrated.

In this context 'consecrated' refers only to Church of England burial grounds. If someone in the nineteenth century wanted to get a private grave or burial ground consecrated he had to get a private act of Parliament passed, which was a very expensive affair. Burial grounds laid out for the use of their own people by atheists, dissenting Christians, Quakers and Jews were not covered by the acts determining the distance from a dwelling house.

In the nineteenth century the very economic success of Britain was a threat to life. Industrialisation and crowded living conditions undermined public health; cholera, typhus, typhoid, diphtheria flourished. Fear of catching cholera was so great that its victims were sometimes buried as little as ten minutes after dying. Not until the 1870s did the death rate decline noticeably further from the eighteenth-century figure, for only at that time did the Public Health Act of 1848 start to be properly administered. This came about as a result of the Local Government Board being established. Then too there was the rise of reforming municipal leaders such as Joseph Chamberlain, mayor of Birmingham and the father of Neville Chamberlain, prime minister just before the Second World War. But even now not everywhere was as advanced as Birmingham. Mass starvation could still afflict parts of the then British Isles where a relatively dense, poverty-stricken population scraped a living from too little land, witness the potato famine in

Ireland and the less well known but nevertheless devastating potato blight in the western Highlands of Scotland.

Cremation in Britain was not made legal till towards the end of the nineteenth century, in 1885 to be precise. The pre-Reformation Christian Church had pronounced cremation a pagan ritual as far back as the eighth century, but among Roman Catholics it was only actually forbidden just after it had been legalised in Britain. To begin with it took some time to catch on among the British and as late as 1902 there were only seven crematoria nationwide and 431 cremations in a single year, whereas in the 1890s there were about 550,000 burials annually. By the end of the first decade of the twentieth century there were thirteen crematoria throughout the country, though in the year 1909 the number of crema-tions, at 855, was still less than 1,000 and only represented 0.14 per cent of all disposals after death.

It is since the end of the Second World War that cremation has really taken off, the numbers of people being cremated rising by between 1 and 2 per cent each year. By the mid-1990s, cremations were outnumbering burials by more than 2–1, or some 430,000–440,000 cases to 200,000. This country is still far ahead of most others in its use of cremation, though available statistics relate to Great Britain (England, Scotland and Wales) only, not Northern Ireland, where burial remains popular hence would probably push down the overall UK figure for cremations as a percentage of disposals.

Population density combined with religion seems to explain why cremation is more popular in one country than another. Japan heads the league, with 97.1 per cent of all dead being cremated. But given the very different culture of Japan it is only in Europe that a more reasonable comparison with the UK can be made. Belgium is as densely populated, yet cremation there is very much a minority activity (19.9 per cent). Belgium is a pious Catholic country, more so than France, where cremations constitute 6.14 per cent of all disposals. France, of course, is much larger and less densely populated than Belgium or Britain. Italy, which pioneered the revival of cremation in the nineteenth century – under the influence of the Risorgimento, with its enthusiastic looking back to classical times, it has been argued – is the only European country to cremate a smaller proportion of its dead than the Republic of Ireland, although the latter is, from my observation, a more pious Catholic country.

In the USA they are not too keen on cremation either (17.02 per cent), but then it is a huge country. About a quarter of the American population is reckoned to be Catholic, so that might have something to do with the infrequency of cremation. But non-Catholic Christian church buildings outnumber Catholic ones (it is inaccurate to call Protestant all the non-Catholic sects in the USA that invoke the name of Jesus). And 'dissenting' Protestants (as they would be called in British tradition), particularly Baptists, predominate in the more conservative southern states, so on a nationwide basis any prevalence of Catholicism cannot be held responsible for cremation's lack of popularity.

On the other hand, the first crematorium in the USA was put into operation in 1876, ten years before Britain allowed them. Easily the most common method of disposing of the dead in America, however, is to embalm them and then bury them. Embalming became all the rage after Lincoln's assassination in 1865, when the presidential corpse was first stuffed with preservatives then trundled by train west from Washington DC to Springfield, Illinois, much as that other legendary wartime leader Alexander the Great's had been from Babylon to North Africa by covered wagon over 2,000 years earlier. Embalming has never fallen seriously out of favour since. It is odd to think that present-day American mortuary customs owe their existence to John Wilkes Booth.

I have already suggested that the divide between the Victorians and ourselves was not as stark as might be thought.

The enduring popularity of Gothic films, novels and even pictures surely binds us in a continuous line to our ancestors. But much of this is a pretty-pretty view of death. Beautiful women declining pallidly, as if from successive sucks of the vampire's fangs, make tuberculosis sexy. So does Violetta's wonderfully tearjerking career in *La Traviata*. Perhaps this is because so few people die of tuberculosis nowadays. Yet the film *Love Story* in the early 1970s did much the same with leukaemia, and that disease is still horribly with us. In reality, tuberculosis is not much nicer a thing to die of than leukaemia.

It may be that in this field the Victorians had the advantage over us, using vague terms like 'she fell into a fatal consumption' or 'he succumbed to an apopleptic seizure' where we would use slightly more clinical language. On the other hand, today's newspapers always say of someone that she 'lost her battle with' cancer, as if everyone everywhere fought tooth and nail to hang on to life. Yet many people, particularly the elderly, can be observed surrendering to death. So in some ways we are just as guilty of euphemisms as the Victorians.

Social changes regarding death may lag behind advances in medicine and public health. It is only since 1945 that most deaths have not occurred at home. Even in America, where to consume medicine is as expensive as to practise it is respectable, half the population were meeting their death in hospitals as late as the middle of the century. If one did not know this one would tend to think of the domestic deathbed scene as purely Victorian. In fact it must have been common, particularly in out-of-the-way regions of Britain, well into the 1930s.

In 1940s Britain state intervention became the fashion. It even muscled in on bereavement, and from 1946 to 1987 the government made a death grant to help people pay for their relatives' funerals. This too had a precursor.

A similar system had been instituted by the Roman Emperor Nerva, who reigned from AD 96 to 98 and decreed that all Romans should be paid a burial subsidy. Professor

Morris (see chapters on ancient Greek and Roman customs), who is usually so ready to see things in context, looking judiciously at every side of the matter, calls this a piece of sucking up to the underprivileged. But might it not equally have been a far-sighted, public-spirited, liberal and statesman-like piece of legislation? What is true of Attlee ought in fairness to be held true of Nerva.

Today, impoverished widows, widowers and lovers, provided these last are of the opposite sex to the deceased, can claim a grant from the Social Fund to meet the costs of their spouse's or lover's funeral. The DSS doesn't put it like that, of course. It talks of 'partners', but defines 'partner' in any role outside marriage as 'the person they live with as though they were married', which would seem to rule out homosexual lovers. The homosexual lover of a deceased person might in practice quality for a grant as the person responsible for arranging the funeral, so it could be argued that exclusion of homosexuals from the category of 'partner' as recognised by the DSS has no practical significance. Homosexual rights campaigners concerned over matters of principle might very well think differently, however. So far no test case has been brought.

The grant is subject to a means test, and the DSS must be convinced that no other person such as a close relative could have borne the expense. The deceased must have been a UK resident and the funeral must take place in the UK. Payments include help with flowers and meeting special requirements of the deceased's religion.

If you need private financial help to pay for a funeral you could try approaching any charities the deceased had links with, such as ex-servicemen's organisations. The precise conditions for getting help from the Social Fund are spelled out in Notes Sheet SF 200, available from any benefits agency. Most social security offices now have a bereavement officer who will help the bereaved claim the appropriate benefits. The better ones offer a private room to discuss these matters which has been booked in advance, thus saving the indigent from having to queue, even if they turn up without an appointment. If a war pensioner dies from his wound or disablement, whether directly or while being treated for it in hospital, or even of something else, provided he was entitled to constant attendance allowance, his personal representative can apply to the state to cover the cost of a simple funeral.

In the 1960s improvements in the technique of manufacturing chipboard meant that coffins came increasingly to be constructed of this unloveliest of materials. Its beauty from the undertaker's point of view was that with a lavish application of varnish it could be made to resemble wood of far costlier provenance. Nevertheless, the cost of conventional funerals is rising steeply in the mid-1990s. Simultaneously there is growing interest in eco-friendly funerals (see the section Go It Alone), including biodegradable coffins, coffins the customer can make for himself, coffins painted in bright colours and the abandonment of coffins altogether in favour of folding wickerwork or just plain shrouds.

In the last few years for which statistics are available, the number of cremations has actually decreased in Britain. That in itself doesn't mean much, for one would have to look at the changing religious and demographic profile of the country before drawing any solid conclusions. Much more interesting is the decline of cremation as a percentage of all disposals, from 69.6 per cent in 1990 to 69.5 in 1991 to 69.2 in 1992. Could the growing enthusiasm for 'green' burial in the garden or, if in a cemetery, beneath a tree, have something to do with it? We have already seen two instances of a wholesale change in methods of disposing of the dead within a couple of generations: cremation to burial in Rome of the second century AD and the other way round in twentieth-century Britain. Change in funerary customs, when it comes, can be swift.

PART II

Religious Attitudes

Introduction

It is something of a paradox that whereas those who have been settled in Britain for many generations tend to be less keen on traditional religious observance (including funerals), newer arrivals are more conservative about their customs and keener about keeping them up. The United Kingdom is one of the least religious countries in Europe, indeed the world, if active church membership is reckoned the test. Of course, the exact criterion for active membership varies from country to country and culture to culture. In Finland, for example, they judge active church membership according to whether people have voted in church council elections, whereas the Roman Catholic Church tends to measure membership by attendance at mass, a yardstick which would put Catholics ahead of Anglicans in the UK.

Again, figures for Baptists and Pentecostalists are supplied to the statisticians by the Baptists and Pentecostalists themselves. Accordingly such figures tend to reflect only the number of Baptists and Pentecostalists who have undergone full adult baptism, for those denominations believe that baptising children is meaningless to the mites concerned since they can have no possible understanding of how solemn a ceremony it is. Therefore regular attendance at Baptist and Pentecostalist religious ceremonies may be much greater than the official figures suggest.

Moreover, there are discrepancies, some of them substantial, between (a) the data given in *Britain 1993*, published by the Central Office of Information, (b) the Central Statistical Office figures, (c) those of the Christian Research Association as given in the latest edition of *Social Trends*, (d) those in the *Multi-Faith Directory: Religions in the UK* and (e) those in the *UK Christian Handbook* for 1994–5. I shall call them *COI*, *CSO*, *CRA*, *M-FD* and *UKCH* respectively, and put them in brackets after the appropriate figures to denote which source gives which. As you can see, it is only if you make certain mental reservations that you can point to the UK as having a mere 15 per cent active church membership among adults in 1990 (*CRA* – the latest year for which figures are available) and the Irish Republic as having the most active church membership in Europe, with 81 per cent (*CRA*) of the adult population involved.

Even within the UK there is a marked difference in attendance figures, not just between individual denominations but between ethnic groups. For instance, the Caucasians (anthropologist-speak for white folk) in the United Kingdom are slack about going to church – around 91 per cent never bother (*CRA*, 1989 figures) – but Afro-Caribbeans are much more pious, to the tune of over 16 per cent (*CRA*) attending a church regularly. As one might expect, teenagers have become less and less punctilious about church attendance over the last ten years, though children under the age of fifteen, who are presumably dragged to divine service by their parents, attend in about the same numbers as ten years ago.

If instead of looking at active membership one measures the much looser notion of affiliation to some sort of creed, the position of the Church of England (C of E) looks a lot rosier than is suggested above for Anglicans, with 46 per cent (*CRA*) of the population calling themselves C of E in 1992 (the latest year for which figures are available), even though this represents a slow but steady decline over the preceding twenty years. Roman Catholics looked to be holding steady at 10 per cent (*CRA*) of the population between 1970 and 1992, but the exodus from the C of E in the last year or two in the wake of that body's decision to ordain women priests will surely have boosted Roman Catholic membership at the expense of the C of E. A Catholic priest I spoke to in late 1994 put the figure at only a few thousand so far, though. It is somewhat absurd that there has been no *official* attempt to ferret out figures for religious affiliation on a national scale since the Census of Public Worship of 1851. Apart from anything else, the UK then was a much more homogeneous place, religiously speaking, so was in less need of such a survey than it is today.

When the *CRA* compiled the 1989 figures for church membership in the UK they divided churches into Trinitarian, Non-Trinitarian and Other Religions (Islam, Judaism etc.). It is not clear to me that this has much utility from a statistical point of view, though I can see that it does from a doctrinal or theological one. At any rate, it seems that in 1992 (again the latest year for which figures are available), the C of E and other members of the Anglican Communion (Church of Ireland in Northern Ireland, for instance, and Scottish Episcopal Church north of the border on the British mainland) could boast 1,810,000 adult members. But Roman Catholics were ahead by nearly 13 per cent, with 2,040,000 active members, and had been leading the established church in this regard since at least the mid-1970s, especially as Anglicanism is not the established church in Scotland, Wales or Northern Ireland but only in England. Next came the Presbyterians, with 1,240,000 members, then the Methodists, with 460,000, then the Orthodox (the *CRA* lumped Greek and Russian Orthodox together, it would seem) with 280,000 and the Baptists with 230,000. The other free churches (for example, the Free Church of Scotland and Scottish Free Presbyterians) were also aggregated by the *CRA* researchers and could boast about 660,000 members between them.

Among the denominations gathered together under the label Non-Trinitarian were the adherents of the Church of

Latter Day Saints (popularly known as the Mormons, though they themselves prefer the lengthier version), with 150,000 members, the Jehovah's Witnesses, with 130,000, and the Spiritualists, with 40,000. The rest of the Non-Trinitarian bunch, which presumably comprised such relatively well-known groups as the Quakers, Christian Scientists and Unitarians, as well as many more obscure sects, accounted for 140,000 members. Harvey Gillman, in his booklet *A Light That is Shining*, reprinted with amendments in January 1994, says there are around 18,000 Quakers in Britain and Ireland. Altogether Christians numbered 37,000,000 (*M-FD*) or 37,600,000 (*UKCH*).

Of the Other Religions, the Muslims were easily first, with 520,000 members (*CRA*, 1992), 990,000 (*CSO*, 1990), 1,100,000 (*COI, UKCH* 1994–5) or 1,500,000 (*M-FD*), depending on which source and date of source you refer to. Whichever figure you prefer, they number more than any other single religious group apart from the Anglicans, the Roman Catholics and the Presbyterians. But of course if you break down the leading Christian denominations it seems only reasonable to try to do so with the Muslims. There are Sunni Muslims as well as Shi'ites, to say nothing of Ismaili Muslims, who look to the Aga Khan as their spiritual leader and number about 11,000 people in the UK. After the Muslims came Sikhs, with 270,000 members (*CRA*, 1992), 300,000 (*COI*, 1993), 390,000 (*CSO*, 1990), 400,000 (*M-FD*) or 500,000 (*UKCH* 1994–5); then Hindus, with 140,000 members (the *CRA* for 1992 and *CSO* for 1990 agree for once), 300,000 (*COI*, 1993), 400,000 (*M-FD* and *UKCH* 1994–5); then Jews (again, no distinction was drawn between Orthodox, Reform, Liberal etc.), with 110,000 (*CRA*, 1992), 111,000 (*CSO*, 1990) or 300,000 (*COI*, 1993; *M-FD*; *UKCH* 1994–5).

M-FD mentioned 120,00 Buddhists, which the other sources entirely overlooked. Buddhists may leave the impression with other people that they are modest and temperate to the point of being self-effacing, but surely not to such an extent that one can 'lose' 120,000 of them between one survey and the next. The *COI* for 1993 and *M-FD* gave a figure of 30,000 for Jains and 5,000 (*COI*, 1993) for Bahá'ís (*M-FD*, 6,000). All other sects, presumably including humanists and possibly even followers of Isis and devotees of Wicca, came to 80,000 (*CRA*, 1992), 23,000 (*CSO*, 1990) or 300,000 (*UKCH* 1994–5) – quite a discrepancy, this last category. *The Times* in late September 1994 reported that there were thought to be about 250,000 British pagans. Since Wiccans claim to be the largest group in the Pagan Federation, accounting for half its entire membership, and are credited with as many as 10,000 followers, this suggests that the Pagan Federation has about 20,000 members. That leaves as many as 230,000 possible pagans unrepresented in any umbrella organisation. *M-FD* alone gave figures for Zoroastrians: 6,000. Not quite as difficult to ignore as the Buddhists, but certainly not negligible.

In general, the differences are so great between one source and another, or even between the same source for two different dates only a couple of years apart, that I wonder if there is accuracy to within even 40 per cent.

Britain is not just a multi-cultural and multi-denominational country but is becoming less and less compartmentalised as regards religion. Thus within a single family there may be a great variety both of funeral practices and attitudes towards bereavement. The close relatives of one friend of mine, for instance, include within a single generation a Catholic woman who was born Anglican but married a Pole and converted; her sister, who is still nominally Anglican but in practice veers between strong sympathy for Hinduism and rather vaguer types of New Age mysticism; their cousin, who is Jewish; and the rest of the family, who vary between humanism and a lukewarm Anglicanism. Buddhism has made inroads into some British families of staunch Anglican origin who a century ago would have professed an intellectualist agnosticism. Many of the great English Jewish families of the nineteenth century have latterly ceased to practise their ancestral religion and married out of the faith. Some members of families which have for many generations professed Roman Catholicism have intensified their doctrinal and liturgical conservatism. Yet the Roman Catholic Church in general has become more liberal in ceremonial matters. Other Catholics have joined up with the 'born-again' brand of Christianity, or simply lapsed. The former pop singer Cat Stevens is the best-known modern male Briton to have converted to Islam – the current (8th) Earl of Yarborough has done so too – but quite a few British women have converted following marriage to Muslims.

Since a death in the family often brings together relatives who may have lost touch with each other long ago, even if only briefly, it is as well to know something of the different beliefs and practices your relations may hold, either now or in the future. Rodney Dennys, in his book *Heraldry and the Heralds*, gives a good example of the sort of awkwardness that can arise. Sir Winston Churchill's funeral was going to be so elaborate that the authorities decreed it should take place on a Saturday, otherwise the disruption to London traffic would be intolerable. What nobody seems to have considered until late in the day was what this would mean for the President of Israel, an Orthodox Jew who could not possibly use a car on the Sabbath, even to get to St Paul's Cathedral for a service of international lustre. Churchill had been a famous Zionist, which makes it all the more disgraceful that nobody seems to have considered the problem in advance. It also gave the matter particular emotional resonance.

Here, then, are how the various religious denominations throughout Britain usually conduct the funeral rites of one of their members, though I must stress that the following accounts are outlines only, whether of beliefs or rituals. If you wish to find out more about any one religion and its attitude to bereavement, go and attend services yourself, study the specialised literature on that religion and talk to a priest or other adept. Moreover, there will sometimes be departures from strict practice in specific cases. For instance, such-and-such a funeral might be organised by a maverick celebrant and/or a wayward congregation, or perhaps the necessary equipment, expertise or knowledge of ritual might not be available to the adherents of a given faith in this country at the time of the death of one of their number, for example because they have only arrived here recently.

Because it would be invidious to list denominations in order of their numbers of adherents anyway – and in this particular case it would be downright arbitrary as there is so little agreement about numbers – I have chosen alphabetical order. It is fortunate that the C of E comes first (being listed under A for Anglicanism), less because of the historical reason that it is the established Church than because what I have to say in the section on it is also valid for funerals conducted under the rites of other denominations, e.g., advice about handling coffins, cemetery and crematoria services and memorials.

It is amazing how many similarities there are in funeral rites and bereavement practices between religions that one would otherwise think had no points in common historically, doctrinally or in land of origin. I don't think this is chiefly because there are only a finite number of ways of disposing of a corpse – burial, cremation, embalming and exposure – though that undoubtedly has some bearing on the matter. Even in little things there are astounding parallels. In the Christian tradition of mediaeval England and post-Reformation Catholicism up to a few decades ago, repeat funeral rites used to be conducted, first seven days after the initial funeral then thirty days afterwards. Compare the Jewish practice of having two mourning periods of seven days and thirty days respectively. Again, in mediaeval England the dead were buried with their feet pointing towards the east so that at the Resurrection they could walk in that direction. Several non-Christian religions lay down similar rules for burial. Ultimately, humans are very much like one another at this most stressful moment in life.

Anglicans

It is possible to be an Anglican and hold the belief (more common among Catholics) that God has power beyond the grave to wash away sins and lift the deceased person into His presence. Hence prayers for the dead are in order. More evangelically minded Anglicans would argue that you earn eternal life by your behaviour on this earth, behaviour that is in accordance with true faith. Such people reject the practice of praying for the dead on the grounds that it is not warranted in scripture.

Every parishioner has a right to burial in his local churchyard, either intact or as cremated remains. The same goes for anyone on the church electoral roll or even a person who simply happens to die in the parish. Unfortunately, many churchyards are full up these days. But the vicar is obliged to hold a funeral service in the local authority-run cemetery for any of his Anglican flock or Anglicans who die within his parochial boundaries. Conversely, anyone who dies in England or Wales, of whatever religious denomination, has a right to burial according to Anglican rites provided they have been baptised and are not excommunicated. The baptism can have been performed according to the rites of any sect.

The local vicar has the final say in what rites are used. A friend of a friend of mine died last year from an overdose of heroin. He had been an addict for some years but had recently been weaned off the stuff. Not sufficiently, it seems, for after being discharged from the treatment centre he rapidly returned to his former ways, which included male prostitution to fund drug purchases.

He was given what they call a 'happy-clappy' memorial service for 'born-again' Christians in an Anglican church (Holy Trinity, Brompton, in London), although he was originally from a working-class non-Anglican Protestant background in Coleraine, Northern Ireland. The evangelist in charge told the congregation that God had loved Gerald so much that it was time for him to go to heaven. The altar was decorated with photographs of the deceased and every time the word 'Jesus' was mentioned the congregation bellowed back His name in echoing unison. A friend of mine in the congregation was a little distracted by an over-excited woman jumping up on her pew from time to time throughout the service.

But the more usual practice is for your vicar to conduct the service using the intensely modern Series 3 from the Alternative Service Book, though even here hymns, the family's favourite prayers, a reading from some non-liturgical work of literature and an address are optional extras. Series 3 is a replacement of the 1928 Prayer Book and has been introduced over the last ten years, though not till after a good deal of heated debate.

If the vicar is high church he might celebrate a requiem at which Communion is taken. Women attending such a ceremony should wear a covering to the head, either a hat or a mantilla, as with a Catholic funeral. If the vicar is low church, he might content himself with hymns and an address to the congregation. It may well have become more difficult to get hold of a copy of the traditional Prayer Book than of the Series 3, so I shall summarise the older office here for the sake of Anglican readers of riper years whose memories may be pleasantly jogged by a reminder of its sublime simplicity, and for the sake of younger ones, to let them know what they are missing.

The service starts at the entrance to the churchyard with the priest and his clerks speaking or singing from the King James version of the Bible – 'I am the resurrection and the life' (St John xi, 25–6); 'I know that my Redeemer liveth' (Job xix, 25–7); 'We brought nothing into this world and it is certain we

can carry nothing out' (1 Timothy vi, 7; Job i, 21). It then
continues inside the church with Psalm xxxix (*Dixi, custodiam*)
or Psalm xc (*Domine, refugium*), or both. Then the lesson (1
Corinthians xv, 20) is read. Then, by the graveside, the priest
would say or sing together with his clerks the passage beginning 'Man that is born of a woman' (often misquoted as 'Man
that is born of woman'). Then the priest would recite the
passage beginning 'Forasmuch as it hath pleased Almighty
God of his great mercy to take unto himself the soul of our
dear brother/sister . . .' while earth is scattered on the coffin.
Shortly after would follow the Lord's Prayer and a little later
the Collect, interspersed with recitals by the priest and culminating in the prayer 'The grace of our Lord Jesus Christ, and
the love of God, and the fellowship of the Holy Ghost, be with
us all evermore. Amen.'

Your vicar is also in charge of the actual order in which the
constituent parts of the funeral service are spoken, chanted or
sung. The normal procedure is for the coffin to be carried into
the church while the congregation and officiating cleric speak
the appropriate lines of the Series 3 service. It is possible for
you to have the coffin brought into the church the day before
the funeral (placing the coffin there for the entire night before
the requiem tends to be a high-church custom) or shortly
before the service, but you must obtain permission in advance
from the vicar. If you do this, you should ensure that the coffin
is placed with its occupant's feet facing the altar, though the
undertakers will almost certainly know this and arrange it
themselves. The only exception to this rule is if it is the vicar
himself who has died, in which case his coffin is placed the
other way round, as if he were still alive and facing his
congregation from the altar rails, as he did when conducting
services in life. The coffin is not usually placed resting on the
floor but on supports. These may be special trestles or stools
or chairs. There is a standard article of antique furniture,
usually dating from the sixteenth or seventeenth centuries,

constructed for this purpose and called a coffin stool.

After the exchange of responses between cleric and congregation, a psalm is usually sung, then perhaps a hymn, then the lesson is read from the Bible, then there is another hymn. You can, however, cut the hymns to one if you wish, or even to none at all. While the coffin is borne by pall-bearers down the nave and out of the church, the congregation may sing the *Nunc Dimittis* ('Now lettest thy servant depart in peace', as it used to be translated). At this stage of the funeral the pall-bearers may be selected from among friends and relatives of the deceased.

If you are organising the pall-bearing stage of the operations, remember to choose people of more or less equal size and strength. Technically, the term pall-bearer applies only to those who hold the edges of the pall, well away from the coffin, as happened in the past, but in modern times it is used of those who actually bear the coffin on their shoulders. If you do not take care over this, the burden will lurch lopsidedly along the aisle, giving a most undignified appearance. Inquire of all your potential pall-bearers whether they have recently sustained any injuries to their hands, forearms or shoulders. I was a pall-bearer at the funeral of the distinguished poet George Macbeth and was assigned the rear near-side position (the back left-hand position of six as you look down on the coffin from above). This, of course, meant that the physical strain was predominantly on my right shoulder, but the manual dexterity necessary to hold the coffin there was to be provided by my left hand. Unfortunately the peer of the realm who was taking the other side of the coffin had recently lost a finger or two from his right hand. Accordingly there was a mildly unseemly reshuffling of assigned places just as we were bending down to lift the coffin.

If the deceased has died of some wasting disease the burden on pall-bearers is likely to be fairly light. Nevertheless, many bereaved persons who have organised a relative's funeral themselves rather than hand it over to professionals say how surprisingly heavy the coffin can be, even when it is that of a frail old lady. If the deceased was a 20-stone bear of a man who was killed instantly, he could prove more than a match for amateur pall-bearers such as friends and relatives, particularly if his coffin is made of one of the heavier woods. Do bear this in mind when considering using non-professionals to carry him from the church, however affectionate a send-off it may appear when planning the ceremony beforehand.

It has become rather the fashion to denigrate undertakers, but some of their professional skills are genuine. In 1965 Sir Winston Churchill's corpse was sealed in lead, which was in turn placed inside an oak coffin. The whole thing weighed over a quarter of a ton. Undertakers had brought it to the lying in state in Westminster Hall, so no layman had any idea of what a burden it would be for the military bearer party which was to carry it from the catafalque to the gun carriage for the procession to St Paul's Cathedral. A run-through lifting of the coffin was attempted at a rehearsal the night before the funeral proper. The bearer party – six burly foot soldiers in the flower of their manhood and at that peak of physical fitness which the army rightly induces in its recruits – simply could not lift it. They had to be shown the technique by the undertakers' men. The next day they very nearly stumbled when carrying the coffin down the steps of St Paul's after the service, even though by now the organisers had prudently increased the number of guardsmen to eight.

What happens next depends on whether you are having the deceased buried or cremated. Let us first assume you have decided on burial, or inhumement as it is sometimes more pompously called (from the Latin *humus*, meaning earth). The funeral cortège will proceed either into the churchyard just outside where the funeral proper has been held or to a cemetery. In either case the grave will have been dug beforehand. (As with the coffin in the church, if it is the local vicar whose funeral is taking place, its occupant may be placed facing the other way from the graves of ordinary parishioners.) A small pile of earth will usually have been left beside the grave so that either the officiating cleric or the cemetery official can scatter a handful on the coffin after it has been lowered into the grave at the moment he intones the words 'Earth to earth, ashes to ashes, dust to dust.' Some relatives of the deceased may like to throw a handful of earth on the coffin too.

The key point of the Anglican funeral service is the committal. If the deceased is being buried in the churchyard, the committal takes place by the grave. If she is being cremated, the committal takes place either in the crematorium chapel or at the church door before the hearse bears the coffin away to the crematorium.

If you never go to church, or if the relative whose funeral you are arranging never went to church, it is unfair to blame an officiating clergyman at a crematorium for getting your relative's name wrong in his address to the congregation, or for calling her a good mother to her children when she had none. If you allow the undertakers to appoint the clergyman you risk similar disappointment, blundering inefficiency, insensitivity, ignorance of the qualities of the deceased – even the appointment of a clergyman of a different denomination to that of the deceased. I have come across instances of every one of these.

It would be going rather far to say that you deserve whatever bad service you get, because a firm of undertakers ought to be able to avoid such problems. Still, there is clearly no substitute for a funeral conducted by someone who knew the deceased very well, at a place of worship, or at any rate in a neighbourhood, where she was a familiar figure. This applies whether she was a churchgoer or not, and whether the funeral is at a graveside in a cemetery or at a crematorium. Unfortunately, today too many people at a critical juncture of their lives want the consolations of religion without the trouble of regular church attendance. Close ties with the clergy formed over years stand you in good stead when your closest relative or spouse dies.

If you all proceed to a cemetery, remember that it may be several miles from the church. Moreover, modern traffic conditions may result in the fleet of cars carrying the mourners becoming separated, so that those attending the graveside ceremony straggle up in twos and threes. If the cortège looks like being very large, it may be possible to arrange with the police some kind of temporary traffic control so that the vehicles are able to keep together. Even so, you should give adequate guidance to precisely where in a big cemetery the interment is to take place. In a place like Brompton Cemetery, the overgrown ground vegetation, numerous trees and multiplicity of elaborate tombs, family burial vaults and miniature mausolea are such that it can be very difficult to see more than a few yards ahead in any direction, particularly in summer.

The Church of England is equally content to have its members buried or cremated. A number of churchyards have a special space set aside for ashes to be buried even if they are full up as regards graves. If the ashes are interred in the churchyard, another short service can be held. Full-size grave-stones or headstones are usually placed only where a dead person has been buried intact, but if the ashes of a cremated person are buried, a small plaque can be used as a commemo-rative marker and set flat in the ground.

The local vicar has some power of veto on monuments in the churchyard, and as we know from the case of the Lancashire parson in 1994 who retrospectively forbade slangy wording on tombstones such as 'Dad' instead of 'Father' or, conceivably, 'Papa' and 'Tom', presumably instead of 'Thomas', this power can on occasion get a bit repressive. The local churchyard in east Berkshire where I wrote much of this book has a recent headstone dedicated to both a 'Dad' and 'Mum', so stuffiness of outlook is not a feature of the Windsor area. Jesus himself would, I think, have found east Berkshire more congenial than Lancashire since he encouraged his disciples to use the colloquial Aramaic word *abba* – the equivalent of the 'daddy' that small children would lisp to their male parent – when addressing God the Father.

In fact, the chancellor of the local diocese is the person with the real say in these matters, a power he enjoys in his capacity as judge of the consistory court, which is the body that hears ecclesiastical cases. But since he would have to grant what is known as a faculty (licence) to each applicant, he usually lets the vicar deputise for him. A vicar may impose not just aesthetic prejudices, in which case he at least has the defence that they are his interpretation of rules imposed by higher authority, but doctrinal ones. There was a case in 1994 of an SAS soldier who was forbidden by his vicar to put RIP (*Requiescat in Pace*, 'May he rest in peace') on his father's gravestone since the vicar was low church and thought it papistical. If the vicar proves difficult, you could try appealing to the consistory court, and beyond that, if the judgement there goes against you, to the Court of Arches if you live in the province of Canterbury or the Chancery Court of York if you live in that province, but however high you appeal, it is unlikely that you will be allowed anything very outré in the monument line, since the policy seems to be conventional tombstones in a 'non-controversial' design and material.

The *Churchyards Handbook*, available from Church House Publishing, Great Smith Street, London SW1P 3NZ (tel. 0171–222 5520), or by mail order from Great Smith Street, London SW1P 3BN (0171–222 9011), making cheques payable to Central Board of Finance, will give you a very good idea of the sort of thing that is likely to be permitted. There is also an advisory committee for each diocese which looks after its churches and churchyards and which will advise both the person applying for a faculty and the chancellor of the diocese. Criteria vary. On one occasion the fact that just over two-fifths of the other monuments in a churchyard were made of marble was the decisive factor in allowing an applicant to put up one in white marble. On other occasions anything in marble has been forbidden, apparently on the grounds that it weathers badly and is too conspicuous. It seems an odd reason for objecting to marble as a commemorative material, since a certain power to arrest the eye is surely what monuments are all about. And when the stone is weathered it can be even lovelier than when it is in pristine condition. How lucky for the Mogul Emperor Shah-Jahan (and the world since) that there was no diocesan chancellor at Agra to object to the Taj Mahal on such grounds in the early seventeenth century.

Another material against which there seems to be some ecclesiastical prejudice is granite, whether black, charcoal or red, particularly if polished. The diocese of Hereford, for instance, forbids all polished gravestones in its churchyards. Photographs on gravestones have been vetoed on several occasions and raised edges round the rectangular area under which the coffin is buried, with or without railings or chains, and whether with chippings inside the raised edges or not, are also nowadays in disfavour, though they were common enough in both cemeteries and churchyards twenty or thirty years ago. The objection today against raised edges is at least based on common sense in that they make it difficult to mow the grass.

The modern trend in the Church of England is to encourage simple and reverent inscriptions on gravestones. Accordingly, many of the poetic epitaphs of the past would not be allowed today. Genealogical research could suffer, since the old grave-stone inscriptions naming a person's parentage and other close relatives are useful sources. It was a long tradition as well as beneficial to scholarship. On the gravestone of an ancient

Greek called Hieropytho some two and a half millennia ago friends or relatives had details of a pedigree inscribed that stretched back fourteen generations.

The alternatives to a wording prohibited by church authority are not always an improvement. Some fifteen years ago a consistory court banned any mention on a dead man's gravestone of the name of his lover, to whom he had not been married. Yet in a stupendous act of ecclesio-bureaucratic absurdity it allowed the legend 'He loved those who loved him'. To anyone who had known about the lover this could have been taken to mean he was rather promiscuous and had several other lovers, whereas in fact he seems to have been rather monogamous, even if within an 'irregular' liaison.

Permission for commemorative tablets in churches is granted very sparingly these days. If the neo-classical sculptor John Flaxman (1775–1826) were alive now he would have a very hard time of it. To get some idea of his genius, go and see the memorial he designed in Westminster Abbey to the 1st Earl of Mansfield ('silver-tongued Murray', the Lord Chief Justice whose house was burned by the mob in the Gordon Riots of 1780). Of course, the Church of England authorities are right in a way to frown on tablets, because there is nobody now alive with the technical skill to match Flaxman's. Church of England bishops have similar powers to control inscriptions on gravestones or other memorials in cemeteries, but only in the consecrated parts.

Take time to decide on what sort of memorial you are going to erect. The thing cannot be got ready in a rush anyway. You might care to consult the more literary-minded members of the family over the wording of any epitaph. You or another member of the family may wish to add a further inscription on the monument in years to come, either in reference to your own passing or to that of a spouse or other close relative of the present occupant of the grave. Around half of all burials still take place in family-owned plots, so this is a distinct likelihood. When approaching a mason to put up a memorial, get an estimate first, with itemised quotes for each service or piece of material, including the VAT that is payable on the whole. The National Association of Memorial Masons (see the Acknowledgements for further details) points out that unless specifically instructed otherwise, the mason will lay out the wording of the inscription according to his own design precepts. In these days of widespread churchyard vandalism you would be wise to insure any memorial against damage. A good mason will inform you of what policies exist for this sort of thing.

Crematoria have a variety of commemorative devices: books of remembrance, stone markers and bushes (frequently roses). They will inform you of their range if you inquire. There are other sorts of memorial altogether: you could endow a scholarship, a book prize, an essay prize, a park bench. I attended a hunt ball a few months after my father's death. One of the prizes in the raffle was the right to have a jump in the country hunted by the pack called after whoever the highest bidder cared to nominate. (The money went to keeping up the jump, restoring brushwood and clearing away weeds and other undesirable vegetation.) I outbid all rivals and asked that my father's name be commemorated. The cost was £100, and cheap at the price. So just as Aintree has Becher's Brook and Epsom has Tattenham Corner, there is some corner of a Shropshire field that is forever Gordon Mosley.

You might prefer to have the entire service celebrated at the graveside rather than in the church. Similarly, some cemeteries have their own chapels. If you follow the former plan, make sure to take into account the likely weather given the current season, particularly where older or frailer mourners may be attending. The early nineteenth-century diarist Charles Greville tells us that at the obsequies of the Duke of York, brother of George IV, in January 1827 the cold was so intense that the Foreign Secretary, George Canning, got rheumatic fever (which may have contributed to his own death some months later) and the Prime Minister, Lord Liverpool, subsequently suffered a stroke from which he never recovered (he resigned his post in February and was replaced by Canning). The Bishop of Lincoln died soon after and no fewer than three dukes, those of Sussex, Wellington and Montrose, caught savage colds.

If you are having the deceased cremated, it is still more important to ensure that all mourners turn up at the crematorium on time, whether they have come from a church service beforehand or are to attend a service in the crematorium chapel itself (supposing there is one). Crematoria work on fairly tight schedules and the actual process of consuming the coffin in the flames is quickly over. If you are having the deceased cremated yet wish to spin things out rather longer – and the sheer efficiency of the cremation process can be a little repellent to those who get more comfort from a long-drawn-out funeral – you can arrange a service while the ashes are interred in the Garden of Remembrance adjoining the crematorium buildings proper. Alternatively, if you wish for an elaborate and lengthy ceremony in the crematorium building, you can book it for more than one session (a session is usually about thirty minutes). Many crematoria have facilities enabling one or two mourners to witness the coffin actually entering the furnace, should that be their desire. Most people seem to find it too gruesome.

At the time of writing, the fees for funerals, burials and monuments in churchyards are set by the Church Commissioners under the Ecclesiastical Fees Measure 1986, itself authorised by the Parochial Fees Order 1993. They are as follows. A funeral in the local church costs £24 payable to the vicar and £19 to the parochial church council; burial in the churchyard immediately afterwards costs £70, payable to the parochial church council. If the body is buried in the churchyard on a different occasion, the vicar gets £15 in addition to the £70 payable to the parochial church council. If the deceased has been cremated and the ashes are to be buried on a separate occasion in the churchyard, the vicar gets £15 and the parochial church council £55. That is only if the ashes are in a container, however. If they are buried loose in the churchyard, it costs £15 for the vicar and £42 to the parochial church council (assuming that this is still a separate occasion from the funeral).

If you arrange for the burial to be carried out in a cemetery on a separate occasion from the funeral you must pay the vicar who officiates £15 unless the local council, or whoever else owns the cemetery, has set a different tariff. Non-residents often have to pay more to a local authority-owned cemetery than if they live in its bailiwick. Greenwich in south-east London charges non-residents four times as much as locals.

The same rule about the local council's tariff overriding the Church Commissioners' one applies if you want the vicar to conduct a service at the cemetery or crematorium, though his normal fee for this would be £43 and nothing would be payable to the parochial church council. If you wish to have the deceased buried in the churchyard without any service by the vicar you must pay him £15 and the parochial church council £70, although if you organise another service by the graveside the full fee for service in church and burial immediately afterwards – £113 – is payable. A burial certificate costs £6. In some crematoria the services of an organist are included as part of the hire fee but use of recorded music (usually supplied by you, the customer, probably in cassette-tape form) is extra. In others it is the other way round. Many crematoria have their own tapes of the more popular choices of music.

The fees quoted above are for the basics. Church bells, flowers and heating in winter (sometimes in summer, too, given the cold of most church interiors), together with music, are extras. The tariff for them is laid down by parochial church councils.

The cost of permission to erect crosses, gravestones, headstones and vases is set by the Church Commissioners. At time of writing it is £5 to the vicar and £3 to the parochial church council for a wooden cross. This should be small, though no exact maximum dimensions are stipulated. A vase of up to 12ins high, 8ins wide and 8ins deep will cost £9 in fees to the vicar and £10 to the parochial church council. A tablet up to 21x21 ins in memory of a cremated person costs £16 to the vicar and £17 to the parochial church council and can be set vertically or horizontally. Any other sort of commemorative object costs £38 to the vicar and £39 to the parochial church council. All these fees include permission to record the original wording of an epitaph. Any subsequent wording (for instance, in memory of a wife who dies a few years after her husband) costs an extra £18 to the vicar. The above fees are simply for permission, of course. The actual vase, slab, cross or other memorial has to be bought and the stonemason or whoever cuts the inscription paid separately.

If mourners have come a long way and the weather is bad you ought to invite them back for some kind of refreshment. You can entertain them at home, which is much the most pleasant venue. Life goes on even after a funeral, so congenial surroundings do matter on such occasions, even if it may seem an unimportant consideration at the time. Alternatively, there are hotels or restaurants who will cater for this sort of thing. Some of the more enterprising crematoria lay on what they probably call 'facilities' for mourners in need of sustenance. If there are many mourners and it is the middle of the day, you must decide whether to include alcohol. Some mourners may have to drive a long distance home. Perhaps you should not put temptation in their way. When Bonnie Prince Charlie's devoted follower Flora MacDonald died on the Isle of Skye in 1790 the mourners drank their way through 300 gallons of whisky, so a proper wake could prove as expensive as a marble memorial. If many mourners are of Celtic stock you can hardly not give them something substantial to drink. Another possibility is to have a select wake the night before for hardened topers and close friends of the family, then a 'dry' collation of sandwiches, tea and coffee for the general mob the next day. That is what Penny Macbeth did at the time of the funeral of her husband, the poet George Macbeth, a few years ago in Ireland.

Bahá'ís

This religion originated in 1844 in what was then Persia but is now called Iran. There are 350,000 Bahá'ís there still – the country's largest religious minority – and in the first few years after the Islamic fundamentalists came to power in 1979 they underwent increasing persecution, though of late this seems to have slackened off following intercession by the United Nations. The word Bahá'í refers to a follower of Bahá'u'lláh, the religion's founder, whose own name means 'the glory of God'. Bahá'ís believe that he was the most recent in a series of messengers from God, among the others being the founders of the rest of the world's major religions, and his writings form the basis of the Bahá'ís' creed.

This creed is monotheistic and it emphasises the oneness of humankind. Indeed, Bahá'u'lláh taught that our present age is the age of unity and during it humankind will unite as a single family, whereupon peace will reign throughout the world. Among admirers of Bahá'u'lláh or the Bahá'í movement, as cited in the Bahá'ís' promotional literature, have been Benjamin Jowett, the celebrated nineteenth-century master of Balliol, Helen Keller and Queen Marie of Romania.

Bahá'ís have no ritual or priestly hierarchy, but they divide the world into regions which come under the guidance of spiritual assemblies. These spiritual assemblies supervise weddings (and divorces, which are allowed, albeit reluctantly), general religious services and the observance of Bahá'í holy days as well as funerals. Bahá'ís claim to be the second most widespread of all the independent religions with a worldwide following. They are teetotallers and make it one of their rules to refrain from party-political activity. Indeed, they hold it as an article of faith that a Bahá'í must be obedient to whatever government is in power in the country in which he lives.

Bahá'ís hold that by submitting to God's will in life one prepares oneself for the afterlife, for humans have immortal souls which travel towards God across numerous planes of existence or worlds. These worlds are conceived of as extensions of the material universe of which we inhabit a small part, although they are not subject to the laws of time and space. Heaven is defined as the soul's drawing closer to God, hell as it failing to draw close, thus being alienated from God. As in most other major world religions, God is seen as the creator and supreme ruler of the universe. Bahá'ís do not go in for a more detailed picture of the afterlife, believing that in the final analysis it and the state of the soul in it are beyond human description. However, they constantly apply the analogy of the foetus inside the womb and its lack of information about the world outside to highlight the unknowability of the next life compared with this one.

There are no particular rites for laying out the body of a deceased person, but as a matter of practicality it is washed and wrapped in a shroud, which may be of silk or cotton. Bahá'ís are against embalming and cremation, though if the law of the land insists on either, that is the end of the matter. Their coffins are supposed to be made of crystal, stone or hardwood, which inevitably pushes up funeral costs. Before placing the dead person in the coffin, Bahá'ís put on his finger a distinctive Bahá'í ring inscribed with the words: 'I came forth from God, and return unto Him, detached from all save Him, holding fast to His name, the Merciful, the Compassionate'. If the deceased is a child of under fifteen, the ring is not used, nor is the prayer for the dead said which is compulsory for all other adherents to the faith.

Bahá'ís also insist that one of their dead must be buried within a single hour's travelling time of the outer limit of the local administrative unit in which he died (which could vary from a village in some countries to a province in others), unless that unit is very large (as in one of the regions in Scotland, say), when the limit runs an hour's journey from the village or town where the deceased died. This article of faith derives from the Bahá'ís' belief that the world is a single country. If relatives try to fly a corpse by aeroplane to a particular cemetery further away than the nearest one, even if they manage to accomplish this in an hour or less, it is still judged contrary to the spirit of Bahá'í rules.

The prayer for the dead is the only compulsory prayer. It is spoken in front of a congregation, though by a single person. The rest of the assembly stand. God is addressed on behalf of the dead person as the supreme embodiment of mercy, the deceased being represented as God's servant. God is asked to be merciful to her. After this the speaker says six times, 'Alláh-u-Abhá; and then nineteen times each of six items of a litany in which those present are described as worshipping, bowing before, being devoted to, praising, thanking and being patient in God. Five more rather longer prayers to God follow, glorifying God and praising his virtues.

If the deceased was the only person in her family who was of the Bahá'í faith, care is taken to explain Bahá'í requirements to her relatives. Moreover, their wishes as to the handling of the ceremony are given a sympathetic hearing as far as is compatible with Bahá'í rules. Clearly, the most important of these is the Bahá'í preference for burial. To that end, Bahá'ís urge their adherents to make a will inserting a clause specifying their desire to be buried according to Bahá'í practice, and also to let their families know before they die that this is what they wish, since sometimes wills are not examined until after a funeral. But in general Bahá'ís are perfectly happy to include in the ceremony any favourite prayers, readings or music selected by the family, even if the readings, say, are from the sacred texts of another religion. If the deceased person's next of kin insist on disposing of her body in a way that runs contrary to Bahá'í practice, the local spiritual assembly is obliged to comply, but they can of course hold their own memorial service on some other occasion.

Bahá'ís are supposed to be buried with their feet pointing towards 'Akká' (the historic Acre in the Holy Land where Bahá'u'lláh is buried). Bahá'ís at local-assembly level have individual members who are experienced in counselling the bereaved, but there is no particular form that this takes other than the general expression of concern and sensitivity which any decent human being would display.

Buddhists

Buddhists believe in reincarnation, but the state of mind and spirit in which people die is important. To Buddhists, death is the entrance to a transitory state, often between one earthly life and the next. To some of them, Tibetan Buddhists, for instance, death is by no means a kindly figure or even a state of nothingness, but an evil being who may spring on his victims at any moment. Yama is the Tibetan god of death and is depicted as having a head like that of a buffalo, although he is otherwise more or less human in shape. He is usually coloured a dark blue shading into black, though portrayals of him as red exist. He has a female counterpart called Chamunda and countless underlings who gather souls for him. When he collects a person he cannot be turned away, but drags them with him down to the underworld, which is thought of as a place without doors or windows and made entirely of iron.

As with many other religions, the dead person's merits and demerits are weighed in supernatural scales, Yama acting as the presiding judge. He is in fact less the ultimate personification of evil than a dispenser of punishment, a judge if you like, albeit an extremely stern one, even a hanging judge – Lord Goddard rather than Stalin, as it were. If a dead person's good qualities outweigh his bad he is returned to life on earth, but if it is the other way round he is consigned to hell. Yama is conceived of as tameable by the Buddhas (enlightened beings) and Bodhisattvas (near-Buddhas, that is to say beings who have very nearly attained the state of enlightenment, or full Buddhas passing themselves off as not-quite-a-hundred-per cent Buddhas so that they will not seem too remote to lesser beings).

There is a British Buddhist Association which recommends certain ceremonies in this country for those who want a Buddhist funeral. In Britain cremation or burial is equally acceptable and white or black clothing may be worn. Chinese Buddhists wear white clothes and hats if members of the family. (The Chinese in Britain, many of whom are Buddhists, prefer burying their dead; they put shoes on the body so that it will be properly shod for walking in the next world.) Prior to the service those attending are encouraged to dwell on certain writings: a passage from *Kindred Sayings*, one of the texts from the Pali canon (referring to the corpus of writings in the sacred language of Buddhism, itself descended from Sanskrit), specifically Book v, 19; *The Light of Asia* (1879), a life of the Buddha in blank verse by the nineteenth-century newspaper editor, poet and schoolmaster Sir Edwin Arnold; a Buddhist scripture called the Dhammapada, a paraphrase of the Dylan Thomas poem, which reads 'Do not go angered into that brief night' and which would appear to have a different meaning as well as a different wording from the usual version; and a meditation by Francis Story, an English Buddhist who became a wandering monk in Burma and Sri Lanka in the decades after the Second World War.

The person conducting the service is called the minister and he opens the proceedings with an address in which he refers to the 'passing' of the deceased and reminds the assembled company that death is in the natural order of things and that it is part of an endless cycle of life, death and rebirth (that is, reincarnation). The deceased is portrayed as the culmination of many previous lives and as henceforward undergoing transition to yet others. Those assembled at the funeral are reminded that the cycle will persist until the disruptive process finishes with the individual soul, in this case that of the person who has recently died, finding repose and fulfilment in ultimate bliss.

A litany is recited by the minister in which he places emphasis on the extent to which what we are now is the result of what we have thought or said in the past, whether good or evil. The inevitability of this is compared with the spinning of the cartwheel as it is pulled behind the horse's hooves or the shadow cast by sunlight.

There then follows further reference to the reincarnation cycle in a series of rhyming verses, with mention of the deceased having died again, just as the mourners have. These verses may be recited by a friend or relation rather than by the minister. At the same time there is a statement to the effect that the deceased chose the circumstances in which he died, almost as if he had willed it, though at the same time the inevitability of his passing is spoken of as well. Future forms which those present will assume in other lives are for them to devise. Death itself is eliminated in a state of namelessness; life does not cease, merely the forms which it assumes.

The minister then recites a prayer. There follows a choice of narratives, depending on whether the deceased was the only member of his family to be a practising Buddhist or whether he was one of several close relatives who are Buddhists. These too may be recited by a friend or relation of the deceased rather than by the minister. The first tells of the death of Sāriputta, one of the principle disciples of the Buddha, the second of Kisā Gotamī, a young mother in India who has not experienced the death of anyone close to her before. In the second narrative Kisā Gotamī's baby son has died and she is in a state of shock. She refuses to let him receive the rites appropriate to the point of death and instead takes him round to all her neighbours trying to procure medicine for him, as if he were still alive and could be saved. The neighbours are almost entirely unsympathetic and unhelpful, but one of them suggests that she applies to the Great Healer or Teacher. She goes to him and he tells her to fetch some mustard seed, one of the commonest substances in an Indian household, as medicine. But he stipulates that this mustard seed must come from a household where nobody has ever died.

Kisā Gotamī goes from house to house and village to village looking for a family in which nobody has ever died. She cannot find a single one, of course. Indeed, the longer she seeks the more it dawns on her that everywhere she goes the dead outnumber the living. She returns to the Teacher, who tells her that she has hitherto supposed herself to be the only person who has ever lost a person close to her. This is not so, however, and all living things are controlled by an unbending law which states that whoever is subject to a desire for worldly goods and attainments is taken away by the Prince of Death, with his ambitions and aims unfulfilled, just as a town may be washed away by a flood.

This causes Kisā Gotamī to attain the first stage of sanctity. She meditates on the various oil lamps burning in a meeting hall, some of them brightly, others flickering feebly as they run out of fuel, others flaring up shortly before they die out, and she reflects that it is the same with the living on earth, some flourishing, others expiring. Only those who have attained Nirvana are unignited, having gone beyond the necessity to burn with either a hard, gem-like flame or a feeble flicker.

Finally, accompanied by a recitation to the effect that it is better to live but a single day, provided one can glimpse the land where death does not exist, than for a century in which one cannot do so, Kisā Gotamī, having had this insight, attains Nirvana.

The next stage of the proceedings, too, depends on whether the members of the deceased's family are Buddhists or not. If they are, a gong is struck and a ritual of homage is either spoken or chanted, with a cantor leading the congregation in the recitation of a litany in honour of the Exalted One, to which the congregation respond with lines expressing honour to Arahant (roughly saint, or one who has attained a high degree of perfection, who has glimpsed Nirvana and acts in a state of pure knowledge) and Buddha Supreme. There follows a passage called 'The Three Refuges', chanted (if it is not recited) on a pitch a tone higher than the preceding passage. The minister leads this stage of the rite with a statement to the effect that he goes for refuge to the Buddha. The congregation then recite three times verses in which they state that they too go for refuge to the Buddha, also to the Dhamma (a support, but here the body of Buddhist teaching) and the Sangha (the spiritual order of disciples and its personification in individual monks and congregations of monks).

Next comes a part of the ceremony called Praise of the Triple Gem. The minister chants or recites a litany in which he lists the qualities and accomplishments of the Buddha, the leader without peer, saying how he is a saint, wholly enlightened, of good conduct, filled with knowledge of all things and all worlds and at peace with himself.

The congregation then chant or recite a text in which they state that they are seeking the presence of the Exalted Teacher, who will be their guide and their means of attaining spiritual uplift and peace. They describe how they will lay offerings and their smouldering worldly desires, their pride, sense of self, ambitions and above all the wearisome burden of the cycle of birth, death and rebirth before his image so that their spirit may attain tranquillity.

Following this panegyric to the Buddha, the minister turns to the Dhamma, reciting how it is completely apprehendable by those who have renounced covetousness and immediately attainable by those who are sufficiently holy. It must be sought out, however, and is a means to reaching the path of enlightenment rather than a destination in itself. It is for each person to undergo Dhamma and practise it himself. The congregation respond by saying that they find in Dhamma relief from hurt, with divine truth, which transcends life and death, acting as a cure for the flaws and distortions of this material world. This divine truth is like a holy place promising tranquillity and purification, slaking the tired and thirsty traveller's parched state.

A section called Sangha follows, in which the minister describes the qualities possessed by the Exalted One's disciples. They exhibit self-control, righteousness and integrity. The Sangha is made up of four couples of saints, each couple in turn representing the path to attainment and attainment itself, totalling eight grades of disciple. The congregation respond with a statement that they seek in such self-control the means of slaking their thirst (their desire for enlightenment). They recite a resolution to keep this desire for enlightenment ever before them, to try to restrain intemperance, whether of the body, speech or thought, and to obey the precepts together with the more exalted state of mind and behaviour which are inherent in the Sāvaka (a particular congregation or group of Buddhists of which those present are members) Sangha.

The minister then invites the congregation to join him in restating the five rules of Buddhism as well as observing them, not just in deed but in thought so that there can be no possible grounds for the mourners to be accused of pharisaical conduct. The five rules, which are recited out loud by the congregation, are: (1) not to harm life, (2) not to take what is not given,

(3) not to indulge in sensual impropriety, (4) not to indulge in untoward speech such as lies, backbiting, malicious gossip and so on and (5) not to indulge in intoxicating substances.

There follows a brief overview of the deceased person's career and accomplishments in life. Before the service a jug of water and a bowl will normally have been put ready for use in the water-pouring ceremony which follows, and if the ceremony is held indoors also a shallow plate, dish or tray on which the bowl can stand so that when water is poured any excess will be caught.

The minister speaks to the congregation, inviting them to join with him in blessing the water with benevolence, both internally and externally, towards the deceased. There follow ten verses recited by the minister which list the qualities of one who is practised in goodness, ending with the observation that once a person has attained virtue and left behind faults and vices once and for all he will escape the cycle of rebirth and death over and over again and never return to earth to undergo them. The minister then asks the congregation to join him in reciting a prayer for freedom from hostility, malevolence and anxiety and a desire that they all maintain themselves in happiness.

Then he describes how, just as the water is poured from the jug, so may those present pour out from inside themselves the benevolence that will envelop their beloved friend and relative the deceased (here his name is mentioned). The next of kin then approach the jug and pour a generous amount into the bowl, while the minister recites a verse desiring that the flow of goodwill from members of the congregation to the deceased may resemble that of water from rivers to the sea. The Triple Gem is seen as the power of the Master, the power of truth and the power drawn from those present, all of which will make the deceased well and happy and allow him to attain Nirvana.

There then follows the actual lowering of the coffin into the grave or the cremation, as the case may be. The minister may already have passed flowers to the chief mourners for them to lay on the coffin before it is buried or burned. Mourners often twist flowers into a circular wreath and label them with the name(s) of the bereaved on one side and that of the deceased on the other. The minister recites a series of verses reminding his audience of the evanescence of worldly existence. The chief mourners then either toss flowers into the grave or place more flowers on the coffin while the minister draws attention to the similar evanescence of floral charms. The service closes with a meditation on the peace of death recited in the first person singular by the minister.

There is a tradition among some Buddhists of burning objects made of paper – banknotes, model houses or items of clothing, for example – to provide the deceased with the wherewithal for existence in the next world. They may also erect an altar at home and burn incense at it. Sometimes they make little graveside offerings of dishes to which the deceased was partial.

Catholics

Historically, Roman Catholics have placed far more impor-tance on ceremony than any other of the Christian denomina-tions apart, perhaps, from high-church Anglicans, who in extreme cases have been known to out-ritualise even that main branch of Christianity from which their ancestors broke away 400 years ago. Certain ways in which the dead are treated reflect Catholic theology, in other words the way Catholics view God and the human race's relations with Him. For instance, prayers at a requiem mass (a mass said or occasionally sung for the repose of the dead person's soul) are supposed to be for the assistance of the deceased in the place to which he has gone.

But in recent years the theology and emphasis on ritual have changed. The saying of masses for the dead to assist the souls in purgatory, which dated back to before the Reformation, was common as recently as the 1950s. Up till 1956 cathedral and collegiate churches celebrated a requiem and office of the dead for all deceased benefactors and clergy at least once a month. In ordinary churches the celebrant added a general prayer for the dead to the usual prayers on such days. The old custom of Gregorian or Trental masses said for thirty days continuously after a person's death was still followed. More recently, the idea has grown up of giving thanks for the life of the deceased; his soul is assumed to be already on its way to heaven. Cumulatively, this is a gigantic shift in emphasis. The church authorities will not thank you for saying so, but along with other liturgical and doctrinal changes it amounts to something perilously close to a second Reformation, only generated from within the Church rather than externally.

The role of laymen as opposed to priests has been enlarged. The local parish may have its own bereavement group in which a number of parishioners take special responsibility for comforting the friends and relations of the dead person. And on an individual basis, a Catholic who is not a priest may assist the bereaved to pray. New funeral rites were introduced in late 1990 and were made official, that is to say compulsory, from Easter 1991. Up till then there had been a fairly wide variety of practices, many influenced by local custom. However, *The Guidelines for Roman Catholic Funerals*, which announced the new rites, stated in its introductory paragraphs that it in no way meant to criticise the practices current up till then.

In the summer of 1994 the periodical *Liturgy*, published by the liturgy office of the Bishops' Conference of England and Wales, devoted much of an entire issue to the subject of lay leaders at funerals. In its editorial it pointed out that prayer sessions were more and more frequently being celebrated by a gathering of parishioners where a lay person presided. Lay people can be of either sex. Although the Church of England's decision to allow women priests has driven many Anglicans over to Rome, the Catholics now allow females as well as males to serve at altars if the bishop of the diocese approves. Inevitably, some bishops do and others don't. A passage in the letter from the Congregation for Divine Worship and the Discipline of the Sacraments to presidents of Episcopal Conferences, in which this innovation was announced, made it clear that lay people carrying out liturgical functions were doing so not as of right but only with the permission of their bishop. In short, their function as readers, eucharistic ministers or servers was almost that of a stop-gap in the absence of clergy. (There has recently been a grave falling off in the numbers of people wanting to be ordained as priests.) Yet at Westminster Cathedral, for instance, lay people undertake these functions when members of the clergy are actually present. In any case, the various minor orders were abolished in 1973. It all amounts to a somewhat contradictory state of affairs.

Catholics tend to divide funeral rites into three parts, which are envisioned as parts of a journey made by the deceased person from life to oneness with Christ. There is first the vigil, then the liturgy, and finally the committal of the body – to the earth if it is being buried in a grave or to flames if it is being cremated. The vigil, or watching over the body, is seen by Catholics as a rite in itself and as a form of preparation of the bereaved for the final goodbye when the body is committed. It is also seen as an act of worship by the bereaved. It may take place in a church, where it should be accompanied by the full Order of Christian Funerals, or at the dead person's home, in a hospice or hospital chapel or at an undertaker's establishment. This part of the rites consists of prayers after death said over the corpse before its removal from the home or wherever by those present, with the priest or a lay figure, if no priest is present, leading the assembly.

Another aspect of the vigil stage is the Gathering in the

Presence of the Body. This is where relations view the deceased together, either at home, in the mortuary or at the undertaker's. The process can generate a good deal of emotion, especially in a close-knit family. A friend, a Tipperary man, who lives in the castle just round the corner of the mountains from mine in Ireland and who is now in his fifties, recalls as a child being led up to the corpse of his grandmother and being told to kiss the dead woman on the lips. There is also a service used when the family is gathered together with the body, again either at home or in a mortuary or undertaker's, just before leaving for the church or the graveyard or cemetery.

At the vigil friends and relations of the deceased are nowadays encouraged to take a modest part in the proceedings – reading from the scriptures or saying a prayer, say – though not if they don't want to. They can say a few off-the-cuff words about the dead person, too, whether reminiscences of his personal life, a sketch of his character or a summary of his achievements. Vigils may be celebrated several times if necessary, for instance if the funeral is not to be held soon after the death. It may be that some relatives have to come from the other side of the world and cannot get a flight immediately. The following scriptural readings are recommended: 'Awaiting the Lord's coming' (Romans xiv, 7–12; Psalm xxvi; Luke xii, 35–40); 'God is faithful' (2 Timothy ii, 8–13; Psalm cxiv–xv; Matthew xi, 25–30); 'God is with us' (Job xix, 1, 23–7; Psalm cxxix; Romans viii, 31–5, 37–59; Psalm lxii; John xvii, 24–6); 'God's faithful will live forever' (Wisdom iii, 1–6, 9; Psalm cxiv–xv; John v, 24–9); 'I am the resurrection and the life' (1 Corinthians xv, 51–7; Psalm xxvi; 1 Corinthians xv, 20–3; Psalm cxiv–xv; John xi, 17–27); 'Life is changed, not ended' (Daniel xii, 1–3; Psalm cii; Romans viii, 14–23; Psalm lxii; John xii, 23–6); 'Our eternal home' (2 Corinthians v, 1, 6–10; Psalm xxii; Apocalypse xxi, 1–7; Psalm cxxi; John xiv, 1–6);

'Our hope of glory' (Lamentations iii, 17–26; Psalm xxiv; Luke xxiv, 13–35).

The above references are to the Lectionary, Vol. III, and the compilation of funeral texts that make up a companion volume to it.

The family of the deceased can decide whether the coffin lid stays open at this stage or to close it earlier. Undertakers usually inquire of the senior family member beforehand which it is to be. If the lid is left open the rites make provision for the deceased person's forehead to be 'signed', that is to say marked with the sign of the cross as an echo of the baptismal process. This may be done by the family and friends present or by the minister (that is, the chief lay figure, or an intermediary personage between priestly caste and layfolk such as a deacon).

The coffin used to be adorned with a raised crucifix on the lid, but the modernising tendencies now prevalent permit just a white pall on which a crucifix alone or a crucifix and a Bible may be laid. Alternatively, the Bible may substitute for the crucifix. Either way there would have to be a flat surface underneath. Flags or flowers can be placed on the coffin on its way to and from the church but are not permitted as coffin coverings within the building. If flowers are brought into the church they may be placed near the coffin, on a table, say, likewise mass cards. These are pre-printed announcements sent by friends and relations of the principal bereaved person to her to say that they are having a mass said for the repose of the deceased's soul.

A variant on the mass card is the altar list of the dead. This would be distributed to parishioners, especially in autumn, when All Souls' Day (2 November) is imminent. It would take the form of a sheet of paper printed with the words: 'Pray for the parents, relatives and friends of:' followed by a dotted line to be filled in with names, then a separate line: 'And the souls of:' plus more dotted lines for all the other people on behalf of whom you might want prayers to be said. At the bottom it might say, 'All Masses on 2 November and on First Fridays of the year are offered for the Altar List of the Dead.'

Coffins are inscribed with the letters RIP and sometimes with an emblem of the Sacred Heart pierced with a dagger or sword. As with high Anglican practice, the coffin is often received in the church the night before the main funeral service. Sometimes, especially in a place where everyone knows everyone else and news spreads like wildfire, and moreover where there is a large body of Catholics, a crowd will gather. At a recent funeral I heard about in Castlecomer, Co. Kilkenny in Ireland, where the deceased had been killed by a falling chunk of scaffolding on a building site only five weeks after his wedding, the cards were parked three deep in the little town's main street and a couple of mobile chip vans had found it worth their while to turn up and do business. But the tendency of late has been for a long vigil service to take place so that local people not directly related to the deceased can drop by and pay their respects more or less in their own time. This also enables those whose busy professional lives prevent their attending the funeral the next day to feel they can put in some kind of appearance to mourn the deceased's mortal remains.

The officiating priest is usually the local parish priest, who has an automatic right to officiate, though he may delegate the task to a curate or another priest, particularly if the deceased has expressed a desire to have a specific priest from another parish officiate over him. The priest will formally receive the coffin at the church porch or the gateway to the church grounds. He sprinkles it with holy water and then leads the way into the church proper. Undertakers are told never to bring the coffin into the church before the congregation is present, and indeed, if it has been arranged that the coffin is to be delivered just before the service, the reception itself forms part of that service. If the coffin has been brought to the church the night before the funeral it rests in a side chapel, often called the chapel of rest, with candles at its head and foot or in threes along each side.

I have already in the first paragraph of this section referred to the requiem mass. The word 'requiem' is the accusative case in Latin of the word *'requies'*, meaning 'rest' or 'repose'. It occurs in the first few words of the introit, or opening act of worship in the mass: *'Requiem aeternam dona eis, Domine* – 'Give them eternal rest, O Lord'. The requiem mass is the usual form of the principal funeral service, but only a priest can celebrate mass, so if no priest is available some other sort of service will have to take place. Sometimes the entire family decide against a requiem, even though they are formally Catholic, because neither they nor the deceased have been regular attenders at mass. Alternatively, only the deceased may have been a Catholic, for instance if he was a convert, or an active Catholic while the rest of the family may not be. The Church authorities do not try to impose a requiem on the family in the latter case but bend with the will of the majority, though of course if the family is evenly and strongly divided, one party for a requiem the other against, it can be a decidedly ticklish business.

At a requiem the vestments worn by priest and other attendants vary in colour depending on how conservative the rite is. Black vestments and candles of unbleached wax used to be the rule but these are very rare nowadays. Only a church such as the Oratory or St Etheldreda's, Ely Place, London would be likely to follow the old practice, which needs the prior permission of the local episcopal conference. In parishes which are somewhat less conservative the vestments will be violet, and in progressive ones they will be white. The last of these colours is supposed to symbolise the paschal significance of Christian death. (Note the very similar gradation of mourning colours from black to white via violet in purely secular mourning customs covered in the historical section.) At a full sung requiem mass in Latin I attended recently the unbleached candles were a pleasant coral colour, but in general candles of any colour or consistency are rare in Catholic churches nowadays. A mass for the dead may be said even if the deceased was not a Catholic, as may prayers, of course. Women attending a Roman Catholic funeral would do well to cover their heads, either with hats or mantillas, however conservative or progressive the rite.

The authorities forbid more than one mass for a single deceased person on the grounds that only one funeral can ever take place. Mourners may prefer an evening mass the night before – many of them may not be able to attend one in the daytime – which is permissible, but in such a case there is on the following day a service consisting only of morning prayer and commendation.

On certain feast days and holy days a requiem mass is forbidden: All Saints' Day (1 November), Ascension Day (which varies depending on when Easter is that year, but is usually around early May), the Assumption of Our Lady (15 August), Christmas Day, Christmas Eve, Corpus Christi (the first Thursday after Trinity Sunday, that is, just over eight and a half weeks after Easter), Easter Saturday, Easter Sunday, Epiphany (6 January), the Feast of the Immaculate Conception (8 December), the Feast of the Sacred Heart (the second Friday after Corpus Christi), Good Friday, Low Sunday (the first Sunday after Easter), Maundy Thursday (also known as Holy Thursday), New Year's Day, St Joseph's Day (19 March), St Peter and St Paul's Day (29 June), Sundays in Advent, Sundays in Lent, Trinity Sunday and Whit Sunday (which again depends on the date of Easter, but is usually mid to late May).

With some local churches there are further restrictions on requiem masses on the anniversary of the specific church's consecration, Ash Wednesday, Candlemas (2 February), days on which the Blessed Sacrament is exposed (when there may be only one priest on duty), the feast day of the saint in honour of whom the church is named, and the Monday, Tuesday and Wednesday before Ascension Day.

There is no prohibition on hymns and in the new rite it is quite common for them to replace certain liturgical texts, but the requiem mass forms a ritual whole and some purists would argue that you should not cut it up by dividing it with hymns any more than you would take a break halfway through burying a dead relative in order to sample liquid refreshment that more properly belongs to the wake. The priest delivers a homily to the congregation rather than a eulogy of the deceased. In the old rite he preached a panegyric while wearing a black preaching cloak rather than the vestments for celebrating the mass. The panegyric was quite distinct from the usual sermon delivered following the gospel.

The latest proposals for funeral rites lay great stress on music, urging that it should be live insofar as is possible. Sadly, music-making in Catholic churches in the UK has tended to be greatly inferior to that in the established Church of England, apart from the great centres of Catholic worship such as Westminster Cathedral or the Brompton Oratory. On the other hand, this is hardly surprising given the persecution and fines Catholics suffered from the Reformation of the sixteenth century up till emancipation in 1829, and the prejudice they suffered even after 1829.

Still more sadly, because so much less forced by circumstances, there has been a tendency of late to match the more fatuous happy-clappy Anglican practices and to introduce pseudo-pop music. Yet some of the most exquisite pieces of music ever written have been settings of the requiem mass: the 'Grande Messe des Morts' by Hector Berlioz (1803–69), and requiem masses by Johannes Brahms (1833–97), Benjamin Britten (1913–76), Anton Bruckner (1824–96), William Byrd (circa 1543–1623), Antonin Dvořák (1841–1904), Gabriel Fauré (1845–1924), Jean Ockeghem (circa 1415–97),

Giovanni Pierluigi da Palestrina (1525–94), Camille Saint-Saëns (1835–1921), Thomas Tallis (circa 1505–85) and Giuseppe Verdi (1813–1901).

Arguably the greatest of them all is the Requiem Mass by Mozart (1756–91), which was left uncompleted on the composer's death and finished by Franz Xaver Süssmayer and two other assistants. The story surrounding its composition certainly outdoes the circumstances in which any plausible claimant to equal greatness was created. According to one version, a mysterious stranger appeared to Mozart and commissioned the work on behalf of an equally mysterious patron. According to another, an anonymous letter delivered by an unknown hand arrived bespeaking a requiem. The mystery is not really so impenetrable. The patron was a Count Walsegg-Stuppach, a dilettante nobleman who liked to pass off others' creations as his own; in this case the biter was bit, for the score he eventually received was not a purely Mozart work. But the death of the Count's wife Anna on St Valentine's Day earlier the same year, which prompted him to commission the requiem, was genuine. A later account mentions Mozart's conviction as the composition progressed that he was writing his own requiem.

It is not true that Mozart was given a pauper's funeral, though it was certainly a very cheap one and such a melodramatic and seductively ironic end is often claimed for him. It was a standard third-class affair and cost 8 florins 56 kreutzer, with a further 3 gulden (a denomination used interchangeably with the florin) for the wagon that transported the body. This works out in modern money at between £24.36 and £60.90, depending on whether you reckon inflation since 1791 has devalued currency twenty or fifty times. Either way, it is a remarkable bargain. The funeral was ordered by Baron van Swieten, another of Mozart's patrons, and was considered perfectly appropriate in a late classical era when simplicity was paramount, and when at one point coffins were replaced by sack shrouds. Besides, Mozart's fellow freemasons were against priest-ridden display. The exact location of the grave, like that of Alexander the Great, has never been discovered. The legend of an unknown figure in attendance in the cortège – Orpheus come to pay homage, according to some mythomanes – is much more seductive than the story of the pauper's funeral. Mozart's requiem was later performed at the funerals of Napoleon and Chopin, among others.

Monk Matthew, in *Comfort for the Bereaved* (Catholic Truth Society, 1980), calls the powers at work on the dead person's behalf which are invoked by the priest in the requiem 'massive'. For some deceased persons, the place they have gone will be heaven. Monk Matthew writes: 'It has been said that there are probably far more who go straight to heaven than we think.' For many dead, the initial destination is called purgatory, which has been called 'the anteroom to heaven'. Another Catholic Truth Society author, Peter Knott, of the Society of Jesus (Jesuits), writes in his pamphlet *Safe in God's Hands* that we have been led to see purgatory as more like a hospital than a prison. Catholics teach that everyone who spends time there is certain to get into heaven eventually. It is some comfort to know that even according to the strictest theologians, there is no absolute certainty that anyone, however wicked, has ever been consigned to eternal damnation in hell.

There is a leave-taking, with friends and family gathering round the coffin in the church (or later at the graveside or crematorium), after which it is taken from the church and the cortège accompanies it to the churchyard, cemetery or crematorium. As David Murphy, general secretary of the Catholic Truth Society, puts it, the theory goes that the dead chap wasn't perfect, so the saying of prayers for him is a bit like a *Times* obituary: it faces up to the character of a person in the round, a man possessing good and bad qualities, who needs praying for even now. He adds that this also gives the bereaved something to do.

126

If the ground in which the deceased person is to be buried has not previously been consecrated, the officiating priest consecrates it then and there. The actual consigning of the coffin to the grave – it will be recalled that this is called the committal, whether to a grave or crematorium furnace – is not a long-drawn-out ceremony, liturgically speaking, if a church service has already taken place. However, if the committal occurs far away from the church – in another county or town, say – or a substantial time after the service, the committal rites are slightly lengthier. Those attending a graveside service will be invited by the priest at the end to sprinkle a few drops of holy water or earth from the grave on the coffin as a final goodbye. The scattering of drops of holy water on the coffin by mourners can take place at cremations too.

At one time cremation did not form a common part of Roman Catholic practice. In fact, it is only since 1965 that it has been permitted, and liturgical texts specifically designed for Catholic use at crematoria have been generally available only since 1972. Even now, cremation is rare among Roman Catholics in Ireland, where there is about the highest rate of churchgoing in Europe, where an overwhelming majority of the population are Catholic and where proportionately the fewest people are cremated. A survey published in the Redemptorist periodical *Reality* in autumn 1994 revealed that 80 per cent of Irish Catholics still preferred burial in a cemetery to cremation. One sees the contrast with Protestant practice particularly starkly in Belfast, a notoriously divided city where religion is concerned. There only around 2.5 per cent of people cremated are Roman Catholic, although Catholics make up a substantial percentage of the population as a whole.

Nonetheless, it is not unknown for Catholic services to be carried out in their entirety at the crematorium (or graveside or cemetery chapel, come to that), rather than in church. The church authorities mildly deprecate this, since all the other rites tend to be either omitted or rendered discontinuous, and a seamless process of leave-taking is central to the Catholic view of how a dead person should be treated. If the deceased has specifically requested a crematorium service only, that is another matter. There is also a purely utilitarian objection to having the whole service at the crematorium: the time element. Crematoria can be busy places and, as we have seen, usually allow only about half an hour for the disposal of each 'client'. A requiem mass takes about three-quarters of an hour.

Now that the Catholic Church has accepted cremation, it has developed a policy with regard to the disposal of the ashes as well. Ashes may be buried, and more and more churches are providing for this in their grounds. But any container should be biodegradable so that the ashes can mingle with the surrounding earth in a natural fashion as they decompose further. The Church does not forbid but does not encourage the scattering of ashes.

Christian Scientists

The full name of this sect is 'The First Church of Christ, Scientist'. Bereaved Christian Scientists seek comfort in prayer. Mary Baker Eddy, the movement's founder, wrote in *Science and Health With Key to the Scriptures* that suffering as the result of bereavement arises from a belief that bereavement has taken place, and that

> there is no cause for grief . . . when our friends pass from our sight and we lament, that lamentation is needless and causeless. We shall perceive this . . . when we grow into the understanding of Life, and know that there is no death.

Christian Scientists reject priesthood and ritual, but if a member of their Church grieves for a 'dead' friend or relative there are Christian Science practitioners who try to soothe away the anguish.

The choice of funeral ceremonies is up to the individual. Relatives of the deceased usually have the body cremated, though burial is permitted and a service can be conducted by a minister of another denomination altogether. At a straightforward Christian Science funeral there tend to be Bible readings and excerpts from Mary Baker Eddy's writings. The only specific rule relating to the dead is the by-law in *The Manual of The Mother Church, The First Church of Christ, Scientist, in Boston, Massachusetts* which states that if a member of the Church dies suddenly without having sustained an injury beforehand or without being ill, then an autopsy shall be carried out by suitably qualified experts. But this, of course, is required by the law in most countries anyway. Another provision of the Christian Science rules is that wherever possible a female corpse should be prepared for burial by another female, but even this, which good taste would tend to dictate in any case, is not mandatory.

Countess of Huntingdon's Connexion

This is the collective name given to Methodists of Calvinistic tendency whose organisation derives from the activities of Selina, Countess of Huntingdon (1707–91). Lady Huntingdon was a great promoter of Methodism, first generally, then of that aspect of it propounded by George Whitefield, which is usually recognised as more unbending than his rival John Wesley's approach. The Connexion, which insists that it is completely separate from and wholly independent of the Methodist Church, nevertheless follows no particular ceremony of its own where disposal of the dead is concerned nor conforms to any pattern as regards beliefs about what happens to the dead. Instead it sticks to the general outlook and rites of the free churches.

Fellowship of Churches of Christ

This group started in the USA in the early nineteenth century as the Disciples of Christ, who at that time constituted an offshoot of Presbyterianism. Members look on the scriptures as the sole source of authority and hold to no other doctrine or creed. What this means in practice is that they do not so much reject doctrine and creed – they subscribe to the content of the historic creeds and they both practise baptism and celebrate the Lord's Supper on Sundays (called Lord's Days) – as reject subscription to a creed as a condition of membership. Their beliefs as to what happens to a person after death are probably as varied as an Anglican's or those of a member of the free churches. They encourage members to come to their own conclusions after reading the New Testament.

They have no literature on funeral rites. Ministers, whether elders, deacons or full ministers, conduct a service for the dead according to whatever form they wish. (Elders and deacons are ordained but earn their living in ordinary ways.) They may even use orders of service from other denominations, for example the Free Church, the Baptists, the Congregationalists or the Church of Scotland (this latter is, of course, Presbyterian, not Anglican in the way the C of E is). As is usual with other denominations of similar origin and outlook, local ministers try to comfort the bereaved.

Hindus

Although most Hindus tend to be confined geographically either to the subcontinent of India or here in Britain (and even in the latter tend to be originally from one of only three regions: East Africa, Gujarat or the Punjab), Hinduism is a remarkably diverse religion, comprising a variety of attitudes and traditions within the main stream.

This book is not the place to describe every detail of Hinduism, since it is about bereavement, not comparative religion, but I would point out that questions of caste as well as of attitude and tradition complicate the funeral proceedings. For instance, some Gujarati castes forbid their women to attend a crematorium, whereas among Punjabis there may be no such prohibition, and the *pagrī* rite involving the use of a turban is observed by Punjabis but not by Gujaratis. Even among Gujaratis there may be differences of emphasis, depending on which of the two principal sects they belong to, and a similar bifurcation is found among Punjabis.

Even the belief in reincarnation is not shared by absolutely all Hindus. For most of them, however, it is a cardinal concept and it makes the Hindu attitude towards death comparatively serene, so that for survivors the period immediately after a person's death is not quite equivalent to mourning as it is traditionally understood in the West. At the same time death is seen as one of the four miseries of material existence, along with birth, disease and old age. The last two would be seen as miseries by the most out-and-out materialist in the West, but birth probably would not. For Hindus, however, it is more material existence itself that constitutes the misery, particularly being trapped in the seemingly endless cycle of having to go through the process over and over again.

A useful metaphor to bear in mind in the context of reincarnation is that of the soul passing from one room to another, for it is the body alone that is shed when someone dies. At the same time the Hindu is striving in the long run to free himself from the otherwise continuous process of birth, death, rebirth (perhaps as a member of another species altogether), death again and so on and on. Only once this liberation has been attained can union with Brahman, the Supreme One, come about. If a person when he dies has his mind concentrated solely on Krishna, the Lord (in Britain probably the most popular avatar, or incarnation, of Vishnu, one of three forms of the Supreme One), he is certain to attain the desired freedom from the cycle. This means that funeral rites are supposed to help the deceased rather than the mourners. In other words, bereavement, however terrible in as much as it touches on the living, is of secondary importance compared to the betterment of the soul.

Yet the bereaved are not expected to grin and bear it. It is considered fitting that they should go through a period of mourning – perhaps 'adjustment in sorrow' might express it better – if only so that they can subsequently continue their everyday lives unimpeded by pent-up grief. At the same time excessive regard for the dead is deprecated as pointless by the Vedas, the ancient Indian writings in Sanskrit from which stems Hinduism, or more properly in its adherents' eyes the *sanatan(a) dharma* (eternal religion). Instead the Vedas teach that one must bow to the will of Krishna, the Lord, accept the inevitable and submit oneself to the temporary nature of all life.

If a person passes his earthly life under the weight of preoccupation with worldly goods and the pleasures of the flesh, after he dies his soul is in danger of becoming entangled, held up, hampered in its progress. Hindus, like Roman Catholics, entertain the concept of a state they call limbo. In the Hindu version the soul may become trapped in limbo as a wandering spirit or ghostly entity called a *preta* (perhaps the Western equivalent would be the 'lost soul', or even the revenant, with its connotation of restlessness). To prevent this the bereaved try to purify the soul of the departed one by preparing consecrated food in rituals known as *śrādda*. Only if the soul is thus purified can it continue its passage.

Hindus regard it as important for a person to die lying on the ground. In Britain the floor may be used if necessary, even if it is on an upper storey of a building, and hospital staff unfamiliar with Hindu beliefs sometimes show consternation at terminally ill Hindu patients struggling out of bed to lie on the floor or being helped from their bed for the same purpose by relatives. In addition to dying stretched out on the ground, a Hindu should be placed so that his head points to the magnetic north, thus aligning him with the earth's magnetic field, though ordinarily this is held to be a most unlucky position.

Suicide, as in most cultures, is considered an extremely undesirable sort of death. Certain other deaths may be inauspicious even though they are not suicides: sudden death, death at an early age, violent death, death that occurs during moonless nights, otherwise known as *panchaka*, and death that occurs during any of the six months between 14 July and 14 January, otherwise the Vedic Capricorn, when the sun is becoming lower and lower in the heavens. This would seem to entail more than half all Hindu deaths being thought 'bad', which on the face of it would seem to contradict the tendency for Hindus to regard death calmly inasmuch as it is considered to be merely a sloughing off of the body while the soul proceeds to another room. Still, such contrasts between theory and practice are widespread in most religions.

The next of kin are supposed to perform the funeral rites.

What follows is predominantly a Gujarati series of ceremonies, but some of these may be mixed with others that are predominantly Punjabi.

If a person has not been put on the ground before dying she should be placed there as soon as possible after death and a *dīva* or *dipak* – a candle – should be lit. These candles are made from the same flour used in chapatti bread, to which is added *ghī* or *ghee*, clarified butter made from buffalo milk. The *dīva* or *dipak* is placed close to the deceased's head on her right side. A little grain is then placed near it. The next of kin should also place themselves on the deceased person's right side and offer up *pindas* to her departed soul, although some observers have remarked that this seems to be a rare feature of Hindu death ceremonies in modern Britain. *Pindas* are small cakes made of wheat flour, sugar and linseed. Ideally, six *pindas* in all are placed either on top of the corpse's chest or on the ground nearby. The number six stands for the entities of body, exit door, crossroads, place of rest, place of cremation and the funeral pyre.

133

If the death has occurred in a hospital, hospice or other establishment outside the family dwelling, the coffin is taken home and opened once there so that the deceased is visible. Mantras (formulaic incantations believed to be divinely inspired) are chanted, such as the Gayātri Mantra (a type of metre twenty-four syllables long, usually set in three sections of eight syllables each, and addressed to the sun savitar as the supreme force of generation). In addition a passage from the sacred scriptures is read, such as chapter XV of the Bhagavad Gītā, which describes the material world, itself held to be a mere reflection of the 'real' spiritual world, much as in Plato's writings the material world is described as being like shadows flickering on a cave wall in comparison with the better, 'real' world outside the cave. The day and month are recited, as are the name and caste of the deceased, in a liturgical rite called the Sankalpa (an announcement of one's resolution to perform a given act; perhaps 'pledge' would be the nearest meaning). Following this the deceased's next of kin strews the body with flowers or dry grass (ideally *kusha*, a species of grass commonly called *darbha*, which is looked on by Hindus as the most sacred of Indian grasses). The next of kin also sprinkles water on the body. Meanwhile the mantra

Aum AAPO HISHTA-MAYO BHYVASTAN URJJE
DAHATAN MAHERANAY CHAKSHASEYO VAH
SHIVTAMO RASAHTASYA BHAJAYTEHNAH
USHTIRIV MATARAH TASMA ARANGMAMAVAH
YASYA KSHAYAYA JINVATH AAPO
JANAYATHA CHANAH

is recited. ('Aum' is cognate with 'om', a sacred syllable which is held to be the root of everything that has existence.) Next an infusion of water from the sacred River Ganges in which leaves of *tūlsi* – an aromatic plant related to basil – have been soaked is poured into the dead person's mouth while the following mantras are recited three times:

Aum KESHAVAY Namah
Aum NARAYANAY Namah
Aum MADHAVAY Namah

Then a *mālā* (necklace, wreath or garland) of *tūlsi* is placed round the dead person's neck, his forehead is smeared with sandal paste and sandalwood and sandal powder are heaped or scattered on the rest of the body. A portion of *ghee* is offered up, accompanied by the mantras:

Aum Prajapataye Swaha Idam Prajapataye Na Mama
Aum Indray Swaha Idam Indray Na Mama
Aum Agnaye Swaha Idam Agnaye Na Mama
Aum Somay Swaha Idam Somay Na Mama
Aum Yamay Swaha Idam Yamay Na Mama
Aum Mriyave Swaha Idam Mrityave Na Mama
Aum Brahmane Swaha Idam Brahmane Na Mama

These are followed by three further offerings of *ghee*, while the mantras below are chanted.

Aum Bhooh Swaha Idam Agnaye Na Mama
Aum Bhuvah Swaha Idam Vayave Na Mama
Aum Svaha Swaha Idam Suryay Na Mama

Next comes the *Havan Samagri* ritual, in which a mixture of aromatic woods are thrown on a fire, accompanied by the mantra:

Aum AYURJAGNEN KALPATAM
CHAKSHUR JAGNEN KALPATAM
VAG JAGNEN KALPATAM

135

ATMA JAGNEN KALPATAM

JYOTIR JAGNEN KALPATAM

PRISHTAM JAGNEN KALPATAM

PRANO JAGNEN KALPATAM

SHROTRAM JAGNEN KALPATAM

MANO JAGNEN KALPATAM

BRAHMA JAGNEN KALPATAM

SVAR JAGNEN KALPATAM

YAGNO JAGNEN KALPATAM

Then a coconut from which the milk has been drained is split open and filled with linseed and *ghee* and placed on the dead person's forehead, after which the mantra

ASOU SWARGAYE LOKAYE SWAHA JAVALTU PAVKE

is chanted. *Ghee* is again poured and is followed by the mantra:

Aum VASOH PAVITRAMASI SHATDHARAM VASOH

PAVITRAMASI SAHASRA DHARAM DEVSTVA

SAVITA PUNATOO VASOH PAVITREN

SHATDHAREN SUPPVA KAM DHUSHAH SWAHA

There are, of course, variations on the above procedure. Sometimes with Hindus settled in Britain, for whom the precise differences between sects back in India may have become blurred, a Vedic fire ceremony observed by one sect will be followed a few minutes later by the ceremony of another sect which back in India purist members of the former would shun. During the offering up of the substances described above the members of the dead person's family may circle the body, touching his feet as they pass. A small-denomination coin may be placed in the deceased's mouth so that he can pay the man who ferries the dead across a mythical river. The domestic part of the fire ceremony may take place after the members of the family have returned from the crematorium rather than before.

Hindus cremate their dead, unless the deceased is a suicide, when the fire ceremony, or *agni sanskār*, which constitutes the Hindu form of cremation, is inappropriate. In such a case the dead person is buried or slipped into a river. In the hot countries from which Hindus either originally came or in which they still live it has become the custom to perform the cremation ceremony within twenty-four hours of death, on the same day if death occurs before sunset, on the following day if after sunset. As with so many other religions, this might seem on the surface to be a reflection simply of local climatic and sanitary conditions. Nevertheless, it has been elevated into a point of doctrine, even in climatically temperate north-western Europe. Accordingly, with Hindus an immediate cremation is necessary if the soul is to benefit to the utmost.

In Britain things are not so easy on this score. Crematoria are busy places, working to tight schedules, so that they cannot book in a 'client' at the drop of a hat. The law may insist on a post-mortem. Many of the deceased's closest relatives may still live in India and have to make complicated travel arrangements to get to Britain at short notice. More-over, not every Hindu priest feels himself qualified to preside at a funeral. Ideally, the services of a *māhapatra* or *māhabrahmin* will be sought, though if neither of these is available an elderly member of a Brahmin family who is familiar with the appropriate mantras may be called in. Because of the frequent delay in cremating a body in today's Britain, the washing and dressing of it are put off until just before the funeral, although in India they would be carried out immediately after death (and used to be in Britain, too, come to that, when the first Indian immigrants arrived a generation and more ago).

Both washing and dressing the body are subject to consid-erations of caste. The family plays an important part at this point, too. Older relatives come into their own on such occasions, being asked for advice about traditions. Any neighbours who help to wash or dress the body must be of the same caste and sex as the deceased. The clothes put on the body are such as would have been worn in everyday life. Ideally, they should be new, which in the case of a whole suit may place a strain on the family finances. If a wife dies before her husband she is dressed in the sari or other costume she wore on her wedding day, rather as some romantically inclined Western women express a desire to be buried in their wedding gowns.

After being dressed the body is taken to the crematorium, where the congregation seat themselves and recite fifteen more mantras. The first likens the allotted lifespan of the deceased to the ripening of a watermelon and implores liberation from the cycle of birth, death and rebirth. The second addresses God and lists his attributes of supreme knowledge, infinity of form and ubiquity of presence. The third likens the passing of the soul from the old dead body to a new living one to a man shedding an old piece of clothing and putting on a new one. The fourth states that the soul is eternal and not subject to death. The fifth recites the invulnerability of the soul, whether to weapons or the elements of fire, water and wind. The sixth is a reminder that the beginning and end are beyond human knowledge, that humans glimpse only transient phenomena and asks why therefore there should be grief.

The seventh offers up the congregation's adoration to God and recites his all-powerful nature. The eighth addresses the deceased and reminds him how his body will merge with the five elements. The ninth addresses God again, as judge, bringer of peace, creator, preserver and destroyer of the universe and implores Him to grant the soul of the deceased person a worthy home. The tenth addresses the deceased and assures him of happiness in heaven in company with his ancestors, though urging him simultaneously to be free of sin so that he may attain grace and enlightenment. The eleventh calls on fire to burn the corpse and the air in the corpse to merge with the air outside it, then prays to the Lord to look favourably on the worshippers' sacrifices.

The twelfth states that everything mortal dies with the death of the body but that *dharma* (moral and religious duty) is the living person's true friend and stays with the soul after the body's death. A prayer that *dharma* may not have died then follows, for if it has it takes the soul with it. The thirteenth recites how the enlightened one, liberated from pride, illusion, attachment to material things, egoism and the dual obsession with pleasure and pain, attains the final everlasting goal. The fourteenth calls on ultimate light to lead the worshippers from untruth to truth, darkness to light and death to immortality. The fifteenth brings the proceedings to an end.

Once the cremation is over, members of the congregation accompany the family home and stay with them there awhile. Sometimes the ceremony of placing aromatic woods on the fire is performed at the bereaved family's home at this point rather than during the funeral proper. There is customarily a time set aside for grieving which is called *shok* (literally 'sorrow'), though an element of ritual impurity is involved too and the living may be subject to the unwelcome attentions of the *preta* of the deceased. This period may last anything up to between ten days and just under a fortnight. During it the principal reception room in the house is cleared of furniture and its floor covered with white sheets. Neighbours and friends call round, offer their condolences, or *afsos*, swap reminiscences of the deceased and stay to take part in readings from holy scriptures such as the Bhagavad Gītā or, for Punjabis, Amrit Varsh. There is also some hymn-singing. With Punjabis the *pagrī* ritual is supposed to conclude the grieving period, but sometimes the *shok* timetable is truncated and the concluding ceremony is brought forward, perhaps because those who are expert in the ritual and necessary for its correct performance are likely to be unavailable after the proper number of days are up and because relatives who have flown in from the other side of the world might have to return there immediately.

Humanists

Humanists are people who see the human species as responsible for its own fate, whether in life or in the future, that is to say for our descendants. They do not have a religious standpoint, though most try to lead their lives within some kind of ethical framework. It might be going a bit far to call them all atheists or agnostic. It would be just possible to hold some sort of belief in what for want of a better word I shall call a deity and still be a humanist. For instance, you might maintain that although some vaguely envisaged supreme being existed somewhere in the universe, he, she or it left human beings and the other inhabitants of this planet to their own devices. Such an attitude is in fact fairly close to that of the ancient Greek poet and philosopher Epicurus (circa 341–270 BC), who features prominently in the list of authors recommended in a British Humanist Association booklet for reading from at humanist funerals.

The British Humanist Association, which exists to propagate humanist ideas, does not, of course, represent all humanists, since to be a humanist is to be very much the opposite of the sort of person who is a slave to the herd instinct and thus a 'joiner'. Nevertheless, it would probably be true to say that the vast majority of humanists hold that there is no God and no afterlife, which are two good reasons why they see humans as responsible for their own lives in the first place.

In any case, from the bereavement and funeral ceremony point of view, the suggestions and information provided by the British Humanist Association are the best the rest of us have got as a statement of the average humanist's position, and they may be taken as broadly representative of the humanist viewpoint in general. Humanism is an optimistic, or perhaps I should say ameliorative, set of principles and views. It aims at improving life for us all by developing the 'good' in people. Humanists hold that this aim can best be brought about by rational discussion rather than superstition and an existence lived according to religious beliefs for which there is no objective evidence.

Humanists maintain that a funeral should be dignified. This is in accordance with traditional religious practice, though I cannot see that dignity is intrinsically desirable from a humanist point of view. For instance, a number of folk ceremonies associated with weddings are not at all dignified – the 'stag' night or the throwing of rice over a newly married couple – even though a wedding is supposed to be just as much a 'rite of passage' as a funeral. Actually, so many marriages end in tears these days that one could argue that a wedding is much more demonstrably a precursor to misery than a funeral, particularly since many humanists would say we don't know what experiences the chief participant in a funeral – the deceased – will undergo later, whether enjoyable ones or unenjoyable ones or simply none at all. So why insist on dignity? It doesn't guarantee happiness for the chief participant, or necessarily for the assembled company. I have been rather beastly to Tony Walter in the Bibliography, but to give him his due he is the only author among those of all the huge number of books I have read in preparing this one who comes near to suggesting that there is no reason why a funeral shouldn't be a 'fun' experience.

The humanist retort to the above is that their funerals are designed to comfort and console the bereaved as much as to give the deceased a decent send-off. This automatically assumes that the bereaved humanist suffers on the same scale as the religious person who has lost a friend or relation. Probably that is correct, though logic suggests that the religious person who believes in an afterlife ought to be less downcast at a funeral than the humanist, who does not. But logic flies out of the window when death looms, grim and lowering, in the doorway. One's humanism has to be very robust to stand up to savage assaults on the emotions – and bereavement unleashes some of the most savage there are.

The British Humanist Association will supply someone to officiate at the funeral ceremony if you do not wish to do so yourself, and undertakers are perfectly happy to carry out a humanist funeral. But if a funeral is avowedly agnostic or atheist and the next of kin want the deceased to be buried in the local churchyard, the vicar's permission has to be sought. In practice the overwhelming majority of humanist funerals are cremations.

The British Humanist Association booklet *Funerals Without God* (see Bibliography) suggests that those officiating at a humanist funeral could allow a religious member of the deceased person's family to insert a prayer, hymn or reading from an overtly religious text into the ceremony if she insists, but only if the person officiating can make it clear that this is a personal contribution, not an invitation to worship for all those present. Another possibility is for the next of kin to give a hard and fast ruling one way or the other about such 'intrusiveness'. After all, the religious-minded can always mount a memorial service on their own initiative on some other date and at some other place if they want a spiritual element.

A suggested order of humanist ceremony is as follows: music, an opening address, readings from poetry or prose, an appreciation of the dead person's life delivered by a practised extempore speaker (or at any rate someone who can read from cue cards, autocues and scripts without seeming to), the committal of the body to the flames in a crematorium or grave in a cemetery or churchyard, some closing words and a final playing of music. Humanists like to stand when the committal takes place.

It is only fair to warn those who contemplate having a humanist funeral service for a deceased friend or relative that it is terribly easy for the event to lapse into banality and insipidity. The result can be infinitely more depressing than the most morbid example of the high Victorian mourning cult. I am sorry to have to say that the booklet *Funerals Without God* gives very little promise that the average humanist 'officiant' will rise to the occasion. It is full of such advice to potential speakers as not to clutter up the lectern with handbags or briefcases. God knows most parsons are dismal enough at preaching these days, but that sort of guidance plumbs new depths of triviality and imaginative poverty.

It is also rather comic that humanists cannot come up with suitably stirring passages from which to quote at a funeral without plundering writings by religious authors. On the first page of the section of *Funerals Without God* devoted to poetry and prose readings there are two poems by Christina Rossetti, one of the most pious Christians who ever lived and an exceptionally glorious pillar of the Church of England. The other two items on that page are entitled 'Requiem' – a wholly Christian institution. True, the humanist content thereafter takes a turn for the better with excerpts from those ferociously anti-religious writers Swinburne and Lucretius, while Shelley continues this note of anti-clerical defiance. But Robert Herrick, who follows, was actually in holy orders though admittedly he celebrated in his works, and to a certain extent perhaps his life, too, a vague paganism. And Shakespeare also is an awkward customer for humanists to claim as one of their own.

A slightly subtler problem with humanist funerals is that participants often cannot make up their minds about (a) how anti-religious they should be or (b) how mournful, as opposed to joyous. It is worth knowing that you can insist on crosses being removed from crematoria assembly rooms (usually called chapels, but clearly the term is inappropriate here). On that score *Funerals Without God* is helpful. It is also useful in pointing out that you can even remove prayer books and hymnals from the crematorium if there is time to gather up what may amount to more than a score of the things and then put them back again before the next lot of clients arrive.

And certainly, as *Funerals Without God* also reminds us, some humanist members of the assembled company may object to organ music on the grounds that it reminds them of church. (My own objection is that it is reminiscent of a 1950s Essoldo on a rainy afternoon.) Indeed, some humanist 'officiants' think that any music is a barrier to strong feelings when the coffin slides into the furnace. This raises the uncomfortable question of how much in the way of strong feelings is desirable. But on music generally the author of *Funerals Without God* gets into her stride at last, discussing suitable music on cassette tapes for inducing solemnity to begin with, then tunes of a very different nature to conjure up a sense almost of lightheartedness at the end. But not every member of the company develops this change of feelings in the same way, at the same pace or even at all. As with any drastic departure from traditional observances, then, humanist funerals bring their own problems. Traditional observances have them too, of course, but they are by no means so inflexible as to prevent modification.

Jains
Like Hindus, Jains cremate their dead, and with the same rites. They are wholly non-violent and have no priests, however, believing that all life is sacred. Thus a Jain will not even step on an insect. In their funeral rites they recite mantras and prayers, their mantra being called *shanti*.

Jehovah's Witnesses
Jehovah's Witnesses are an adventist sect started in the USA by Charles Taze Russell (1852–1916), a Pittsburgh draper who

was brought up as a Congregationalist. 'Adventist' denotes a preoccupation with the Second Coming, something Russell became convinced would occur in 1874, followed by the end of the world in 1914. The outbreak of war that year boosted his reputation. Jehovah's Witnesses believe that Jesus was not divine, although he was the son of the God of the Old Testament, Jehovah. By now, of course, over eighty years have passed since 1914, but they hold that Armageddon is still to come. On that day Satan will be cast into servitude for a millennium and the elect, that is to say all Jehovah's Witnesses, whether dead or alive according to conventional ideas of what constitutes life, will enjoy a terrestrial paradise in an exclusive resurrection. The rest of humanity face extinction.

Jehovah's Witness funerals take place at the nearest kingdom hall, the buildings in which their assemblies take place. Among other features of the funeral, a member of the kingdom hall's committee delivers an address. Burial in cemeteries and cremation are equally common.

Jews

Unlike all the previous denominations or faiths, being Jewish according to traditional law is not a matter of what a man believes, in the way it is in Christianity or Islam, but of descent. And not any old descent, either. Not a Jew's father's descent, for instance, even though that father is of the line of David himself, if he married out of the faith so that our man's mother is not Jewish. It works the other way round, too. If your mother was Jewish you are, according to traditional law, also Jewish, whether you are a practising believer or non-practising, or believe wholeheartedly or half-heartedly. Thus the Earl of Snowdon counts as Jewish according to this criterion since his mother, Anne Messel, was of a Jewish family, but his son and heir Viscount Linley would not be because only his father was Jewish, not his mother, Princess Margaret.

You would still be Jewish in the traditional law's eyes even if you were actually an atheist or agnostic or a paid-up member of some wholly distinct faith. Thus the British Humanist Association can speak in slightly quaint terms of the advisability when planning a humanist funeral of placing the coffin in a crematorium chapel before the mourners enter if the family 'has a Jewish background'. And Disraeli, who was baptised a Christian as a child, is still referred to as Britain's first and so far only Jewish prime minister. Even St Peter, who extended Christian Church membership to Gentiles and is popularly (if perhaps unhistorically) credited with being the first pope, was Jewish 'within the meaning of the act', as it were, though his Jewishness is seldom stressed by Christian writers. Most peoples would have cause for congratulation after having produced the founders of one religion of world importance. Judaism has produced the founders of two – a colossal achievement.

Anyone meeting the above definitions of Jewishness has among other things the right to be buried in a Jewish cemetery. The position has become complicated since 1983 by the decision in that year of the Central Conference of American Rabbis, who constitute a nationwide gathering of Reform rabbis in the USA, to look upon sons and daughters of a Jewish father or a Jewish mother as Jewish. No other branch of Judaism has agreed to this, however.

That is a crucial proviso, because there are several sects within British Judaism, ranging from the highly orthodox, such as the Chasidic and Lubavitch Jews, through the more or less middle-of-the-road United Synagogue to the progressive wing represented by the Reform Jews and Liberal Jews. It is in the latter groups that female rabbis such as the broadcaster and newspaper article-writer Julia Neuberger are found. Conservative Jews, and still more so Reform Jews, also impose less strict rules for accepting Gentile converts to the faith than do the orthodox. This means that some converts and subsequently any children they may have are accepted as Jews by some Jews but not by others. Some of the extremely orthodox Jews, particularly in Greater London, where the majority of Jews in the UK live, seem to find it difficult even to recognise their more progressive brethren as co-religionists. The latter in their turn sometimes deprecate what they see as the inward-looking, even narrow attitude of the orthodox.

What unites, or ought to unite, Jews in this country is that they are still labouring under a collective bereavement – that of six million of their kind, many of them close relatives, slaughtered in the most nauseating fashion by the Nazis.

Even now, nearly half a century after the Second World War, some individual memories are impossible to eradicate. Indeed, now that the generation that suffered in concentration camps is entering its seventies, the sense of horror is in many cases stronger than ever, for just as elderly people who have led the most ordinary of lives cast back in their memories to their early days rather than their more recent ones, so do those who have undergone ghastly ordeals.

The Jewish Bereavement Counselling Service is a pan-Judaism body, that is to say it operates across all sects within British Jewry. It has found that not only is the generation of concentration-camp survivors under greater psychological pressure than ever but that their younger relatives are increasingly alienated, shocked, distrustful or resentful of their elders when the latter have refused to talk about their experiences.

Jewish ideas about what happens to the dead have a long and varied history. There are references in the Old Testament to a place where the dead go: sometimes a pit, sometimes the earth opening up and absorbing them, their permanent dwelling place being an underworld called *sheol*. A later rabbinic tradition in Judaism derived a word *gehinnom*, meaning hell, from an Old Testament word for a valley where children were sacrificed to pagan gods. (The better known variant in English is probably gehenna, which occurs in the New Testament.) The rabbis also evolved the idea that in an afterlife obedience to divine law in this one would be rewarded and disobedience punished.

Some commentators also came up with the concept of resurrection, which is not mentioned till late in the Old Testament. As the Messianic age comes to an end, the resurrection of the dead will take place and they will be reunited with their souls, whereupon there will be a final judgement, or so says the Talmud (a collection of legal commentaries on the Mishnah, which itself is a summary of the Torah She-Be-Al Peh, which in turn is the Jewish religious legal code handed down from generation to generation by word of mouth). The good will go to heaven, the bad to everlasting punishment. The debt owed to this concept by Christian doctrine is obvious.

An ancient rabbinical commentary called the Midrash Konen describes heaven (*gan eden*) as containing five halls for each of five classes of the saved: one of cedar with a crystal ceiling for sincere converts to Judaism; a second, also of cedar but with a silver ceiling, for sinners who have repented in time; an especially sweet-smelling third hall of silver and gold studded with pearls for what one might call the crème de la crème among the saved; the fourth of olive wood, for religious martyrs; and the fifth, again of gold and silver but this time studded with precious stones, for the Messiah (literally 'the anointed one', that is to say chosen leader, or redeemer) of the line of David, of the line of Elijah and of the line of Ephraim.

One picture of hell describes sinners being tormented by angels of destruction, some hung up by their eyelids, some by their ears, some by their tongues, some by their feet, with long black worms crawling all over their bodies.

These are essentially historical concepts, however, and have been unequivocally rejected by Reform Jews, for example on the occasion of the Pittsburgh Platform of 1885, which is one of the principal formulations of the Reform position. Among both Reform and other Jewish groups they have largely been replaced in modern times by the doctrine that the soul is immortal and will eventually attain spiritual ecstasy.

Anybody present at the moment of death should join in saying the prayer 'Tziddukha-Din' ('justification of the judgement'). After someone has died his eyes and mouth should be shut and the jaw tied shut if necessary, as with the usual procedure in other religions. The corpse is then placed on the floor and a sheet is draped over it. A candle is lit and put near the head. The corpse should not be left alone and ideally someone will watch over it, reciting psalms. If the brother, father or husband of the deceased does this he has performed *mitzvah* (a good deed), and is excused having to take part in prayers or donning the phylacteries (*tefillin*) till the time of the funeral. *Tefillin* are small boxes made of leather, inside which are excerpts from the Torah. They are strapped on to the left arm and forehead by thin leather thongs and worn for morning service unless the day is the Sabbath or one of certain festivals. Whether the deceased has died at home or in a hospital or hospice, all the mirrors in his private dwelling should be covered over and any containers with still water in them should be emptied.

It is desirable that the body be disposed of promptly (usually, but not always, by burial, which we shall come to), but this is not always possible. For instance, the death may have occurred on the Sabbath or just before it; at the Jewish New Year (Rosh Hashanah), which falls in early autumn; on the Day of Atonement, which falls shortly after the New Year and is reckoned the most sacred day of the Temple year; on the opening and closing day of pilgrim festivals – so called because originally Jews made a pilgrimage to the holy city of Jerusalem – such as Passover in spring; and Tabernacles (Sukkot), a kind of harvest festival at the end of the summer.

All of the foregoing are sacred and no funeral can take place on them.

Most practising Jews are members of a burial society and fellow members look after the corpse and get it ready for the funeral by washing it and putting it into a shroud of white linen, then into a coffin (which among the traditionally minded should be made of wood only, without handles or decorations of metal, not even name plaques). Alternatively, the corpse may be lifted on to a bier, always face upwards, without the use of a coffin. The deceased is buried in his *tallit* (prayer shawl) if he is a fully grown man, although it will deliberately have been slightly damaged, either by a slight tear to a fringe or by the removal of a tassel, so that it is not whole and cannot be used again.

Each synagogue belongs to a burial society. The rabbi conducts the funeral service. Orthodox Jews insist on burial rather than cremation, though very occasionally a person's cremated remains are allowed to be buried in an orthodox cemetery. If so, they are placed in a full-sized coffin first. In family law as interpreted by the orthodox, a widow whose husband has disappeared – lost at sea, say – is forbidden to remarry until absolute proof of her husband's death is forthcoming. This has proved particularly trying for women whose husbands have been taken as hostages in the Middle East. Some have not heard news of whether their husbands are alive or dead for years on end. A man in the same circumstances is under no such restraint.

Reform Jews tend not to object to cremation or even embalming. Indeed, their rabbis often conduct services at a crematorium, having led a procession there or to a cemetery while reciting the appropriate liturgy. Funeral processions may halt en route so that mourners can grieve as uninhibitedly as possible, including tearing their clothing, though in some Jewish traditions this should be done on first hearing the news of a person's death or after the funeral. There is none of the insistence on a supposed decorum that one finds in Western Christianity or, for instance, Islam. Nor, among Reform Jews, is there such a need for haste with burial, if that is chosen instead of cremation, in the way there is with the orthodox, although it is still Reform practice to dress the deceased in a shroud and *tallit*.

Among all Jews suicides are nowadays entitled to equal treatment with those who died involuntarily, though at one time the orthodox opposed this while their Reform brethren did not. But in general suicides and other transgressors against God's law are not subject to mourning under the full set of rules set out below. Provided they are halachically Jewish (that is, by inheritance through the mother), even those who marry out of the faith are still entitled to a Jewish burial, even an orthodox one, or indeed a Jewish funeral according to the rites of any other community that recognises the authority of the Chief Rabbi and the Beth Din (court of the Chief Rabbi) in London.

One of the principal mourners often delivers a panegyric over the coffin as it is lowered into the grave or perhaps at the funeral chapel. The late George Jessel, who was of course Jewish, brought to a fine art this feature of the funeral proceedings – and not just for the Jewish dead, either. After the deceased has been consigned to the grave, several of the men present cover him up with earth. All males attending a Jewish funeral service should wear skull caps or hats, whatever their religion. At the obsequies of the late Lord Delfont, one of the two barons of the powerful Winogradsky dynasty, there were press photographs of many distinguished non-Jews – what a character in Disraeli's *Tancred* calls 'flat-nosed, bustling Franks' – wearing skull caps. Putting the tile in Gentile, as it were, or here perhaps 'on' would be more accurate. Lord Forte wore a trilby, which some press commentators observed was more suitable for a race meeting.

Those present say a prayer for the dead known as *kaddish*,

151

together with other prayers in memory of the deceased. The nearest kin – parents, siblings, spouse or children – are offered condolence by other mourners and everybody, whether he has helped fill the grave or not, is supposed to wash his hands before going home to where the deceased lived. There the members of the immediate family eat a round bread roll and a hard-boiled egg prepared by non-family members. The shape of the roll and the egg itself are both symbols of life and to symbolise mourning it used to be the custom to dip the egg in ashes.

Many rabbis in the United Synagogue branch of British Jewry are nowadays schooled in pastoral care, not excluding bereavement counselling, as part of their vocational training. Reform Jews claim that their rabbis tend to be better at consoling the bereaved. Barbara Borts, an American feminist who as an ordained rabbi looked after her own flock until 1988 out at Radlett and Bushey in what was for urban types the remote location of Hertfordshire, is quoted in Stephen Brook's book *The Club* as saying that her Reform Jews have the edge over the United Synagogue in lots of ways and that Reform rabbis are more proficient at dealing with bereavement, whereas some orthodox rabbis are extraordinarily lacking in sensitivity on the subject. Doubtless the orthodox would retort that tradition confers its own strong framework, and in such a secure manner that the necessary sensitivity is conjured up almost automatically, certainly naturally and organically. Besides, the orthodox communities see their society as an extended family rather than the small unit of father, mother and two children dubbed 'nuclear' by sociologists, so that the whole community offers condolence and support. Accordingly, as they see it, bereavement counselling is virtually redundant.

In Jewish tradition the friends and more distant relations of the bereaved person, be she spouse, sister, daughter or mother (or, if male, brother, son or father) of the dead person, rally round and more or less take over her household for a week following the death. This period of seven days is known as *shivah*, and technically it starts with the burial rather than the death, though the former normally takes place on the same day as the death or at most the next day. The friends and more distant relations take care of all the domestic chores, in particular the shopping for groceries and the cooking. They may even spoon-feed the bereaved person, treating her almost like a small child. The principal bereaved person is not supposed to take part in any recreation at all, including religious feasts, or to wear leather shoes or clean clothes. Male bereaved are forbidden to shave. Neither sex may bathe, have sex or cut their hair. And between the actual death and the funeral the principal mourners are excused various religious duties such as prayer. At home they perch on low stools or cushions on the floor.

The idea of taking the domestic tasks off our hypothetical widow's shoulders is to get her to appreciate that she is not alone in her bereavement. Nowadays, with doctors tending increasingly to administer sedatives, this has in some cases become a thing of the past, and *shivah* is anyway most frequently and minutely observed among orthodox Jews, who, for instance, would also recite morning and evening prayers if a *minyan* (quorum) of ten men can be gathered together.

After the period of *shivah* is over – it comes to an end on the evening of the seventh day after the burial – there is a comparatively low-key time of mourning called *sheloshim*, literally 'thirty', which, as one might expect, lasts for thirty days. The prohibition on shaving, hair-cutting, donning new clothes or attendance at festivals continues. There is some divergence among Jews as to whether the end of *sheloshim* brings mourning to a close as far as most of one's relations are concerned. Even the more relaxed attitude holds that parents should be mourned for almost an entire year and the stricter tradition enjoins this prolonged period of mourning for all relatives. The *shivah* period can be shortened if certain holy days and feasts fall in the middle of it, for example the Jewish New Year, the Day of Atonement and Passover or the Festival of Weeks (Shavuot). Conversely, if the burial is carried out in the middle of certain other holy times, such as the Feast of Tabernacles or Passover, the full *shivah* comes into effect once that holy time finishes.

A year after a member of one's family has died one would recite the *kaddish* and a reading from the prophets known as the Haftarah, peruse the Torah and set memorial illuminations going.

Lutherans

In the UK Lutherans are often of Germanic or other Central European background. Their doctrine as to what happens to a person after death is broadly similar to that of the other chief Protestant denominations and they are equally comfortable with cremation or burial. As with Anglicans, the minister meets the coffin, which may be covered with a pall, at the entrance to the church. He calls down blessings on God and reminds the congregation of the implications of Christian baptism and the Resurrection. The congregation then sing a psalm or hymn, typically Psalm xxiii, 'The Lord is my shepherd'. Then there follow prayers, a reading of the lesson (typically Job xix, 23–7) and another hymn, psalm or anthem, followed by a second lesson (Isaiah xxv, 6–9).

Other lessons can include Romans viii, 31–5 and 37–9; 1 Corinthians xv, 12–26; Revelations xxi, 2–7; John xi, 21–7; and John xiv, 1–6. Then there is a sermon, which should deal with the dead person's character and perhaps aspects of her life. There follows a recitation of the creed and the intercession, led by the minister with the congregation responding 'Hear us, Lord' after every paragraph. More prayers follow, with either Holy Communion followed by the commendation ('Into your hands, O merciful Saviour . . .') or a recital of the

Lord's Prayer. The choristers then precede the coffin out of the church, while the 'Nunc Dimittis' is sung, if it has not already been sung during Communion.

The committal at the graveside or in the crematorium can be accompanied by sung psalms or readings from the Bible: Job xix, 25–6; Romans xiv, 7–8; John xi, 25–6; John xii, 23–6; 1 Corinthians xv, 51–7; or Philippians iii, 20–1. The same service may be used in modified form for a memorial or for when the body of the deceased is not present.

Mar Thoma Church

This is a Christian denomination – indeed, its members were once best known as being among the Malabar Christians, that is, Christians living in south-west India (where Malabar Coast was a geographical term in former use). The Mar Thoma Church is so named because it claims to have been founded by St Thomas the apostle, 'mar' meaning 'saint'. St Thomas is perhaps best remembered as 'Doubting' Thomas from his calling into question the news of the Resurrection, though what is less well known to lay people is that in saluting the risen Christ as 'My Lord and my God' he is the first human in recorded history explicitly to recognise Christ's divine status.

The Mar Thoma Church and their fellow Christians of south-west India claim that after the sequence of events that included the Crucifixion and Resurrection, St Thomas went to India (they place the precise date as being in AD 52). There he made the first converts to Christianity in the subcontinent and was martyred at Mylapore. Roman Catholic tradition maintains that he died at a place called Calamina (which is sometimes identified with Mylapore) and his relics are allegedly at Ortona, in the Abruzzi region of central Italy, where they are still venerated.

The original Malabar Christians split into three main groups from the late sixteenth century onwards, two of them ending up more or less in communion with Rome, the third becoming closer to the Anglican communion. The Mar Thoma Church, which is in full communion with the Episcopalian churches of North America, the C of E and the respective churches of north and south India, calls itself a reformed church and acknowledges the importance to it of both the Reformation proper and the revivalism of the last century. It describes its worship as Eastern and its tradition as episcopal (that is, it has bishops) but its administration as democratic. It also claims to be ecumenical in outlook. Worldwide it has 875,000 members. In 1988 it created a diocese of North America and Europe, which currently consists of about 13,000 adherents, though in the UK specifically there are probably only about 600.

The funeral service is in three parts, one at the home of the deceased and his family, a second in church and a third at the graveside. Some sections of the liturgy are chanted and are composed in Malayalam, which is the language used in the Indian state of Kerala. In part one the priest starts by invoking God, followed by excerpts from Psalms xxxix, xlix, xc, ciii and cxv, then comes the first of the chants in Malayalam. These last call on the Lord as Messiah and glorify Him principally in terms of the Resurrection and forgiveness of sins. The priest says more prayers and a second chant celebrating the Resurrection is offered up.

The next prayer is called a 'supplication of Mar Jacob', referring to the St James who was 'the Lord's brother' and is known as St James the Less (as opposed to St James the Great, the apostle and one of the inner circle around Christ that witnessed the Transfiguration and the agony in the Garden of Gethsemane). St James the Less was Bishop of Jerusalem in the very earliest Christian times and is credited with the composition of a liturgy that is used by the Syrian Jacobites, who were direct precursors of the Malabar Christians in terms of the rites they used.

The Syrian Jacobites take their name not from the Latin version of St James the Less, although that is indeed

'Jacobus', but from Jacob Baradaeus (circa AD 500–78), who was active throughout much of what is now the Middle East as a wandering monophysite. A monophysite holds that Christ made flesh had a single, divine nature, whereas the principal Christian denominations in the West, including the Roman Catholics and the C of E, believe that after the incarnation Christ had a double nature, divine and human. The Copts, Abyssinians, Armenians and Syrian Jacobites are monophysites, and some of the Malabar Christians united with the Jacobites in the mid-seventeenth century. The Mar Thoma Church is monophysite too, though that does not prevent it being in communion with the C of E.

Bible readings follow, such as Genesis l, 1–13, which is used for male dead, or Genesis xxiii, 1–20, which is used for females. A third lesson, 1 Corinthians xv, 12–19, may be used for either sex. This part of the rites finishes with the Lord's Prayer and a blessing.

At the church the priest opens the proceedings by invoking God. Then he recites an extract from Psalm ciii. Next come more invocations by the priest to God, which differ slightly depending again on whether the deceased is male or female. Thereafter much the same pattern follows as at the private dwelling, with prayers, chants in Malayalam and readings by a specially appointed deacon from the epistles.

Finally comes the procession to the grave and the committal of the body to it. (Mar Thoma Christians do not utterly object to cremation, but they prefer burial if possible.) Chants in Malayalam and more invocations are recited before and after a series of readings from the Bible (John xi, 25–6; John ii, 17; Job v, 7; Ecclesiastes vii, 1; 1 Timothy vi, 7; Ecclesiastes xii, 7; Job i, 21; Ecclesiastes vii, 29; Numbers xxiii, 10; Ecclesiastes xiii, 3; Ecclesiastes iii, 1–2; Ecclesiastes xi, 8; Psalms vi, 5, xxx, 9 and xxxix, 6; and Ecclesiastes xii, 13).

Then the coffin is lowered into the grave and covered over with soil. One passage that can be read either at the graveside following the committal or beforehand while the assembled company are still in the church may be of particular interest to those Christians from other traditions. It consists of a vision of hell expressed in terms of the graves of various powerful men whose footprints are nothing more than marks leading to annihilation, for all the might on earth of those who made them. The footprints are so barren that ugly spiders have spun their cobwebs in them. The moral hardly needs pointing out.

More prayers are said, then the Nicene Creed is recited and the service ends with a blessing. Afterwards the bereaved are offered pastoral care and counselling for as long as it may take for them to adjust to their loss.

Moravian Church

This is a Protestant denomination, sometimes known also as Moravian Brethren. It dates from 1722, when Count Nikolaus Ludwig von Zinzendorf (1700–60) allowed Protestant refugees from Austria (which, of course, was an almost entirely Catholic land) to settle on his estates in Saxony. These Protestants were spiritual heirs and in some cases direct descendants genealogically of the Bohemian Brethren, who, back in the fifteenth century, two or three generations before the Reformation proper, had formulated a simple and almost anarchistic form of Christianity. (For instance, they refused to swear oaths and to undergo military service.)

The colony flourished and became known across continental Europe as Herrnhuter, from the village of Herrnhut, which they built on Zinzendorf's land, rather than Moravian Brethren. The Count spent some years in the early 1750s in England proselytising on behalf of the Moravians. An act of Parliament had recognised the Moravian Episcopal Church as early as 1749 and bishops, presbyters and deacons are still part of this denomination's hierarchy, though not with the formal powers that they have in other churches which retain those institutions.

The Moravian Church has had a strong influence on Methodism, and like Methodism it emphasises simplicity, evangelical fervour and rejection of complex doctrine and liturgy. In earlier times the word 'died' was never used by Moravians of one of their number. He was spoken of as having 'fallen asleep' or 'gone home and been laid in the grave'. Instead of graveyards or churchyards for burial the Moravians speak of 'God's Acre', where deceased Christians are deposited to wait for the resurrection. They established their own burial grounds from an early date. These were subdivided into square plots, each of which was designated for specific occupants. For instance, dead women, whether married or widowed, are placed in one section; men, whether still married or widowers, in another; single men on one side of a third section and boys on the opposite side of the same square-shaped plot; single women and girls in a similar pattern inside a fourth plot.

The idea that people who in life had interests and occupations in common should be buried next to each other is common among nearly all faiths, but with most denominations it usually boils down in practice to members of the same family or income group. With Moravians it is more marital status and sex that are the determining factors, though they express the idea in terms of association in life and shared responsibilities and interests. The Moravians tend to live in simple rural communities, so the concept that single women and girls have more in common than either group would with married women or even males is comparatively plausible.

A member of the Moravian Church is not forced to bury his next of kin in one of the areas called 'God's Acre'. He or the deceased before her death can direct that burial take place in a conventional cemetery, and where there is no God's Acre already in existence, for example because the Moravians in the district are very few, church members use the conventional cemetery as a matter of course. But Moravians look on burial in God's Acre as a privilege. It has been the custom to cordon off a God's Acre on an eastward-facing hill slope and to bury the dead with their feet facing east.

The Moravians do not use monuments but just a marble slab set on top of the grave flush with the surrounding earth, bearing the deceased person's name, birth and death dates, and a short quotation from the Bible or similar scriptural epitaph. All adults have the same size slab. Children's, also uniform in size, are slightly smaller.

There are services for use in the home, church and by the grave. The officiating minister opens with a prayer and continues with more prayers interspersed with Bible readings. A hymn and an address may also feature and the Lord's Prayer is recited. As with many other denominations, there is a slightly different form of service for the funeral of a child. In addition victims of fatal accidents get an individually tailored service, whether they were killed singly or as part of a mass disaster such as a ship sinking or a plane crash.

In Moravian tradition there is also a service at Easter which takes place in a graveyard. It dates from the early Herrnhut years and can be traced as far back as 1732. Some youths spontaneously decided to celebrate the Resurrection of Our Lord at sunrise on Easter Sunday and since the disciples had congregated at a place of burial the Moravian young men decided to follow suit. To this day in Winston-Salem, North Carolina, where there is a substantial Moravian settlement, large numbers of people gather as early as 2 a.m. on Easter Sunday and Moravian bands play chorales.

Mormons (Church of Jesus Christ of Latter Day Saints)

I have entitled this section Mormons and for brevity I shall use the term throughout, for the sake of easy recognition by the general reader, although as they point out in their promotional literature the full and correct title is the Church of Jesus Christ of Latter Day Saints. Mormons urge their followers to choose burial rather than cremation, though they accept that the relatives of the deceased person may prefer the latter and of course if the law of the land demands it there is an end of any dispute in the matter. They regard baptism as making important references to burial, which is why they prefer it to cremation, and they hold that resurrection will take place quite literally and in a physical sense, with a person's corporeal and spiritual aspects united in an inseparable and perfect form. It follows that death is simply the separation of the two elements, physical and spiritual.

Mormon funerals take place in an LDS (Latter Day Saints) meeting house (the abbreviation LDS is one commonly used by them). Sometimes this happens after a gathering of the immediate family to view the corpse with a prayer to follow before the coffin lid is screwed down and the mourners proceed to the meeting house proper. If a deceased Mormon visited the Temple in her lifetime (the Temple is the chief place of Mormon worship in the world and is situated in Salt Lake City, Utah, USA), she is dressed in sacred clothing, in particular a set of ritualistically significant undergarments. The dressing is done by fellow Mormons in a chapel of rest or similarly private chamber set apart from the main meeting house assembly room (it may of course be done at the undertaker's provided privacy is maintained). An ordinary Mormon is not required to wear anything special.

Mormons are episcopalian and have bishops, although their stake area, which is the equivalent of a diocese, may have as many as eight to ten bishops to serve it, these being lay preachers rather than ordained prelates of a church hierarchy. A bishop or branch president of the local congregation officiates at a funeral. The rites are simple. There is an invocation, a blessing and a sermon based on the New Testament. A musical accompaniment is usual. Afterwards

161

the cortège proceeds to the cemetery, where a prayer is said beside the grave.

Muslims

One of the principal tenets of faith in Islam is *akhirah*, or the idea that there is life after death. As Muhammad the Prophet has said: 'The grave is the first stage of the journey to eternity.' Muslims see *akhirah* as either reward for a person's good deeds in life or punishment for his bad ones. Every member of humankind is held by Muslims to be accountable to Allah for his behaviour on earth and there will eventually be a Day of Judgement, when the dead will be resurrected and dealt with as they deserve. A passage from the Koran reads:

> Every soul shall taste of death; you shall surely be paid in full your wages on the Day of Resurrection. Whosoever is removed from the fire and admitted to Paradise shall win the triumph. The present life is but the joy of delusion.
>
> *Chapter iii, Verse 182*

Another reads:

> Does man think that We shall not assemble his bones? Yes, surely, yes. We are able to restore the very tips of his fingers.
>
> *Chapter lxxv, Verses 3–4*

One of Allah's purposes in sending prophets and messengers among humankind is to warn them of this impending Day of Judgement so that they can regulate their behaviour according to Islam's precepts.

In the West some Muslims have been subject to laying out procedures for their dead which run contrary to the regulations of Islam. As recently as the late 1980s, two-fifths of

Muslim dead in Britain were buried in ground that had been consecrated according to Christian rites and even in exclusively Muslim areas of a cemetery seven out of ten graves were not pointing towards Mecca, the importance of which we shall come to. In consequence there has grown up a movement for special Muslim cemeteries. Indeed, Haji Taslim Muslim Funerals, of the East London Mosque, 45 Fieldgate Street, London E1 1JU (tel. 0171–247 2625/9583), operates one of the cheapest funeral services anywhere, though only for Muslims, as well as supplying one-off items such as coffins and free advice to those who want to go it alone (see that section in Part III); they will even bury the very poor free in a private grave.

In fact Muslims are traditionally enjoined to bury their dead in special Muslim cemeteries anyway. (Cremation is not practised at all.) The dying or recently dead person must be positioned in such a way that he faces towards the Ka'abah, which is the large black cubic stone (*ka'abah* means cube) draped with a black cloth in the Grand Mosque at Mecca, the supreme holy city for Muslims in the centre of Saudi Arabia. He can either be laid on his right side so that his face is towards Mecca or on his back with his feet pointing in that direction and with his head slightly raised, as if looking towards the holy city. The Muslim authorities prefer the former. While a person is actually on the point of death, watchers by the deathbed will keep up a recitation from the Koran or say prayers, but once the last breath has left his body those present stop their recitation, as the practice after death is not sanctioned either by tradition or the corpus of deeds and sayings of the Prophet Muhammad known as the Sunna.

Next someone closes the dead man's eyes, secures his jaw so that it does not loll open and places a weight on his stomach to prevent it swelling up with intestinal gas. Muslims believe that the soul stays in the corpse for some time after death and even

163

that the corpse can feel pain. Therefore the deceased's body must be handled with great sensitivity. After undressing him, those who are preparing the corpse cover his entire body with a sheet so that no part is exposed, not even the feet or head. (An exception to the wholesale covering of the corpse is made in the case of a person who has died while on the pilgrimage to Mecca, something which all Muslims are supposed to make at some point in their lives. The idea is that on the Day of Judgement a pilgrim will be resurrected in his capacity as a pilgrim. Nor is anything sweet-smelling introduced into such a person's presence at this stage of the funerary process, unlike the recommended procedure with ordinary Muslims.)

A family friend, relative of the deceased or other bystander lets potential funeral mourners know that the death has occurred and pays any of the dead person's debts still out-standing. If the deceased was destitute and the relatives or friends he relied on for support cannot meet the funeral expenses there is usually a Muslim public treasury which will defray the cost; alternatively more prosperous Muslims in the community will bear the expense. Islam urges its followers to bury their dead with the minimum delay, certainly within twenty-four hours and ideally before sunset on the day of death itself. This can lead to difficulty in the UK, where the authorities often close cemeteries at weekends and on public holidays. It is another reason why Muslims are enjoined to provide their own burial grounds.

Loud or physically vigorous lamentation such as rending clothes, rocking back and forth in an ecstasy of grief, flailing of a mourner's arms against her body or head is prohibited, but no Muslim in authority will reproach a relative who merely cries softly. Only Muslims may wash the corpse and they must use clean water or sand if water is unavailable. The dead person may have allocated the task of washing to a relative before dying. Otherwise the people whose duty it is are (a) the deceased man's father, or if he is not available (b) his grandfather, then the next closest relative on his father's side and so on in descending order. If none of them are available, then the closest relative on his mother's side is indicated and so on down the line. A man's widow may wash him instead of any of these. For a woman it is exactly the same except that they must be female relatives, and with the corresponding exception of her husband as the sole male permitted to perform the task. If the dead person is a boy or girl, then persons of either sex may wash the body. If, despite these fairly wide-ranging stipulations, it is simply impossible to find someone to wash the body who is either of the same sex or the deceased's spouse, then a member of the opposite sex can cleanse the body but he or she must do it with sand and cover his or her hand to protect it from coming into contact with the naked body.

There is a ceremony to the actual washing. As with such procedures in virtually all religions, it must be carried out in private and with decorum, the dead person's body from his lower trunk to the thighs being covered. First the mouth is wiped, then the rest of the body, then the teeth, then the nostrils. The same rite is followed as when a Muslim says prayers (see the description of *ghusl* below), though in this case care is taken to see that no water enters the deceased person's mouth or nose. If he has hair and a beard, they are also washed. Camphor or powdered lotus leaves as well as soap may be used to freshen up the water. The washing process is then repeated. It is part of the Prophet's teachings that this should be done an odd number of times, up to five or seven in all. Once the washing is completed, the dead person's hair and beard (if any) are treated with a sweet-smelling substance. A woman's hair is arranged in three plaits down her back before her body is shrouded. Ideally the scent should be camphor, but there is no particular prohibition on what should be used except that it must not be saffron. As well as

165

facial hair and the hair of the scalp, the ears and armpits are treated, also those points of the body that come into contact with the ground when a Muslim says prayers, namely the feet, forehead, hands, knees and nose.

The ritual washing after death is called the *ghusl*, or greater ablution, and it may be necessary not just for the corpse but for any living person who has come into contact with a dead body before he can pray or touch a copy of the Koran. Some Muslims, however, hold that *ghusl* for living persons after they have come into contact with a corpse is only recommended, not mandatory.

When a living person performs the *ghusl* on himself he splashes water over his head, trunk, arms and legs, always the right one before the left, the upper part before the lower and the front of the body before the back. Water is held cupped in the right hand. The navel is rinsed out eight times, nor are the parts between fingers and toes neglected. The mouth and nostrils are washed too, in the same way as those of the corpse. A less strict interpretation of the *ghusl* regulations current among some Muslims holds that a shower is sufficient. Whether the *ghusl* is used for a corpse or mourner it may be followed by *wuḍū*, or the lesser washing ritual, known in Farsi as *abdast*.

Apart from various prayers and other linguistic formulae (which I have omitted in the purely physical sketch of both kinds of ritual washing, but which may be studied in detail in any good book on Islam) the *wuḍū* involves putting first the right hand then the left under running water, rubbing the hands together thrice; washing out the mouth, also thrice, using a cupped right hand; rinsing out the nostrils, once again thrice, using the right hand to insert the water and the left to expel it by pressing against the side of the nose; washing the face, again thrice, this time using both hands; washing the right forearm with the left hand and the left forearm with the right hand, each time thrice; slightly moistening the head, either with the right hand while the left one lifts any headgear (usually, of course, a turban), or with both hands if no headgear is worn; rinsing both ears, inside and out, with the index finger, while the thumb steadies the ear behind the lobe; and finally washing both feet, the left one first using the right hand, then vice versa.

Unbelievers, still-born children and aborted foetuses are not washed, nor are badly mutilated corpses. Above all, no warrior who has been killed in a holy battle – that is to say a battle in which he has been fighting to uphold or promote Islam – is ever washed. The Muslims maintain that such a person goes straight to paradise, which is one reason why Muslims have proved so formidable in battle down the centuries. The tradition of leaving dead warriors unwashed goes back to the Battle of Mount Uḥud, or Ohod, in the year AH 3 (AD 625). Mount Uḥud is north-west of Medina, in what is now Saudi Arabia, and the fight there was between Muhammad and his followers, the proponents of the new religion of Islam, on the one hand, and the citizens of Mecca, who at that time were still pagan and who had been defeated by Muhammad and his adherents the year before. The result appeared to be a defeat for the followers of Muhammad, but fortunately for them, the Meccans were content to kill only that number of the enemy which they themselves had lost the year before and they returned home without following up the victory. The Prophet decreed that those on his side who had fallen at Uḥud should have the status of martyrs and be interred just as they were, all covered with blood.

Those mourning a warrior killed fighting on behalf of the faith take away his weapons and other martial accoutrements and bury the corpse in the clothes he wore while fighting, placing up to three men together in a single winding sheet and grave if there are not enough of either to go round, as may well happen at the site of a battle. Unlike the procedure with the ordinarily deceased, no prayer is said over a warrior killed

167

in a battle to promote the faith and he is buried where he fell if possible.

The shroud consists of up to three winding sheets coloured white for men and as many as five (shift, waist-wrapper, winding sheet proper, head veil and loincloth) for women. It is the custom to cover the female dead more thoroughly than male dead and this extends even to the grave, which ought ideally to be covered with a sheet once the dead woman's body has been interred there. One winding sheet will do at a pinch provided that the whole body is covered. If not even a single sheet is available, grass or paper may be used to cover the legs. It is essential that the private parts be covered even if no other part of the body can be. Incense is used to perfume the shroud, which is then wrapped round the body, first over the right side then the left.

If the usual winding sheet is used it is knotted at the end before the body is placed in the coffin, the use of which is more usual in the West. In Muslim countries, although there is no prohibition on coffins, the corpse is often buried just wrapped in its winding sheet or sheets. If a coffin is used there is often no plate on the lid and the name of the dead person is simply written on it in longhand. Handles are rare; instead the pall-bearers lift or lower the coffin with ropes. If the deceased's remains are to be sent overseas, as happens quite often in Britain, the coffin may have windows inserted for viewing, but of course it will be hermetically sealed.

A Muslim who has put his affairs in good order before dying will have designated someone to say the appropriate funeral prayers over his corpse, bearing in mind that the chosen person must be of good moral character and orthodox religious opinions. If the deceased has not arranged his affairs properly, for example because he dies suddenly or in extreme youth, then the task of saying the appropriate prayers falls to the following in the order given: the ruler (only if of an Islamic state, of course) or a person deputising for that ruler, the

deceased's father, grandfather, great-grandfather, son, grandson, great-grandson, then other relatives on his father's side in
order of closeness of kin.

The dead body is carried through the streets on a bier by
mourners chanting the *shahādah* (literally in Arabic 'testimony', the Muslim profession of faith: 'There is no god but
Allah; Mohammad is the prophet of Allah'). The procession
goes either to the cemetery or to a mosque. If the latter,
prayers will be said over the body before the funeral party
goes on to the cemetery. Prayers for the dead can be recited
in a mosque whether the dead body is present or not.
During the funeral procession God-fearing bystanders may
come up to the cortège and give temporary assistance to the
pall-bearers.

When there are a number of mourners the *imam*, or
prayer-leader, stands at the front of the gathering and the rest
of those present pray behind him in an uneven number of
rows, usually three. It is quite common for funeral prayers to
be recited in a mosque after the normal daily prayer session.
The chief person praying recites the words 'God is most great,'
called the *takbīr*, then the first chapter of the Koran, called the
Fatiha, then, raising his hands, he repeats the *takbīr*, then the
prayer of Abraham ('O God, bless Muhammad and his family,
as You blessed Abraham and his family: You are the Benign,
the Exalted. Grant Your benediction to Muhammad and to
his family, as You granted it to Abraham and his family; You
are the Benign, the Exalted'). Then, raising his hands, he
repeats the *takbīr* for the third time, then the traditional
prayer for the dead ('O God, grant forgiveness to our living
and our dead, our present ones and our absent ones, our
young and our old, our men and our women. O God, to
whomsoever of us You give life, let it be as a Muslim, and
whomsoever of us You take unto You, let it be as one of the
Faithful. O God, deprive us not of the recompense for our
departed one, and do not subject us to trial as a result of his

death'). The *imam* then raises his hands a third time and the *takbīr* is recited a fourth time. At this point the assembled worshippers turn first to the right then to the left, but they neither bow nor prostrate themselves in the way they would do at ordinary prayers.

There follows either a short silence or else the *imam* repeats a passage from the original prayer for the dead: 'O God, deprive us not of the recompense for our departed one, and do not subject us to trial as a result of his death.' The *imam* finishes with the words 'Peace be upon you.' It is most important that all mourners say the words 'God is most great' four times. Accordingly, if anyone is late for the prayer session he must recite this passage after the prayer-leader has delivered his final benediction until he, the latecomer, has made up the shortfall.

Muslim funeral processions are unusual in that they move at a smart pace, even though mourners are supposed to follow the bier on foot unless they are so infirm that they have to ride in some conveyance, when they are supposed to travel a little way behind the procession proper. The Prophet himself is supposed to have said, 'Convey the deceased swiftly, for if he was a good man, then you are taking him to good things, and if he was not, then you should lower the evil from your shoulders as soon as possible.'

Mourners who have prayed over the body of the deceased at the session led by the *imam* as set out in the preceding paragraphs are not obliged to follow the procession to the grave, and even if they do they are not obliged to do more than witness the committal of the body to the grave then go away. Nevertheless – and a show of concern for the deceased on this level is held to call down the greatest reward from God – mourners can attend both the procession and the burial, then offer up prayers on the dead person's behalf after the committal to the grave, asking God for His forgiveness towards the deceased, asking God that He fortify him in his faith and beseeching Him to have mercy on the dead man's soul. At this point mourners are supposed to contemplate their own eventual demise and possible fate after death, having regard to both their own characters and that of the recently deceased. Those present should stand while the dead person is lowered into the grave.

The grave should be roomy and dug to such a depth as would contain a man of average height to the level of his chest if he stood in it upright. Among the Prophet's teachings is one to the effect that a hollow should be made in the side of the wall of the grave that lies in the direction of Mecca and that the corpse should be placed in this hollow, head first if possible, lying on his right and with his face pointed towards Mecca as described earlier. Alternatively, a trench can be cut in the floor of the grave – its proportions would in such a case be so considerable that the trench would virtually constitute a grave within a grave, as it were – and the body placed in that instead, then covered over.

As with the washing process, there are rules about who may lower a body into the grave. Dead females should be handled only by male relatives who are within the accepted degrees of kinship, for example a husband and brothers, for such people are the only males who would have been allowed to see the woman and even travel with her when she was alive. If no such male relatives are available, elderly males present may perform the task, even if they are not close relations. The deceased is placed in the grave accompanied by the words 'In the name of God, and in the faith of the Prophet of God', and is secured in her niche by a little ridge of earth to prevent her rolling backwards, together with a barrier of canes or bricks made of dried mud to protect the corpse from falling earth. Before the grave is covered mourners scatter a handful of dust over the cavity, making three passes of the hand.

A small ridge is often raised above the surface of the grave to alert strangers to its position and induce them to say a short prayer on the deceased's behalf, for example, 'May God have mercy upon the person whose grave this is.' Gravestones are not forbidden, but no more elaborate structure such as a mausoleum or memorial is allowed. Not even a mosque should be erected above a grave and commemorative lamps are also prohibited, the Prophet having said, according to one account, 'May God curse women who visit the graves and those who erect mosques and light lamps over them.' Men are encouraged to visit graves, however, when they should pray to God for his forgiveness towards the dead and recite the words 'Peace be upon you. O believers and Muslims who dwell here; we shall, God willing, be joining you. We ask God to grant wellbeing to us and to you.' Praying to the dead or asking them to intercede with God is forbidden, as is any idolatrous gesture towards the grave itself, such as caresses.

The friends and more distant relatives of the dead person condole with the immediate family for three days and nights following the death, saying 'May God make your reward abundant and your solace great, and grant forgiveness to the departed.' Those condoled with are supposed to respond with the words 'May God hear your prayer, and have mercy upon us and you.'

Widows traditionally observe a full mourning period of four months and ten days They are expected also to undergo various abstentions. Forty days after the death a memorial service is held in which various litanies are recited.

Non-Conformists

This term comprises what are sometimes also known as the free churches, that is, the Baptists, Methodists and United Reformed Church. The last of these was formed first by the union of Congregationalists and Presbyterians in 1972, then by the addition of the Churches of Christ in 1981. The treatment of the deceased is so uniform among all the non-conformist groups that a minister of one often officiates at the funerary rites of another. The service will consist of hymns and an address by the minister. In this respect there is a similarity to the funeral rites of the smaller groups known collectively also as the free churches, namely the Evangelical Free Church, the Four Square Gospellers, the Salvation Army, Strict Baptists and Unitarians. The Strict Baptists forbid cremation, however.

With the non-conformist groups the coffin tends to be brought into the chapel from one direction and taken out after the service another way. During the service it is positioned crossways at the fore end of the chapel. There are other, subtler differences between the various denominations in this group.

Baptists
In their beliefs as to what happens after death, as in their funeral ceremonies, Baptists most closely resemble the Methodist and United Reformed Church. Ministers of one of these other churches sometimes officiate at Baptist funerals.

Methodists
Currently (that is to say roughly from 1991 to 1996), Methodists are introducing certain features into their funeral ceremonials, but it is intended to be a trial period only. Some features have a long Christian tradition. There is for example the vigil; a two-part funeral service, the first at the crematorium or cemetery and a second in church, which, as the explanatory paragraph of the booklet introducing the changes observes, is a throwback to pre-Reformation practice; optional use of a white funeral pall, symbolic of baptismal garb; a service forty days after the death which symbolises a death-resurrection-ascension pattern. It is not, I think, putting matters too strongly to argue that these features amount collectively to a Catholicising tendency, liturgically speaking. It is odd that over roughly the same period (though in a much more

long-drawn-out fashion, and starting way back in the 1950s) the Catholics should have developed a less formal array of rites – that is to say a move in completely the opposite direction.

A Methodist funeral opens with prayers, then a hymn, then more prayers. Next comes the ministry of the Word, with a prayer in standard form by the officiating minister, Psalm cxxx, then Psalm xxiii or ciii, 8–17, or both, either spoken or chanted. Next comes John xiv, 1–6, 27; 1 Peter i, 3–9; 1 Corinthians xv, 1–4, 20–6, 35–8, 42–4, 50, 53–8; then Psalm xc; 2 Corinthians iv, 16–v, 10, or Revelation vii, 9–17 or xxi, 1–7. Afterwards there may be a sermon, followed by the Apostles' Creed, the thanksgiving, a hymn, the commendation, another prayer, the Lord's Prayer and lastly the committal. The John xiv passage is also suitable for incorporating into the prayers conducted by a minister or pastoral visitor on calling on the bereaved after a death in a hospital or at home. The office of commendation, which is for when mourners have heard news of a death or for the day of the funeral if the latter is held elsewhere, incorporates a hymn, the Lord's Prayer and readings of Psalms xxiii, xlii, xliii, cxxi, cxxx and cxxxix plus Bible readings from John xi, 21–7, xiv, 1–3; Romans vi, 3–9 and Philippians i, 20–6. The vigil may incorporate Psalm xxvii, 2 Corinthians v, 1, 6–10 and Luke xii, 35–40. The two-part funeral incorporates excerpts from John ii, 25–6; Matthew v, 4; John iii, 16 and Lamentations iii, 22-3. Psalms cxxx, xxiii and ciii (8–18) may feature here also. There follow John xiv, 1–6, 27; John vi, 35–40, 1 Corinthians 20–4, 1 Peter 3–9 and Romans viii, 28, 31–5, 37–9. In the second part of the ceremony at the church there is an excerpt from 1 Peter i, 3–4, hymns, a sermon and a blessing. For a church service followed by a committal the same Biblical excerpts are recited as in the first part of the two-part ceremony as regards Matthew v, John iii and Lamentations iii, but in addition there are readings from John xvi, 33 and Psalm xlvi, 1. Moreover, on the occasion of a scattering or burial of ashes, the officiating minister or some other person may read from Revelation vii, 16–17, Colossians iii, 3–4 and Romans vi, 8–9. Prayers are also said.

Methodists usually employ the full name of the deceased, both forename(s) and surname, when the ministry of the Word is introduced, but the forename only at the committal. If the body is not present – because it has been lost at sea, say, or because the deceased died abroad – the procession and committal are dropped. The commendation is the name of the service on such an occasion. No body should have more than one commendation and committal. If a memorial service is held later, therefore, and these have already been celebrated at the funeral, they would be omitted.

The Salvation Army

Salvationists, the adherents of the Salvation Army, speak of someone being 'promoted to glory' rather than dying, or even the relatively mealy-mouthed 'passing away'. Because Salvation Army followers were originally from among the most destitute of the population, early references to heaven were couched in terms of precious metals or jewels. Accordingly, one comes across metaphors such as 'streets of gold' and 'gates of pearl', which to outsiders might sit more comfortably in an Asprey's or Tiffany catalogue, used to describe what is 'up there' in heaven.

A still more martial metaphor was the habit of describing a dead comrade as 'another warrior passed safely through the enemy's lines', the enemy being not so much human (although Salvationists were persecuted in their early days) as death itself. When the movement's founder, General William Booth, died in 1912 he was described as having 'laid down his sword'. Salvationists in mourning rejected crape, hearses, undertakers' men in attendance and black clothes before anyone else in Britain. Indeed, far from going into mourning in the accepted sense of the word, Salvationists adopt a positively triumphalist attitude when one of their number has been promoted to glory. The only sign of bereavement they have favoured has been a white band, with a red cross on it and a crown on top of the cross, though a black band will do at a pinch. If black, the band often has a red 'S' for 'salvation' on it.

After a Salvationist funeral it is common to have a memorial meeting in the local Salvation Army hall. Neighbours and colleagues of the deceased are encouraged to attend and an address is given in which an overview of the dead person's life is sketched. It must not be thought from the foregoing that the Salvationists take a narrow or pseudo-militaristic view. In a sample funeral address I came across while researching this book there was a reference to the pre-Reformation German mystic Thomas à Kempis (1379–1471), though it is true that he has been cited by Christians of all denominations, not just Catholics.

Orthodox (Greek)

There is a broad similarity in outlook as regards bereavement between people of the Greek and Russian Orthodox faiths. But as far as funeral services are concerned the Greek rites are considerably shorter. Orthodox Christianity teaches that humans are made up of both soul and body and that in death the two are separated. However, in the resurrection the two come together again, with the difference that this time the body is perfect and incorruptible. At the same time human personality is restored.

Funeral services start with the priest donning his stole, called an *epitrachelion*, which reaches down to about his knees. Having robed, he then proceeds to recite prayers, either in the home of the deceased person, in church or at the graveside. Burial is the usual way of disposing of the dead, and some cemeteries have a section set aside specially for Orthodox Christians. Although there is no prohibition on cremation it is relatively rare, and an Orthodox priest would not attend one.

The initial prayers for the dead are called the Trisagion, a word which has connotations of 'threeness'. The Trisagion consists of, among other things, the words 'Holy God, Holy and Strong, Holy and Immortal, have mercy upon us', recited three times. Also recited three times are the words '*Kyrie eleison*' (a phrase familiar in the mass of Western Christianity). This part of the service ends with a version of the Lord's Prayer that is virtually identical to that said in the West.

Next comes the Troparia, in which a lector and the priest take it in turns to recite a text whose main concern is with rest for the dead person and remission of his sins. At one point there is an interesting contrast with Western rites, in that the Old Testament patriarchs Abraham, Isaac and Jacob are invoked, and also 'the holy and righteous Lazarus, the friend of Christ'.

The funeral proper is ideally celebrated in the church. Here the priest wears not just his stole but a garment over it called a *felonion*, which is roughly equivalent to the chasuble in use in the West, though higher in front and longer at the back. It is a band of material meeting in a circle round the front of the priest's neck, from where another band depends rather like a tail to the letter 'O'. Only married priests wear these, but the monastic communities aside, nearly all – some 90 per cent – of Greek Orthodox priests are married.

In Orthodox churches there is a barrier, called the icon screen, between the main body of the church where the congregation gathers and the inner holy of holies in which the priests perform their offices. The priest faces the congregation from a step in front of the three central doors of this screen. Three stanzas follow in which God is invoked once more. Next follows the Evlogitaria, which is more or less a litany in praise of God, the Trinity and the 'pure Lady', the *theotokos* (literally 'God-bearer', though in later Western tradition the term Christ's mother has been used as an equivalent). Then comes the offering of incense, called the Kontakion, with special hymns of St John of Damascus (St John Damascene).

The principal theme of this part of the service is the temporary nature of worldly goods: riches, pomp, luxury. Then come the beatitudes, which are very similar to those recited in Western Christian services, e.g., 'Blessed are the poor in spirit', 'Blessed are the meek', etc. Introduced here is a slightly gruesome element, one which will be unfamiliar to Western Christians, which follows on from the beatitude about being blessed when men revile you and persecute you, viz a mention of man being 'but naked bones, the food of worms and stench'. There is also a reference to the Apocalypse: 'Woe to those who seek to see the terrible day of the Lord. It will be dark, fire will test the universe.'

Then follows the offertory, or *prokeimenon*. There is a reading from Thessalonians iv, 13–17, and during it the priest offers incense. After references to the Resurrection, there is a reading from John v, 24–30. Just prior to the dismissal of the congregation the priest offers the deceased person a kiss and each member of the gathering follows suit, while the lector chants the words 'Come, O brethren, to give the last kiss to the departed, he [or she] has left his [or her] family marching hastily to the grave. There is no more care for vanities and the stirrings of the flesh. Where now are his [or her] relations and friends? We have already parted from him [or her]. Let us pray to the Lord to grant him [or her] peace.'

In addition to this regular funeral service there is a rather more elaborate set of prayers which may be recited by a bishop, either at a funeral service or a memorial service. Neither a memorial service nor burial are permitted in the case of a suicide.

The coffin is usually adorned with a Latin cross on the lid and a candle is placed at its head and foot. Often the coffin will be left open during the funeral service. Indeed, the final kiss of farewell from the priest and congregation would lose much of its impact otherwise. An alternative to kissing the deceased is to kiss an icon held in his hands. If the deceased has died of a contagious disease, however, the coffin lid will be screwed down beforehand. As in the West, tributes of flowers from mourners are allowed and may be brought into the church during the service.

Members of the congregation often hold candles throughout the service and an experienced undertaker will provide these, also little trays to catch the melted wax. The committal of the coffin to the grave is accompanied by the priest shovelling earth in the shape of a cross athwart the lid. Members of the dead person's family may also throw earth on the coffin. A final feature, one which is probably unfamiliar to Western Christians, is that the priest pours out the remaining oil from one of the lamps that are so much a feature both of Orthodox churches, where they burn in front of icons, and cemeteries, where each grave is furnished with a lamp burning in the equivalent of the Eternal Flame, together with any ashes still in the censer which contained the incense.

Orthodox (Russian)

There are two principal funeral rites, a short one called the *panichidia*, which is in the nature of a memorial for the dead generally, and the funeral service for a specific deceased person. There are also other services for dead children and priests. The *panichidia* is chiefly concerned with the soul, the funeral service with both soul and body. The Orthodox Christians hold that for the first three days after a death the person's soul hovers near the places he has known in life, possibly even revisiting them. In this way the soul is imbued with associations to do with life for when it comes before God shortly afterwards. During these three days the bereaved on earth are supposed to pray, celebrate the *panichidia* and dwell in their general thoughts on their relations with the person

179

who has just died, ideally purifying their hearts of any lingering enmity or resentment towards him so that they can say to his soul in earnest, 'Go in peace.'

Women who attend an Orthodox funeral should cover their heads, just as they would at a Roman Catholic ceremony.

Pagans

There are six main pagan groups in the UK at present: Druidism, Men's Traditions, Odinism (also called Asatru and the Northern Tradition, Asatru being more accurate in that it means 'belief in the gods' rather than just Odin, who is only one of the Norse gods), Shamanism, Wicca (also called Witchcraft) and Women's Traditions. They combined together in an organisation called the Pagan Federation in 1971. This exists chiefly to inform the outside world about the various beliefs that constitute paganism and in particular to clear up any misconceptions that linger in the public mind, notably the suspicion that it is just an excuse to have a good orgy. The federation acts as a liaison between one group and another, and also between European pagan groups and others in other continents. Lastly, it agitates for the right of pagans to conduct their religious ceremonies without restriction, citing the Universal Declaration of Human Rights, Article 18. The United Kingdom is a signatory to this.

Anyone who is over eighteen can join the federation provided he subscribes to the following principles: (a) that there should be respect, even reverence and love, for Nature, seen as a life force, though subject to a cycle of life and death and then life again which is eternally renewed; (b) the pagan ethic, which invites initiates to follow their own desires completely provided they harm no one. This translates into self-fulfilment, though in concert with Nature, and would not only not preclude an orgy, provided everyone present was a consenting adult, but can be interpreted as encouraging orgies. The third principle (c) is recognising that the 'divine reality' has both male and female aspects and honouring these. Some events organised by the federation are open only to members; others are open to the wider public.

Pagans look back to pre-Christian gods and goddesses and find them in all living things. They are in effect virtual pantheists, and tend to be highly ecologically minded. They reject the concept of dogma or revealed religion. Among the most frequently worshipped deities are the Triple Goddess of the moon (the waxing phase, the full moon and the waning moon) and the Horned God of the woods and beasts (emphatically not to be confused with the beast worshipped by Satanists, pagans stress). Although deities of either sex can take many forms, they are ultimately seen by some pagans (but not all – not Wiccans, for instance) as avatars of a single divinity. Here one may perhaps see a resemblance to Hinduism.

Anyone interested in further details of the history and specific beliefs of the groups making up the Pagan Federation is strongly advised to consult the federation's information pack (see the Bibliography for details). Here I have space only to describe beliefs and practices to do with bereavement. The Pagan Hospice & Funeral Trust, at BM Box 3337, London WC1N 3XX, will also give further information. It exists to make pagan rites available to the dead at 'funerals and cremations' (I take this to mean burials and cremations; elsewhere it is stated that pagans accept both methods of disposal); to set up pagan burial places; to look after ashes of cremated pagans until they can be buried in pagan cemeteries; to set up and look after memorials to dead pagans; and to promote pagan beliefs about death and associated rites and laws. A leaflet on pagan funerals is planned, also a publication called the *Pagan Book of the Dead*.

The information pack speaks of 'requiem rites' for the dead, which Christians might regard as blasphemous since the word requiem is a specific term from the Roman rite. Pagans generally compare the human life cycle to the succession of the seasons and harvests. A particularly important festival marking death and renewal that Christianity did not manage to suppress but instead incorporated is, of course, that which falls on 31 October, known as Hallowe'en and by pagans as Samhain (pronounced as 'sow-in'). In the Christian calendar it is strictly speaking the day following Hallowe'en, All Saints' Day, that is important. The end of October used to be the time of the Celtic New Year and was thought to be a moment when the boundary between the realms of life and death was open and passage between the two realms eased. Pagans regard Samhain as a feast of the departed, recognising death as a mystery and commemorating those who have died.

Wiccans, who claim to be the largest group in the federation with some 10,000 followers, accounting for half its total membership, celebrate Samhain from dusk on 31 October to dusk the next day. They would also appear to be the only group in the federation with a coherent set of rites for dealing with death. Wiccans hold that the soul of a dead person spends some time in the 'summerlands' and is then reincarnated. They also hold that the individual has some power over her destiny and can use ritual to ease her spirit's path to the summerlands. A bereaved friend or relation of the deceased is seen as a possible hindrance to the progress of the latter's soul, hence part of the Wiccan ritual aims to release the grip of the bereaved on the departing soul.

A Wiccan possesses an athame, a knife, which is not used to cut anything and should never be handled by anyone except the owner. The idea is that the owner concentrates her mental powers on the athame. Other objects connected with Wiccan ritual include statuettes of the appropriate god or goddess, or less formal representations of gods and goddesses such as stones, and a disc marked with the form of a pentacle. Wiccans ascribe some importance to what they call the four elements of air, earth, fire and water, and to deal with air they wield incense and an open blade such as a sword or knife; for earth they use the disc/pentacle; for fire a candle and wand; and for water a chalice to hold the liquid in.

In the rite for a departed soul, a Wiccan consecrates water and salt and a space is cleared in which to conduct the rite by drawing a circle. Worshippers step into the circle and are purified, typically by being anointed with oil. Each of the four elements is then invited into the circle from one of four compass points and lastly the appropriate deities are beseeched to enter the circle too. The celebrant delivers a eulogy of the deceased and words of comfort to the mourners. The rites are designed to speed the soul of the deceased to the summerlands. After the ceremony the deities and other powers are thanked and bidden goodbye, cake and wine (or non-alcoholic drink for teetotallers) are blessed by the celebrant and consumed by the congregation and the circle is 'deactivated'. A post-ceremony feast is an optional extra.

Plymouth Brethren/Strict Brethren

There are minute differences between these two sects, of great importance to their respective adherents, naturally, but broadly speaking their attitudes to funeral services are not dissimilar. Coffins are simple in design, with the words 'Asleep with Jesus' or 'With Christ' invariably inscribed on the plate, along with the basic facts of the deceased person's age, date of death and name.

Unlike the dead of other sects, the Plymouth or Strict brother is kept in his home or in the home of another brother till the day of the funeral. The Brethren prefer to act as coffin-bearers themselves and they remove the coffin to a meeting room for the service, following which the cortège proceeds to the cemetery. It is customary for Brethren to sing a hymn by the graveside and partially to fill in the grave themselves.

183

Quakers (Society of Friends)

The Quakers are particularly important in the history of bereavement and how it has been viewed in Britain. Way back in the seventeenth century they had burial grounds of their own. Indeed, these were their first forms of property, before even meeting houses. Their interest in acquiring plots of land for burial arose because they refused to entertain the concept of consecrated ground which formed such an important part of the orthodox Christian attitude to disposal of the dead. To Quakers the ceremony associated with this attitude was alien and pointless; in addition they resented having to pay for burial in consecrated ground. The Quaker plots of land were more or less exclusive to Quakers themselves, although from the eighteenth century they allowed close relations (who were sometimes lapsed Quakers) and those who had become frequent attenders at their meetings but who were not themselves full Quakers to be buried in the plots as well. In the nineteenth century the next of kin of suicides found the Quakers more accommodating than the established Church, although it was only in 1832 that the Yearly Meeting (the most important forum for setting rules among the Friends – now known as the Britain Yearly Meeting) allowed non-Quakers to be buried in Quaker burial grounds. Permission was granted provided that the procedure was in all respects conducted as if for the burial of Friends. Non-Quakers are still allowed to be buried in Quaker burial grounds, but the Friends prefer that in such a case they are buried with the same ceremony – or perhaps one should say studious lack of what most people mean by ceremony – as if they were Quakers.

In the early days of Quakerism, the Friends' attitude to burial aroused hostility among the orthodox. Thomas Ellwood (1639–1713), the Quaker friend of Milton who put up the poet at his cottage in Buckinghamshire so that he could escape the plague in 1665 – and who after reading *Paradise Lost* in manuscript said, 'Thou hast said much of *Paradise Lost*, but what hast thou to say of Paradise Found?', thus inspiring the poet to write *Paradise Regained* – records in his autobiography how an attempt at a Quaker burial in the Chiltern village of Amersham was prevented by Ambrose Bennett, a local JP, together with some constables.

Quakers are strictly speaking to be lumped with non-conformists, but they do not share the general non-conformist tendency to emphasise the autonomy of local congregations. Thus all Quaker meetings are conducted according to the dictates of the 'discipline', though at the same time there is local freedom of manoeuvre in non-essential matters. In practice this means that the way Quakers conduct funeral ceremonies will vary from place to place, but the overall approach and intent should be identical.

In general, however, it is customary to give thanks for the life of the departed person. This is especially the case since Quakers have no official doctrine as to what happens to us after we die. Some believe in a survival of the individual personality in an afterlife, sometimes in a series of states, with progression from one state to the next. Others believe in a conglomerate oneness of all humanity after death; others still in virtually nothing at all apart from love. Some Quakers hold that the good and perhaps evil a person has done in her lifetime carries on in the lives of those who survive her. It is even possible to be a Quaker and believe in reincarnation. Any life that may exist after death is not seen as a reward or punishment in any case.

The person responsible at meeting house or crematorium chapel (the funeral of a Quaker can take place at either) is the local elder, who may feel it desirable to cut the meeting short when time is important, for instance at a crematorium. He will also superintend the consignment of the coffin to the grave if the deceased is being buried, for minor procedural differences can vary from locality to locality. In general, however, responsibility for supervising funerals rests with the Monthly Meeting, which is the principal meeting of the Society of Friends concerned with business. Each elder is appointed by the Monthly Meeting.

Quakers gather either in the presence of the coffin or without it, though the deceased person may have requested that he be buried or cremated without any accompanying meeting at all. If they do congregate, they nevertheless remain silent unless moved to speak, testifying, for instance, to the qualities which the dead person by the grace of God displayed in life. A Quaker meeting, which lasts perhaps half an hour, could be entirely silent (though this is rare), as few as one or two of the assembled number in all could give tongue or there could be a fairly substantial colloquy. A prayer or prayers may be spoken aloud, as may a passage from the Bible. The end of a session is marked by a shaking of hands. Elders are asked to consider their ministry at a meeting for burial: total silence could be hurtful to the friends and relations of the deceased.

If for whatever reason a cremation or burial needs to take place soon after death, the Friends may hold a memorial meeting for the deceased at a later date. Quakers have no objection to the scattering of a dead person's ashes in one of their burial grounds which is still in use. They keep their own records of burials which have taken place in Quaker grounds set aside for that purpose, though of course these are no more a substitute for official records kept by the state than those of any other religious denomination, and Quakers here comply with normal civil procedure.

Gravestones are allowed, but they must be plain and put up under the Monthly Meeting's supervision. Quakers go to great lengths to achieve uniformity of design, shape and size of gravestones, to say nothing of the wording on them and the materials of which they are made. This is not at all because they value conformity, for individual Quakers vary as much as members of any religious group – rather more so in the latitude permitted them where beliefs are concerned. Rather it is because they are anxious that there shall be no indication given by a gravestone as to how rich or poor the family of the deceased person is or how important the individual was felt to have been in life.

This may seem a little odd to the rest of us, since one of the least significant clues to a person's worldly wealth is usually the size or splendour of his tomb – outside famous and highly extravagant examples such as the Mausoleum of Halicarnassus. In fact, until recently the poor in Britain were notorious for spending proportionately much more of their entire worldly wealth on funerals than did the better off.

I was struck when researching the various denominations' attitudes to death by the greatly superior literary quality of Quaker writings on the subject. There are in fact various collections of useful passages of such work which can be quoted at a meeting for burial. Anne Hosking, administrative secretary of the Quaker Home Service Department of the Religious Society of Friends, says:

> The 'testimony to the grace of God as shown in the life of XX' [is] . . . an important way of embodying the story and tradition of our Quaker faith, and the recording of them, and the reading of some extracts at [Britain] Yearly Meeting are significant to our life and worship together. I have found that helping to write one is a form of service, of love, that has helped me in my own growth . . . [Testimonies] are different from an obituary, which is descriptive, and one person's work.

Here, then, are some excerpts from Quaker writings on the subject of bereavement:

> The funerals of Friends should be held in a spirit of quiet peace and trust. Natural sorrow there will be, especially for friends taken away in youth and in the strength of

their days, but often our thought will be one of a great thankfulness for lives which have borne witness to the upholding power of Christ.

Drafted by the 1925 Revision Committee

In relation to the last sentence of the passage I have just quoted, readers might care to note that Quakers tend to shun mourning colours such as black.

Friends should not adopt any rigid pattern for the conduct of funerals. In some cases it is best to hold, separately from the committal or cremation, a 'meeting for worship on the occasion of the death of our Friend', at a weekend, when Friends are free to attend and there is time for the spirit of quiet trust and dependence on God to overcome natural grief. In other cases the brief meeting for worship at the crematorium is all that is either possible or desired . . . If Friends really believe that all meetings of every kind are meetings for worship in which the presence of Christ is with them and that they are in unity with the living and the dead, they will not experience difficulties or find the occasion of a funeral imposing a pattern of unbalanced eulogy of the deceased. Arising from a gathered meeting, messages of a general character, even from those who have not known the deceased, will enrich the worship of all who are there.

Berks & Oxon Quarterly Meeting Ministry and Extension
Committee, 1951

A feeling of hesitation as to speaking at funerals is most natural, for great wisdom and tenderness are required. On the other hand, these gatherings give opportunities of a very special character, and we urge all on whom the gift of the vocal ministry has been bestowed to consider whether it may not be their duty and privilege to use it on these occasions, even if in some degree contrary to their convenience and inclination. There is also need for the presence of others, and [their] attendance in a living and sympathetic spirit is a very real service.

Warwickshire North Monthly Meeting Ministry Committee,
1912

The value of vocal prayer at a funeral can hardly be over-emphasised. If offered under guidance it will touch hearts too much distressed to listen to an address and will bring real comfort. This is above all to be borne in mind where there is some special ground for sorrow, when the anxious mourners may thus be helped to open their hearts to the healing stream of divine love.

Warwickshire Monthly Meeting Elders, 1960

Quakers do have something very special to offer the . . . bereaved, namely that we are at home in silence. Not only are we thoroughly used to it and unembarrassed by it, but we know something about sharing it, encountering others in its depths and, above all, letting ourselves be used in it . . .

Quoted by permission from Diana Lampen, Facing Death, *Quaker Home Service, 1979*

Seventh-Day Adventists

A Protestant group originating in the early nineteenth century and recognising the scriptures as their guide, the Seventh-Day Adventists observe Saturday (actually from sunset on Friday to sunset on Saturday) instead of Sunday as the chief day of the week for rest and worship.

They stand more or less inside the main stream of Protestantism in their beliefs about what happens to the dead: the resurrection of the body and of Jesus Christ and the Second Coming to raise those who, in the similar phraseology of the

189

United Free Church of Scotland, have 'fallen asleep'. Where they go beyond many Christians is in firmly holding the soul to be mortal, hence the need for the resurrection.

In Seventh-Day Adventists' eyes, to grieve is painful but probably a necessary transition process following separation from a loved one. The local minister offers condolences and comfort, as with similar denominations. The Seventh-Day Adventists publish a minister's manual for those conducting funerals. This document advises ministers to respect local traditions unless they run counter to Christian beliefs, the exception being if the Christian belief comes too close to embracing the immortality of the soul.

Ministers are advised when visiting the bereaved to say little but do much, for example offering a hug or joining hands in a prayer circle. That idle and commonplace remark by someone offering condolence – 'Let us know if there's anything we can do to help' – is, surely rightly, rejected by Seventh-Day Adventists. Instead the minister is urged to make specific suggestions to the bereaved person, such as offering to tell her friends and relatives about the death, answering the telephone for her, looking after her children, even doing some of the housework. Ministers are reminded that a funeral is a fruitful time for evangelising since serious thoughts are in the air, even for someone who is ordinarily among the most alienated members of society.

A typical service would consist of a reading from scripture and a prayer of thanksgiving to God for the deceased person's life, solace for those who mourn and the hope of eternal life. A hymn may follow, also an overview of the person's life, though not too eulogistic. Then there is a sermon and another prayer and finally a solo hymn or song of hope. Ministers are advised never to assume that the dead person is lost, even if he was not a believer, though the minister should never assume that such a person is saved, either.

Seventh-Day Adventists are equally happy to see the deceased buried or cremated, their belief in the mortality of the soul and the need for the resurrection of the body being no bar to cremation in God's eyes. After all, they argue, He had no problem over lack of raw materials when He created all living things.

Sikhs

Officially, Sikhs take the line that it is part of God's purpose that we all die. On the other hand, given human nature, it is more or less inevitable that the close relatives of a dying or recently dead person will give way to grief. Nevertheless it is Sikh policy to put them in a more accepting frame of mind by reciting the Psalm of Peace, called the Sukhmani, and quoting from the scriptures to the effect that everyone who is born must die, that this is God's will and that we must abide by it. Sikhs regard death as a period of sleep only, and of short duration at that, so for believers the period of mourning should theoretically be a time of quietude, if not perhaps exactly of hope.

The notion of death as a kind of sleep is underlined by the priest, or *granthi*, from the local temple, or *gurdwara*, reciting a bedtime prayer, called Sohilla, at the climax of the funeral. Another reminder of the Sikh view of death as a species of sleep rather than physical extinction is their complete prohibition of any kind of memorial. As far as commemoration is concerned, they hold that a person's virtuous deeds constitute a link with those still alive and, together with his words, stand as his true memorial.

Sikhs cremate their dead unless the law of the land forbids it, in which case they usually choose burial, though sometimes in India they place the body in a river or even in the sea. Here in Britain they use both coffins and the services of mainstream undertakers. Cremation is carried out as soon as possible after death. Near relatives, having first closed the eyes and mouth of the dead person immediately after his last breath, straightened his arms either side of him and covered him with a white sheet, undertake the bathing and dressing of the corpse. The washing and dressing of the body should be performed by members of the same sex. The five 'K's form an essential part of the dead male's bodily adornments: the *kaccha*, or knee-length shorts; the *kangha*, or small comb, which holds in place the *kesh*, or uncut hair; the *kara*, a steel bangle; and the *kirpan*, a small sword.

Mourners then carry the corpse either directly to the place of cremation or first to the *gurdwara* and then to the crematorium. They carry the body on their shoulders, either by means of a bier, which is itself covered with a pall, or in a coffin, also covered with a pall. As they walk in slow procession they chant the word '*waheguru*', meaning 'wonderful Lord'.

A member of the deceased person's family who was particularly closely related to him is given the task of lighting the funeral pyre. While it burns, a communal prayer, or *ardas*, is recited, either by one of the mourners or by the local priest, in addition to the Sohilla already mentioned above. The members of the family who bathed and dressed the corpse also undergo a ritual bath to purify themselves of the pollution that is supposedly contracted from having handled an unclean thing such as a dead body. Even ordinary mourners wash their hands, feet and faces.

There is a brief reading from the sacred scriptures, which are of general rather than specific application since prayers for or to the dead form no part of Sikh religion, and special food called *karah prashad* is handed out to the assembled company. This symbolises the necessity for ordinary life to go on, although on the actual day of the person's death no cooking is done at his home. Those who are not members of his family then leave, but they will come back to visit the next of kin for several days following the funeral, during which period the cycle of readings from the sacred scriptures is completed. This takes ten days in all. The day after the cremation the family gather the deceased's ashes and strew them on the surface of a nearby river – in Britain they often keep them until they can take them back to India on their next trip there.

United Free Church of Scotland

This denomination follows New Testament doctrine on death and resurrection as set out by other mainstream Protestant churches, though what happens to people after they have died but before the resurrection of the body on the last day is another matter and subject to a variety of views. One of the leading United Free Church spokesmen, the Rev. J. G. McPhee, senior principal clerk of that body, states that a position which is widely held among his church's members is that believers fall asleep in Christ and while waiting for the resurrection are at rest.

Ministers of the United Free Church use various services and can follow any form they wish. A common liturgy is that from the Book of Common Order of 1928. Here the minister starts with a prayer, said in front of the assembled congregation. God is addressed as the Heavenly Father and credited with the power to 'turn the shadow of death into the morning'. He is beseeched to grant those praying to him submission and patience and to lift them above their darkness and distress to light and peace in His presence. The minister then reads from the scriptures. Stress is laid on the power of God to transform grief to joy and affliction to comfort, misery and tears being of short duration. Psalms xxiii, xxxix, xc and ciii are recited, then there follow readings from John xiv, 1 Corinthians xv, Romans viii, 1 Thessalonians iv, 1 Peter i and Revelation vii, xxi and xxii. Some different readings are given for the burial of a child or an old person.

These days cremation and burial are equally acceptable, with cremation proving more popular. Only in the remoter areas of Scotland is burial still the norm, and there it is as much because of the lack of nearby crematoria as out of doctrinal conservatism.

If the deceased person is buried there is a service at the grave, again often with scriptural readings. There are slightly different forms of wording depending again on whether the dead person is a child or whether the burial is at sea. Again, if cremation is used there are specific forms of words, one for the cremation proper, the other for the burial of the ashes afterwards.

Ministers of the United Free Church of Scotland would usually visit the bereaved family a few times between the death and the funeral. How often would depend on the length of time this interim period lasted. They would call on the family after the funeral, too, giving spiritual solace, helping with practical tasks and joining in prayers.

Zoroastrians

Zoroastrianism is named after its founder, Zoroaster (sometimes also referred to as Zarathustra), who is thought by one of the latest writers on the subject to have lived somewhere very roughly around 1600 BC, though other authorities have argued that he lived as late as the second half of the sixth century BC. The religion to which Zoroaster gave his name is dualistic, that is to say it regards the principle of good and that of evil as independent of each other and equal in strength, though one may enjoy a temporary supremacy over the other for a period of up to a few centuries. This is a development that came about after the time of Zoroaster himself, however; he taught instead a slightly different doctrine that evil is present at all times, even when good is prevalent.

Zoroastrianism is thought to have originated in central

Asia. Subsequently it became the chief religion in Persia
(now Iran), though at the zenith of Persian power the lands
controlled by its kings were hugely more vast than Iranian
territory today. Latterly Zoroastrianism has become perhaps
best known in the West for adherence to it by Parsees, a
light-complexioned, diligent and highly sagacious people of
Persian territorial origin who migrated in relatively great
numbers to India, particularly Bombay and its environs,
where many of them became successful merchants and under
British imperial rule were on several occasions awarded
baronetcies.

The popular picture of Zoroastrians is one of fire-
worshippers. From a bereavement point of view, their chief
interest is in the way they have traditionally exposed their
dead on towers to be picked at by vultures until the flesh is
entirely removed from the bones. Exposing the dead is not
unique to Zoroastrianism: Professor Ian Morris thinks it
was probably quite common in the second century BC in
western Europe. But Zoroastrians have been most closely
associated with the practice at all other times. Zoroastrianism has a word, *dakhma*, which originally meant grave but
later came to be used of a 'tower of silence'. The dead were
put at the top of these towers to make it easier for the
vultures to get at them, though there seems to have been an
intermediate period when a bare mountainside would do
provided it was sufficiently a wilderness for there to be no
water, plants or easily cultivable soil.

If a corpse comes into contact with earth it is held by
Zoroastrians to render the earth unclean. In the early fifth
century AD one of the kings of Persia of the Sasanian dynasty,
under whom Zoroastrianism had become the established
religion, allowed Christians in his dominions to bury their
dead. He became known among his own people as 'the
Sinner', probably because to orthodox Zoroastrians this practice was tantamount to polluting the earth. At the same time

195

they had no objection to interring the bones of their own dead once these had been picked white by beasts and scoured and dried to a state of antiseptic purity in the harsh sun of the Middle East.

In the immediate aftermath of death, however, the corpse of an orthodox Zoroastrian was deeply, appallingly unclean, not so much from the nature of the deceased person as from the crowd of malign influences clustered around it, an idea that goes back to Zoroaster's original teaching. Indeed, the better a person had been in life the worse the risk of pollution after his death. This was because a good man would attract an unusually heavy concentration of evil beings trying to overwhelm him. In this way the fresh Zoroastrian corpse was actually treated with more repugnance than old, dried bones, and only those whose job it was were supposed to touch one – undertakers existed in those days, too.

Yet the Sasanian dynasts themselves, like their predecessors as rulers of Persia the Arsacid dynasty, treated their own dead wholly differently from the way their subjects did. Royal personages were embalmed after death and laid to rest in mausolea rather than being left in the open air to provide sustenance for scavengers (dogs, for instance, as well as vultures) in the way the common people were.

Zoroaster's teachings on what happened to humanity after death were less exclusive than those of his pagan predecessors. Pre-Zoroastrian beliefs about the afterlife seem to have had a lot in common with those of the classical civilisations of the Greeks and Romans in the Mediterranean basin: a non-corporeal spirit went to a shadowy realm of the dead beneath the earth, crossing a dark river at some specified place such as a ford or ferry. Consequently the dead needed to be provided with food and clothing by their living descendants in this world. But according to those who speculated on the afterlife in pre-Zoroastrian times, only a select few would enjoy an elevated and sunny existence in heaven, chiefly priests and military heroes.

In contrast Zoroaster extended hope of attaining paradise to anyone, including women and the servant class, basing entrance qualifications for all on how well they had behaved in life rather than their wealth, caste or occupation. One's good deeds were weighed against one's bad ones in a celestial pair of scales at a judgement seat before three divine justices: Mithra, Sraosha and Rashnu. Paradise could be attained provided one's good intentions, speech and actions throughout life outweighed the bad, in which case one's soul was conducted by a lovely girl, representing the conscience of that self-same soul, over a bridge and on into heaven. Nevertheless, perfect bliss was not to be found in heaven at this stage, but was only attainable at the moment of resurrection following the Last Judgement, after which life everlasting and faultless would take place under a divine rule on an immaculate earth rather than in a far away and non-material paradisiacal realm.

If at the initial judgement following one's death the basket of one's bad deeds, words and thoughts was the heavier of the two, one was clutched by a hideous witch while crossing the bridge, which itself shrank to a knife-edge, and dragged down to hell. There was also a kind of limbo for those whose good and bad qualities cancelled each other out, and while not as unpleasant as hell, it was a tedious, characterless place.

Zoroaster's teachings as to there being a judgement after death of a person as an individual led to the idea that you were responsible for your ultimate fate. If you had behaved well overall you were well treated; if badly you paid for it. This concept of individual responsibility, together with a resurrection of the body, Last Judgement and eternal life for soul and body joined together again was unprecedented. But I imagine that to most of us all those concepts will sound familiar. They were in fact adopted by two of the leading world religions that came afterwards, namely Christianity and Islam, and also by Judaism, which may or may not have originated before Zoroastrianism. But it was Zoroaster who came up with these concepts and formulated them, and it has been argued that his version is the most rational and consistent.

In the 1930s the then Shah of Persia persuaded the remaining Zoroastrians in Iran to stop exposing their dead on towers. They were now in a minority – indeed, they had been ever since the conversion of most Persians to Islam – and besides there had grown up reforming tendencies in Zoroastrianism itself. The Shah was concerned that the ancient tradition of exposing the dead was out of keeping with modern civilisation. Shortly before the Second World War, the progressive elements among the Zoroastrians of the capital city of Tehran instituted a cemetery. This was in stark contrast to the wild and desolate places where the dead had traditionally been exposed, being fertile, well-wooded and lush, but corpses were still not allowed to come into contact with the earth. The Zoroastrians ensured this by shoring up the sides and bottoms of their graves with a layer of cement, then placing the coffin of the dead person inside so that he was hermetically sealed against the soil.

By the mid-1970s, on the eve of the fundamentalist Islamic revolution in Iran, there was only one centre of any importance there where the old ways were still respected. Even now that fundamentalist Islamic zeal has started enforcing conformity on Iranians with slightly less rigour, most Zoroastrian towers of silence in that country have fallen into disuse. Only perhaps on Malabar Hill in Bombay, where the Parsee community is powerful, wealthy, respected and relatively numerous, does this ancient custom maintain its sway, and even there the proliferation of high-rise buildings round about, which are lived in by non-Zoroastrians with intensely modern notions of what is seemly, has led to tension.

The Zoroastrians in Britain have a section of Brookwood Cemetery near Woking in Surrey reserved for them. This probably first came into use early this century. Before that, Zoroastrians who died in the West were taken back to Persia or Bombay for disposal. The ceremony for the dead is recognised as being in reality more for the sake of the bereaved, since the soul is assured of its future.

PART III

Practical Matters

Regulations Surrounding Bereavement

So far we have looked at the rules for disposing of the dead and for mourning set by the leading religious denominations. Now for those set by the state.

It can be both a great help and a great nuisance in your time of bereavement that the law imposes a whole array of tasks. It may be a help because it not only gives you something to do but erects a structure and timetable in which to do it. But it is more likely to be a nuisance because you have to deal with all sorts of officials who, however kind, sympathetic and considerate as individuals, could well, like many officials, have a limited and unimaginative outlook. Besides, you have never met them before so, with the best will in the world, any helpfulness, sympathy and consideration they exhibit will have an impersonal quality compared with that of friends and relations.

Worse, a lot of travelling is involved, to strange and highly institutionalised places such as registrars' offices, hospitals, crematoria or cemeteries – perhaps even coroners' courts and offices for interviews to do with probate or inheritance tax. The timetable for accomplishing all these visits is set by officialdom, not you, and can involve a tight schedule. If you are the next of kin or an executor you cannot delegate the obligation to attend these interviews. Nor can you put them off until better weather or a warmer season. If you don't have a car it can be a real hardship.

If you find someone dead you should inform the next of kin, a doctor and possibly the police and a cleric. Whether you also get in touch with an undertaker, and if so which one, depends on such factors as the existence of a pre-paid plan, which we shall come to later, and your attitude to go-it-alone funerals (see Part III). You need not inform the police unless the death is suspicious, that is, due to violence (including self-inflicted violence) or an accident or if it seems to have no obvious cause. In the last case we are talking of the death of someone previously in good health as opposed to a person who had been suffering from a serious illness or was very old.

More deaths than ever take place in hospital nowadays, though very recently there have been disturbing reports of terminally ill elderly patients being shunted into nursing homes so that their families or councils, not the NHS, will bear the cost of looking after them. The councils are obliged to means-test patients before giving help, which scarcely cheers up a sick old person's last days, however necessary it may be given the importance of curbing public expenditure. If death occurs in a hospital the ward sister will break the news to the next of kin, unless the patient died while being visited by the next of kin (as happened with my mother when my father was present), when it is the other way round. The next of kin is simply a person nominated by the deceased before she died: it need not be a relative.

If you are the next of kin, find out whether the deceased has subscribed to a pre-paid funeral plan. These have begun to be sold very assiduously in the last few years, and the National Association of Funeral Directors (NAFD) reckons that more than 100,000 people in the country have bought one.

Also try to find any will as soon as possible, not only because this may contain wishes for a certain sort of funeral but because it may ask that some of the dead person's organs be donated, or the entire body presented to a medical school. In the last two cases you often have only a few hours in which to act before the organs or body are useless for such purposes. Currently medical schools are burdened with a glut of cadavers and could well decline to accept any more.

The great advantage of presenting a body to a medical school is that they will bury or cremate it free after using it for study, though only in a simple ceremony. Most people intending to donate parts of themselves carry donor cards these days, but even then staff at the hospital where the deceased passed his last days will notify the next of kin before removing organs. In the case of an entire body, telephone the London Anatomy Office (0171–387 7850) if in Greater London; the local medical school's anatomy office if outside Greater London; or the official Inspector of Anatomy (0171–972 4550) if there are any difficulties and/or it is outside working hours.

If the police need to be called then the coroner may well have to be notified as well, in which case his consent has to be obtained if organs are to be removed or the entire body donated to science. Coroners are listed under the letter 'C' in the phone book; hospitals and the police also have their addresses and phone numbers. The coroner or his officer will advise about further steps to be taken in connection with the report to a coroner. In practice, given the time element, any need to report a death to a coroner means that however much the deceased might have wanted to benefit others it will be impossible for organs to be removed.

Anyone has the right (and everyone has a duty) to get in touch with the local coroner if he is unhappy about the circumstances of a death. Suspected foul play is the most obvious reason, but a contributory factor as seemingly innocuous as an old war wound or industrial disease may be relevant, especially if the deceased was not regularly attended by a doctor. For example, a widow's pension and family's right to compensation could be affected. If the person died in hospital during an operation or even when coming out from under anaesthetic (up to twenty-four hours after an operation, in practice) the coroner is informed, as he is if drugs or any other poison or sheer physical neglect may have been involved; if suicide is suspected; or if there is a possibility that an abortion might recently have been performed on the deceased. If the dead person was in prison or held by the police at the time, a coroner must also be informed.

If you find the body at home, whether your own or the deceased's, and wish to have it removed by an undertaker you must get the doctor's permission first. Not all doctors attend immediately on all deaths, particularly if the death has been expected and was peaceful. If the deceased is to be cremated, the doctor must be informed since both he and another doctor, who must not have attended on the dead person or been involved in caring for her or treating her, must examine the corpse beforehand. And if you apply to have a body cremated you must get your application countersigned by a householder who knows you.

Up till 1965 the countersigner had to be an MP, JP, minister of religion, doctor or dentist, barrister or solicitor, bank manager, policeman of sergeant's rank or upwards or the secretary of a trade union. Considering how many of those occupations have fallen into disrepute since, particularly that of MP, it is probably just as well that a householder will now do instead. It's amazing that one never hears of a crooked undertaker (apart from one offstage in the short story *Totentanz* by the late Sir Angus Wilson), crematorium official or registrar, considering what a heavy public responsibility they bear.

Only an executor or the next of kin may normally apply for cremation, although someone else can sign the application form if he can both satisfy the cremation authority that he is an appropriate person to do so and give a good reason on the application why he rather than an executor or the next of kin is applying. Any application for a cremation whatsoever can be turned down by a medical referee and he does not have to give a reason. A medical referee is nominated by a cremation authority and appointed by the Home Office. He must be a doctor and have other relevant qualifications and experience. Although an executor is not obliged to obey every wish in the will as regards conducting the funeral he must do so where the deceased expresses a desire *not* to be cremated.

It is important to remove a pacemaker before cremating someone as it could explode otherwise. In or before 1977 something like that did occur, which is why in that year crematoria were allowed by the Home Office to ask additional questions to those they already posed. The medical certificate Form B, which the dead person's regular doctor fills in now, makes the rather obvious statement that radio-active implants are a health hazard and asks whether the deceased was fitted with one. This sounds alarming at first but is nothing to worry about. It refers to one of two possibilities. First, in the very early days of pacemakers the manufacturers produced ones powered by atomic batteries which were fitted to about fifteen patients in the USA as an experiment. As far as the UK is concerned any radio-active implant is much more likely to be the second possibility, a radium chip or needle inserted in cancer patients to deliver a minute amount of radiation locally to a tumour. These are routinely removed, along with pacemakers, by hospital staff in the case of anyone who dies in hospital. The risk of one remaining in the body of anyone dying elsewhere is slight because a person whose cancer is so far advanced as to need a radio-active implant is likely to be a hospital inpatient already. And any risk arising from the radium chip not being removed before cremation will fall to crematorium staff, who remove all metal objects from the ashes, not to the next of kin or executors who eventually take possession of the ashes. But having said that, at least one case has allegedly come to light of crematorium staff failing to remove pieces of shrapnel from the ashes of a dead man who had long before suffered a war wound so that the next of kin,

207

on being presented with the cremated remains, later did so themselves using a domestic magnet.

Every death must be registered within five days, and if you are the informant who supplies the registrar with the basic facts about the deceased you must do so in person at the registrar's office. But for the registration to take place the registrar (whose address and phone number will be found at your doctor's surgery, local library, police stations and post offices, as well as being procurable from a Citizens' Advice Bureau or the council) first needs a completely separate certificate stating the cause of death. This would be filled in and signed by the deceased's doctor if the person died of a reasonably drawn-out illness. The doctor will usually put the certificate in an envelope with the name and address of the appropriate registrar on it.

Registration may be delayed for up to a fortnight from the moment of death if the registrar is given written confirmation that the doctor has signed that certificate. In very exceptional cases the registrar might visit you at home. There used to be a fee for this but it was abolished in 1968.

If someone dies suddenly or unexpectedly, such that the doctor has not attended in person on her in the last fortnight before death (or four weeks in Northern Ireland), he is prohibited from signing the certificate and the matter must be reported to the coroner, whose staff may look into the cause of death at the coroner's mortuary, possibly even to the extent of instigating a post-mortem. Some post-mortems are done by the hospital where the death occurred. This is not the same as a coroner's post-mortem and needs the next of kin's permission. If the coroner orders a post-mortem he does not need the family's permission, but they can contest his decision and fight it legally as far as the High Court. This will, of course, entail delay and expense.

It is worth discussing with the registrar by phone the most convenient time of the working day from your point of view to register the death, even though few registrars are said to operate an appointments system. Many are located in parts of the local town that are difficult to get to even with a car, parking spaces being at more and more of a premium these days. If the death occurred in a hospital the registrar in whose district the hospital lies will normally be the one you must go to, not the one in whose district you live.

You will find the business of clearing up after a death quite time-consuming enough without having to hang around a registrar's waiting room while the parking meter a few streets away ticks up an ever-growing sum and the garrulous couple of middle-aged women in front of you discuss their aunt's deathbed, as happened to me. It is important that officialdom be made to realise that they are there to serve us, the consumers, not the other way round. Your taxes pay their salaries. If you are not seen soon after arrival do not shrink from expressing your irritation to the registrar. They should be used to emotional outbursts from the bereaved, anyway.

The certificate of cause of death lists the categories of those who can go to the registrar's office and provide the simple information (the deceased's birthplace, date of birth, maiden name if a married woman, date and place of death and former occupation) without which it is impossible to register a death. Nobody else may do so. The registrar issues you with a death certificate, which is technically a copy of the entry in the register.

You may need more than one copy, and the price of extra copies (currently £2.50 each) goes up (currently to £5.50 or if after two years and by post to £15) if you put off requesting them till the volume your relative's death was registered in is full – a month or so afterwards on average. Most financial institutions need a full copy of the death certificate (not a photocopy) before they will release money to the executor, but they are quick at returning them. I made the mistake of getting ten after my father died for what in aggregate amounted to that number of insurance policies, building society accounts and probate. I need not have bothered to get more than three at the very most, as it turned out.

If the coroner holds an inquest members of the family may be present and if they have the permission of the coroner they can cross-examine witnesses or employ a lawyer to do so on their behalf. They cannot get legal aid for this. If your relative died following an accident which might give rise to your subsequently suing someone for damages you would be well advised to have a lawyer represent you at any inquest which takes place. Next of kin are not always told the result of a post-mortem and may not even be notified of the precise date of the inquest, a deplorable state of affairs which ought to be rectified.

To be fair, the timing of the inquest is not a straightforward matter since some investigations take longer than others and the police have many calls on their time. Then again, if the death is the result of a major disaster or connected in any way with an alleged crime such that an investigation or crown court trial could ensue, the inquest will probably be adjourned. Meanwhile, you can get an interim document from the coroner certifying that the death has taken place and thus start dealing with any monies due and other administrative matters affecting the estate.

Nevertheless, I hope not many others experience what I went through when my father committed suicide. This was as follows. First I was told by the police that they would arrange a closed inquest (not open to the public, particularly the press). Subsequently it was from the newspapers, rather than any other source (I was never officially informed at all), that I learned not only of the inquest's verdict of suicide, but that the inquest had been held in the first place. I wrote letters of complaint to the Chief Constable, the Home Secretary, my local MP and various other appropriate bodies but got no satisfaction. The police were unable to say whether the leak to the press had or had not come from them. Still, if more people did this when it happens we might all get somewhere.

In one respect the police were excellent. While the undertakers were first laying out and then removing my father's body, a local constable kept me chatting in the kitchen, distracting me from the grisly activities upstairs and the cumbersome manoeuvres of bearers struggling with the bulky body down the narrow and steep stairs and out of the door. He said nothing very sensationally amusing or interesting. He was not even – thank God – 'understanding'; just good old-fashioned conversation about day-to-day topics such as you might strike up with any stranger in a pub or railway carriage. This seems to me the essence of pastoral care. One only wishes the police collectively would show more of it when a householder is hit by crime.

The timing of a funeral is governed by law in certain circumstances. You cannot bury or cremate your dead friend or relative till you get a disposal certificate from the registrar or, from the coroner, an order for burial or certificate for cremation. If you yourself as the person charged with disposing of the body are unavoidably detained elsewhere (in hospital, for instance) you can get from the registrar a certificate for burial even though you have not yet gone along and personally given him the information required for the formal registration of death, but this does not apply to cremation.

If a person has died of one of six 'notifiable' illnesses (cholera, plague, relapsing fever, smallpox, typhus or AIDS), he comes under the provisions of the Public Health (Control of Disease) Act 1984 and the Public Health (Infectious Diseases) Regulations 1985 Statutory Instrument 1985 No. 434 Regulation 2. (It was the latter that added AIDS to the list of other diseases.) A JP can then order that the body be taken to a mortuary or immediately buried, if keeping it in a building would put the health of others there or in neighbouring buildings at risk. If anyone suffering from these diseases dies in hospital his body can be ordered to be taken direct to a mortuary or buried or cremated. It seems odd that burial is permitted along with cremation since the latter would on the face of it seem to be more hygienic, but there it is.

If the death of someone from one of these six illnesses has occurred in a place other than a hospital, then no unnecessary contact with the corpse must take place. 'Unnecessary' in this context refers, of course, to what is deemed medically important rather than what may be culturally or religiously important. Luckily the Commission for Racial Equality can recall no cases of any conflict between the customs of an ethnic minority group and the law of England and Wales, Northern Ireland or Scotland over this.

As Section 45 of the 1984 act puts it (in a prose style only a little less impenetrable than Joyce's in *Finnegan's Wake*):

It shall not be lawful to hold a wake over the body of a person who has died while suffering from a notifiable disease; and the occupier of any premises who permits or suffers any such wake to take place on them, and every person who takes part in the wake, shall be liable on summary conviction to a fine not exceeding Level 1 on the standard scale.

Dead bodies are not property in the sense of having owners, but someone, usually an executor or next of kin, can be 'in possession of a body', which isn't quite the same as owning it outright. It would seem that the crown has the power to take possession of a body, though whether unilaterally or with the agreement of the next of kin is not clear. In 1852 Queen Victoria decreed that the body of the recently deceased Duke of Wellington should be taken into the possession of the crown. She was planning a hugely elaborate funeral, yet according to Lady Longford in her biography of Wellington, the next of kin were not too keen on the idea and knuckled under with some reluctance. Normally the executor or executors have a right of both possession and custody.

The executor or whoever else is 'in possession' has quite considerable powers over the body: she doesn't have to obey the provisions of the deceased person's will (unless, as already noted, the will expresses a desire not to be cremated). Common decency, unlike the law, does dictate that you observe the dead person's wishes. But remember that sometimes these wishes don't form part of a will, drafted, one hopes, in a mood of calm reflection and assisted by the testator's lawyer, but instead have been expressed orally, perhaps on his deathbed. In that case he may have been under the influence of powerful painkilling drugs or neurotic fears about the future such as one comes across in a mentally confused OAP. The problem here is that common sense can conflict with common decency.

The local council may have to organise the disposal of a body if no other person turns up to take responsibility (for example, in the case of a down-and-out), acting usually through the aegis of the social services department. In such a case it is obliged by law to respect the clearly expressed wishes of a person now dead if they involved a repugnance to burial as opposed to cremation, or vice versa. But if a specific desire for some other means of disposal was expressed by the now deceased person and after his death the authorities consider this is unsuitable, then according to one interpretation the social services can force through either burial or cremation but according to another the council must respect those wishes. There also appears to be a contradiction in the law between whether the authorities can force those in possession of a body to dispose of it or whether it can be kept 'on any premises' for an unusual length of time, perhaps for embalming or other form of preservation.

If a firm of solicitors has been appointed as executors be

213

prepared for very steep charges, on average between 1.5 and 2.5 per cent of the total estate. Things are even worse if a bank has been appointed executor. The bank usually appoints a solicitor anyway but may charge anything up to 5 per cent of a major part of the estate. Richard Bark-Jones, a Liverpool solicitor quoted by the press from time to time, is on record as saying that banks sometimes even charge 6 per cent of the estate. There is a neat little short story by A. A. Milne, better known as creator of Winnie the Pooh, about a solicitor who draws up a will for a client and then marries his client's daughter. The wedding is a very quiet one owing to the sudden death of the groom's father-in-law, felled like an ox on perusing the solicitor's bill of costs. Be warned. It is bad enough having to deal with the death of one member of the family without having to guard against apoplexy in another soon afterwards through overcharging by institutional executors.

If the deceased was foolish enough to have made no will the personal representative must share out the estate according to certain rules. The surviving spouse gets the lion's share, but factors come into play such as whether or not there are children and how big the estate is. If there is no surviving spouse the children get equal shares unless a child or children has predeceased their intestate parent, in which case that child's share goes to his children, if any. If neither spouse nor children nor children's children survive the person who failed to make a will, first his father and mother, then his siblings and nephews and nieces, then his grandparents and finally his uncles and aunts and cousins (if uncle or aunt has died first) come in for a share.

If the person who has died has no relatives the crown gets it all. You have a right to a share of the estate of someone who made no will even if you are not related to him provided you were being supported by him in the period immediately prior to his death.

Undertakers

So far you have been guided through dealings with the official world. Its very impersonality makes it comparatively easy to deal with at a time of charged emotions. When newly bereaved you also come into contact with another occupational group you may not have encountered before: undertakers.

The undertaker has this century started calling himself a funeral director, though even then not invariably. I saw a notice in the deaths column of *The Times* in May 1994 in which inquirers were asked to contact the firm of McLeod, redundantly described as 'Funeral Undertakers', of Inverasdale, Ross-shire. In any case, the undertaker's emotional stock-in-trade has remained much the same, hovering uneasily between the lugubrious and the smarmy. Cheerfulness may break through but easily transmutes into familiarity or facetiousness. The truth is, you need the diplomatic skills of a Talleyrand combined with the genuine concern for other people's feelings of a Mother Teresa and most undertakers simply haven't got either, let alone both.

Though many of them strive to be helpful and I think often are, they are nevertheless businessmen, not members of a 'caring' profession such as doctors, psychiatrists or clerics, all of whom have usually had some kind of higher education. Undertakers are not even fired by general benevolence in the way nurses seem to be. The rest of us only ever have dealings

215

with them when we are unusually vulnerable, just as we usually only see much of nurses in a similar condition. But patients grow to adore their nurses; the bereaved do not grow to love undertakers. I am sorry to say that there is a great deal of evidence of overcharging by undertakers, or at the least a tendency to encourage people to use services such as limousines that they would not normally contemplate. No less an authority than Ken West (see the Go-it-Alone section) is quoted in the *Sunday Telegraph* (15 October 1994) as saying that many bereaved families feel ripped off: 'Funeral directors can get the standard coffin for around £50 but some will charge people around £350.'

Now, every person in business is entitled to sell as much of his wares at as high a price as the market will bear. But in other fields involving a degree of emotional pressure on the consumer – hire purchase, door-to-door life insurance – there is a legal cooling-off period in which the consumer can reconsider his decision to incur considerable expenditure, or a legal obligation for the salesman to disclose what commission he is getting. The average funeral in the UK costs just over £1,000, yet 96 per cent of all estates, including immoveables such as houses, amount to less than £150,000. If you take away the value of the family house, which is usually the single biggest item in a family's portfolio and is not easily realisable, it could well be that the average family is spending something like 5 per cent of its entire movable assets on a funeral.

It is facile to argue, as some defenders of the elaborate funeral do, that we spend a lot of money on a wedding, so why not a ritzy celebration of death too? True, if the consumer wants ceremony he should be allowed to pay for it. Cribb's, the family undertaking firm of Canning Town in east London, report increasing demand for their glass-sided, horse-drawn Victorian hearse. One would respect them more if they did not give out misleading information: 'Can you be buried in your own garden?' Ysenda Maxtone Graham, of the *Sunday*

Telegraph (28 April 1991), asked a man at Cribb's. He said no. He was wrong. (See the Go-It-Alone section for details.)

A wedding is entered into by two living people of their own free will and whoever pays for it, usually the bride's father, does so with a grimace perhaps but still of his own free will also. In contrast, the cost of the funeral is recoverable from the estate of the one person who, being dead, has little real say in the matter. He cannot even get his wishes for a certain kind of funeral always enforced by law, even if he has expressed them with the utmost clarity in his will.

Until recently the commercial myopia of undertakers was astonishing. Some of them in the early years managed to wrest business away from the heralds, but in the nineteenth century, although often adroit at persuading their customers that a simple funeral would be socially demeaning, they never showed much gumption. They never expanded into coffin furnishings, stationery or jewellery to do with mourning, crape production and sales or cemetery management. There were too many of them in London for huge profits, although individual firms went in for gigantic mark-ups, sometimes as much as 500 per cent. In the country communications were so bad that an undertaker seldom had much custom beyond the parish boundaries.

Things are changing. I recently saw a play in Dublin about an old lady whose relatives want to put her in a nursing home so that they can get their hands on the money tied up in her large house. An enterprising undertaker was among the advertisers in the programme. Other professions connected with bereavement are showing similar vision. The Institute of Burial and Cremation Administration is urging that graves older than 75 years be disinterred (subject to permission from living relatives, if traceable) so that they can be reused and bodies buried deeper, with more placed on top. This would not be a new practice, as John Luby of the City of London Cemetery and Crematorium said in August 1994, being merely a repetition of what churchyard authorities used to do in the nineteenth century.

Most tradesmen organising funerals continued to call themselves undertakers until shortly before the war. The British Institute of Undertakers existed from 1898 to 1905, when it rechristened itself the British Undertakers' Association. In 1935 it took on the more pompous title of National Association of Funeral Directors (NAFD).

A parallel organisation, the British Institute of Funeral Directors, started up in 1982, for the undertaking trade is split into two rival camps nationally. There is nevertheless considerable concentration of forces in the market. Co-operative Funeral Services claims 25 per cent of it, Plantsbrook is said to have around 9 per cent and Great Southern, taken over in August 1994 by the American group Service Corporation International, 5. Britain is an attractive country to undertakers. It is a compact place with an ageing population. The future looks rosier than in the USA, where undertakers persuade their clients to spend much more on funerals but arrange fewer per firm.

The NAFD has a code of practice by which its members must offer full information on prices, written estimates and detailed invoices, client confidentiality and a mechanism for handling complaints. A number of authors have written books and newspaper articles questioning how closely that code is adhered to and in 1993 the Co-operative Funeral Services broke away from the National Association on the grounds that the code was a dead letter, setting up the Funeral Standards Council instead.

As if to make matters more complicated, there is also a Society of Allied and Independent Funeral Directors at Crowndale House, 1 Ferdinand Place, London NW1 8EE (tel. 0171-267 6777), which speaks for small family firms. At the same time some of the small men are members of the NAFD too.

Undertakers may have a difficult time of it in an era like ours which is both anxious for more involvement by the bereaved and yet still often shrinks from the consequences or necessary preconditions of that involvement. Nevertheless some of the stories of undertakers' blunders do not make attractive reading. These include losing coffins from the back doors of hearses and failing to prevent a deceased woman's gold tooth 'disappearing' at some point between removal of the body from the family home (which allegedly took place a day earlier than arranged) and the funeral proper.

I myself once attended a funeral where the plate on the coffin gave the wrong date of death for the deceased and where the emblem on it was a sacred heart pierced by a dagger together with the letters RIP, whereas the deceased, if not exactly a staunch Protestant, had at any rate been given a funeral in the local Anglican cathedral. That was in the Republic of Ireland, however. Cases have been reported in Britain of the cost of embalming being concealed in the general account, not itemised separately.

At the time of writing, the Association of Burial Authorities, the Memorial Advisory Bureau, the National Funerals College and the National Association of Local Councils, plus individual local councils, are getting together to draw up something called a Dead Citizen's Charter. It is hoped that this will deal with consumer dissatisfaction, and not just dissatisfaction with undertakers but also with the clergy, for instance over the recent ban by a vicar on the words 'Mum' and 'Dad' on gravestones. It is a misnomer, of course. Dead citizens can't lodge complaints or receive apologies, let alone compensation. This will be a live citizen's charter, if it comes off. The very fuzziness of the thinking surrounding it is one more bit of evidence of how contradictory people's attitudes to bereavement remain.

The Go-It-Alone Approach

As you have probably noticed from the historical sketch earlier in this book, most of our laws and regulations about disposal of the dead in this country date only from the last few centuries – they are certainly post-mediaeval. Since undertakers in modern times (as opposed to their equivalents in Roman Britain) started operating only from the late seventeenth century, it is not surprising that they are, strictly speaking, a superfluity. After all, if millions of people managed to dispose of their dead between AD 410, when the Roman occupation came to a shamefaced end as the legions sailed back to Italy to stem barbarian invasions there, and the 1670s, when undertakers first came on to the scene, they cannot be that vital.

The argument in favour of using undertakers is that they remove the bother of arranging distressing and sometimes grisly details from your shoulders at a time when you are feeling particularly fragile. In the Middle Ages people lived so close to subsistence level, being beset by stink, plague, murderous violence and low life expectancy generally, that they evidently didn't need undertakers. They also had the Church, which the British by and large are now happy to do without on a day-to-day basis. It is a testimony to the advanced technical state of our civilisation that most of us nowadays need hardly encounter physical unpleasantness and can pay others to deal with it. Perhaps we do as a result lose some sense of immediacy or involvement in the death of a relative, to say nothing of oneness with nature, but that is always part of the price of civilisation.

Nevertheless, there are some members of the public who are quite prepared to tackle the challenge of doing an undertaker's work themselves on a one-off basis. They choose to go it alone because they (a) resent paying undertakers' fees, or (b) are naturally independent-minded, or (c) find that the activity takes their mind off the loss and helps prevent them brooding, or (d) are enthusiastic about the supposedly 'green' benefits of disposing of a body in an unorthodox fashion, such as by burying it in the garden, or (e) a combination of all these.

Burial outside a churchyard or cemetery is neither a new idea nor even a new practice. Some of the dissenters from the Church of England in sixteenth- and seventeenth-century England carried it out in places like orchards and traditionally suicides were often buried at crossroads, together with a stake through their hearts to stop them 'walking' (becoming revenants). A prosperous provision merchant of Stevenage in Hertfordshire left instructions on dying in 1724 that his coffin should be stored in the roof-space of a barn rather than buried, and seems to have been obeyed. He apparently feared that bodysnatchers would get at him otherwise. The ploy worked well enough for nearly two centuries, but during the First World War skylarking soldiers purloined his bones.

If your motive for organising the proceedings yourself is that you resent paying undertakers' fees, stop to consider whether you are actually saving yourself money. You are going to have to set aside a great deal of your time over the next few weeks or months anyway if you are a close relative of the deceased; perhaps much more than a few months if you are an executor. If your time is valuable ordinarily this will represent quite enough disruption to your professional life as it is. You cannot avoid certain expenses such as fees for doctor's certification anyway.

I got a basic conventional funeral (cremation) done professionally for my father for something like a little over £600 in south-east England in September 1993 (it may have helped bring the price down that he negotiated with them – or at any rate secured a quote – a month or two before he committed suicide, though I could not bring myself to ask). That is surely quite reasonable considering that it involved transport of the body, laying out, encasing the body in a receptacle ready for cremation and the hire of the crematorium. All my sister and I had to do was turn up at the crematorium and supply the management with a cassette tape of Purcell's 'Music for the Funeral of Queen Mary', which in its opening sequence is scored for kettledrums and trumpets and is much the most moving piece I know of for use on such occasions. The three minutes' playing time exactly matched the time it took for the coffin to slide out of sight into the furnace. This funeral took place just outside Greater London, so would probably be cheaper still in more remote areas of the country. Certainly costs vary from region to region of the UK.

Conventional religious or semi-religious services are not necessarily to be despised just because they are conventional. Nearly everybody is familiar with Psalm xxiii even if they never go to church any more. That is a great advantage: those present know the tune and just because it is recognised it is often sung with fervour. The same goes for the one or two hymns which feature on these occasions. Unless you can rehearse everybody likely to attend a funeral in advance, and possibly on several occasions, a deliberately unconventional funeral can be shambolic, even degenerate into farce. Do consider these points.

Nor are Go-It-Alone funerals particularly cheap unless you want a very hole-and-corner affair. I mean this almost literally: you use just a shroud – no coffin – and bury the deceased in a hole in a corner of the garden. Much of the basic equipment for a funeral, even one you conduct entirely yourself as regards ceremony and the handling side of the operation, has gone up substantially in price over the last two years.

Take the joint winner of the Natural Death Handbook Award for the Most Helpful Funeral Director, Gibsons Funeral Service, of Bolton, Lancashire. Gibsons' cheapest fully fitted coffin was priced in the latest (1993) edition of the *Natural Death Handbook* (hereafter *NDH*) at £45, whereas two days before Christmas of 1994 I was quoted £90. *NDH* mentions Gibsons as quoting a local delivery charge of £10, whereas at Christmas 1994 it had risen to £30 (and although *NDH* says delivery nationally is negotiable, Gibsons explained to me that 'nationally' in this context was restricted to England and Wales). *NDH* also mentions Gibsons as quoting advice for do-it-yourselfers at £10 an hour whereas by Christmas 1994 it had risen to £15 an hour. According to *NDH*, Gibsons quoted their basic funeral at £260, whereas by Christmas 1994 it had soared to £650. When *NDH* researched the matter Gibsons operated no pre-paid plan; they do have one now, though for people in the Bolton area only. *NDH* gives their horse-drawn funerals as ranging from £450 to £850, whereas by Christmas 1994 it was £650 to £950. These are very substantial increases in a time of low inflation, but Gibsons explained to me that the price of wood and doctors' and clergymen's fees had risen.

Similar arguments may apply to the independent-minded, and unless your sense of independence is overwhelmingly strong, you can probably assuage it by simply ringing round to find the lowest quotation and then giving detailed orders to the undertakers as to how you want the funeral conducted down to the minutest particular. Incidentally, since, according to a number of reliable sources, notably Jane Spottiswoode (see the Bibliography), undertakers are extremely cagey about giving a breakdown of their costs, you could try the threat of going it alone so as to induce them to be a little less reticent.

It is only where the reasons mentioned in categories (c), (d) and (e) are uppermost in your mind that you will probably want to break away from all conventional methods and deal with the matter entirely without professional help. For the information of the ecologically minded and those with multiple reasons for wanting to go it alone, I would point out that according to the *Guardian* of 10 December 1994, British crematoria burn their way through 437,000 wood coffins a year. (The source doesn't say whether this includes Northern Ireland. Strictly speaking it shouldn't, since Northern Ireland is outside Britain though within the UK.) On the other hand, cemeteries are reckoned to occupy a total of some 16,000 acres and the more than 15,000,000 cremations since 1885 have probably prevented a further 6,000 acres being swallowed up by cemeteries.

An essential point to make about arranging funerals off your own bat is that they may need to be planned a long way in advance. Unless the deceased has taken a long time to die or has been so frail in health for so long that the end has been in sight for an appreciable period, that factor alone could prevent a wholesale individualistic approach, such as arranging for the body to be buried in your garden. *NDH* lists a number of undertakers all over the country who will dispense free advice to anyone wanting to arrange a funeral with the minimum of professional help.

Let us suppose that you do in fact want to bury the body in your garden. First you should be aware of a case in 1973 in which unorthodox disposal of a dead body resulted in prison sentences which were sustained on appeal. A few people had got together and hidden a corpse under some paving stones. They were found guilty of conspiracy to prevent a lawful and decent burial. In 1983 three people who had disposed of a body by rolling it up in a carpet and some plastic sheeting and tying up the parcel with a washing line before burying it in a ditch were held to be guilty of (a) preventing lawful and decent burial, (b) trespass (the ditch) and (c) contravening the Births and Deaths Registration Act 1926, though it was also held that it would be for a jury to adjudicate on whether the use of the ditch constituted decent burial.

On the other hand, in early January 1995 Wolverhampton Council was ordered by the local government ombudsman to pay a widow's legal costs of £1,000 after it had mistakenly informed her that she could not bury her husband in her garden on public health grounds (for example, soil conditions and the rising water table – the National Rivers Authority had not objected to the widow's proposed 'green burial'). The Wolverhampton ratepayers might have had to fund their council's liability for a great deal more than £1,000 in the form of compensation for distress to the widow, but she had herself died by the time the ombudsman made his decision. To the layman this might seem like the ultimate in prima facie evidence of distress, but the law doesn't work like that.

Next look at the title deeds of your house to make sure that there is no restrictive covenant on such activities. It is unlikely that there will be, but you need to be sure. Even if there is you could try to get a court order quashing it, but to do this you would need to prove that the original purpose for which the covenant was drafted no longer holds good, if that is indeed the case. As with almost any legal ruling, a court order of this sort cannot be obtained overnight.

There may be local by-laws restricting your use of an unorthodox site for burial. The local authority's planning department, chief executive or legal department will have a register of any such rules. They too could need some time to check their records. Even if there is no restriction on burying a body in your grounds, there may be a legal obligation to dig the grave to a certain depth lest a nuisance or health hazard be created. This tends to be more the case in areas of longstanding human settlement, for example, York as opposed to Harlow New Town, though where a settlement is so old that it has been abandoned, as at Silchester on the Hampshire–Berkshire borders, or Dunwich in Suffolk (one is an abandoned Roman city, the other a mediaeval town long swallowed by the sea following erosion of the coastline), anyone living in the environs should not have too much of a problem.

A number of the older towns have by-laws insisting that coffins must be buried with at least 2½ft of earth between the top of the lid and the ordinary level of the ground. Manchester, which, though it greatly expanded from the Industrial Revolution onwards, is an old settlement, used at one time to specify 4ft, but since 1977 this has no longer been a requirement. Cemeteries run by the local council have since 1977 had to bury coffins to a minimum depth of 2ft from the top of the lid to the ordinary level of the ground if the soil permits and in some cases to a minimum of 3ft where the soil is less suitable. If you do not use a coffin the measurements are calculated from the top layer of shroud instead of the coffin lid.

It has been suggested that one way of getting round the restriction on the depth of burials beneath a top layer of soil could be to build up a tumulus or mound of earth above a lightly buried body. You should scrutinise the wording of local by-laws very closely before doing so and probably take legal advice, but historically this has been a perfectly acceptable way of coping with health problems where there is very stony or closely packed soil.

Only if there is going to be what the planners call 'material change of use' will you need planning permission for a grave in the garden or other grounds of your property, or even an unobtrusive memorial stone. Many children bury pets in the garden and put up some kind of commemorative device and the heavens don't cave in. Some writers who have looked into the subject suggest that the same applies to human burials. It might nevertheless be a good idea to get some kind of documentation from the local authority saying that what you are doing is not against the law if you would otherwise worry about being harassed by officials or officious neighbours. The usual form of this is called a Certificate of Lawfulness.

J. B. Bradfield, in *Green Burial* (see the Bibliography), is adamant that this is not necessary and takes *Which*'s *What to Do When Someone Dies* to task for asserting that permission from planning authorities must be obtained. The passage in the *Which* publication certainly reads as if planning permission is invariably necessary, and a slip of loose paper inserted in my copy, although not called an erratum or addendum slip, states that though planning permission isn't a legal requirement advance permission is highly advisable. A press officer from the Department of the Environment has made it clear that planning permission is not required when one or two persons are being buried in back gardens. I take that to mean that burying more than one or two bodies might constitute a different case and that burial in the front or side garden, or a roof garden of a block of flats, might be a trickier business too.

If you wish to keep the deceased person's body from decomposing while you sort out these problems, a practical solution is to store it with an undertaker. *NDH* gives a list of undertakers prepared to accept a body for cold storage. They are reasonably widespread throughout England (no such establishments are listed for Northern Ireland, Scotland or Wales) and usually vary between no charge and £15 to £20 a day. But elsewhere in *NDH* it is suggested that this sort of service would be available only for a few days, especially among the undertakers who make no charge. Yet legal problems might take weeks to resolve. *NDH* also suggests the hospital mortuary if the deceased person died there; the cellar or other cool room in your home; ice cubes in some such covering as plastic bags; or dry ice. None of these is practical for any length of time. And some bodies decompose more quickly than others, depending not just on the age of the deceased at the point of death, but on the cause of death itself.

Even if you are planning to bury a relative or friend in a local authority-run cemetery or churchyard rather than in privately owned ground but want to conduct the proceedings yourself, you must inform the vicar or cemetery officials beforehand. In the latter case you would do so by getting formal permission from the council under whose jurisdiction the cemetery comes. If you wish to bury a dead person without the Anglican rites you may do so if you give forty-eight hours' notice in writing, signed with your name and address and with the words 'Notice of Burial' on the envelope. You should state the proposed time and day of the burial, which unless arranged otherwise between you and whoever is in charge of the burial ground should be between 10 a.m. and 6 p.m. from 1 April to 1 October and between 10 a.m. and 3 p.m. for the rest of the year, excluding Christmas Day, Good Friday and Sundays, which are off limits entirely.

It would appear that you or someone appointed by you can either conduct any type of Christian funeral, which is defined as every religious service used by any church, denomination, or person professing to be Christian, or organise a burial involving no religious service. What you cannot do is bring into contempt or obloquy the Christian religion, or the belief or worship of any church or denomination of Christians, or the members or any ministers of any such church or denomination. Nor may anyone utter a public statement to the assembly which is unauthorised. It is not clear whether, for instance, a pagan ceremony would fall into the prohibited category.

Cemeteries owned by private companies have their own rules as to such matters as time and place of burial, how much advance notice must be given, fees to be paid up-front and whether you can carry out a burial on Sundays and public holidays. Many of these rules depend not just on the particular cemetery but also on such points as whether the person to be buried is an adult or child (and if a child, whether stillborn or otherwise) and whether the burial is of cremated remains or an intact body.

Cemeteries and crematoria have set opening times for the public to visit graves and memorial plaques or rose bushes or whatever. A typical schedule is 9 a.m. to 4.30 p.m., Monday to Friday from 1 October to 31 March, and 9 a.m. to 8 p.m. Monday to Friday from 1 April to 30 September. Under rules of this sort the authorities typically might decree that anyone turning up after 4 p.m. in winter or 7.30 p.m. in summer would be refused admission. On Saturdays, Sundays, Good Friday, Christmas Day, New Year's Day and other public holidays a cemetery or crematorium might also decree that the grounds open at 10 a.m.

This sort of restriction on when you can visit the place your loved one is buried seems to me the best reason of all for burying her in the garden. It is intolerable that local bureaucracy should dictate when you can and cannot commune with the dead. The romantically inclined lover may want to strew flowers on the grave of her dead fiancé and have a good cry over him in the moonlight; the busy executive to offer up a silent prayer over his deceased mother early one sunny morning on his way to the office; the harassed housewife to think fond thoughts of her late husband after picking the children up from school in the late afternoon. By mid-March sunset is well past 5 p.m., yet the cemetery gates have clanged shut. There is an hour of daylight well before 9 a.m. throughout the year but still the gates remain closed till some oafish council employee finds it convenient to unlock them.

The central question when deciding whether to apply for planning permission is what the word 'material' means in the context of 'material change of use'. J. B. Bradfield in *Green Burial* mentions the case of a couple living in rural Scotland who wanted to bury some of their better-loved relatives and friends in a bit of land they owned and used for grazing. The matter became fairly complex when treated by the planning authorities, but the upshot was that planning permission was not deemed necessary in the first place (nor would it be in identical circumstances in England and Wales, even though the legal system in those places is different from that in Scotland). It seems that this particular case didn't constitute a legal precedent, however.

We do at least know what 'material change of use' is not. It is not brought about by the use of 'any . . . land within the curtilage [the area immediately surrounding the house and including outbuildings] of a dwelling house' when that use is 'for any purpose incidental to the enjoyment of the dwelling house'. The Town and Country Planning Act 1990 specifically states that anything falling into that definition does not amount to material change of use, though on the very day I wrote this paragraph in November 1994 there was a report in the newspapers of a man being obliged to demolish a tree house he had built for his children because he hadn't got planning permission beforehand. So the Town and Country Planning Act is fairly narrow in its terms.

Mention of legal advice and applications for documentation giving permission for home burial is a reminder that these things are not free – certainly not legal advice, though local council permission may be. Even so, a proper Certificate of Lawfulness will cost over £50 and planning permission well over £100. There is likely to come a certain point when one wonders if it is worth paying out money to lawyers and council officials just to spite undertakers by denying them their traditional disbursements.

There are legitimate safety considerations, and a council would not be unduly stuffy if it insisted that when you dig a grave you should be accompanied by one or more associates in case of emergency. Geological circumstances affect your case, too. For instance, certain soils are likely to collapse on diggers who make a deep grave and to be easily swept away by rain and storm if a shallow grave is dug. Talking of rain, you must clear the choice of privately owned burial site with the local water company and National Rivers Authority lest the human remains contaminate an underground stream or other water supply.

In practice this means that apart from anything else you should dig graves at least 170ft from a well or borehole and about 40ft or more from water at or near ground level, whether still or running. Since most town and many suburban gardens are not much more than 50ft long, this would surely preclude private graves in them, since the public water supply is a running one. Presumably even something as trivial as a goldfish pond in your garden could constitute still water 'within the meaning of the act', as they say, and you would have to site a grave well away from it.

On the subject of the public water supply, clearly any digging at all must avoid underground cables and pipes, whether they conduct water, electricity, telephone wires, gas, cable television or anything else. Even if you know where these are, you ought to dig about 5ft away from them at least. If you don't, try to find out by looking at local maps and plans. Don't just rely on the latest ones, either. Cases crop up every year of gardeners, whose excavations seldom extend beyond turning over the uppermost foot or so of topsoil on the rose bed, accidentally striking drains, cables, Second World War bombs and abandoned cellars or air-raid shelters, all of which had long been forgotten about. Deeper delving, of the sort you'd want to do if you were constructing a home-made grave, could bring to light still more serious discoveries. If you uncovered an Anglo-Saxon burial site, for instance, you might have to contend with archaeologists sifting through earth for months on end, a box at a time.

What you have to think about on a more personal level is whether a home-made grave in the grounds of your house will make it more difficult to sell the property, perhaps in quite a few years' time, long after your enthusiasm for bucking the system has evaporated, when memories of your close relation or spouse are, if not fading exactly, nonetheless not so vivid as to necessitate his remains being quite so close to hand, and when you may need quite urgently to realise capital so that selling the house is not something you have much choice about.

At the time of writing the housing market has for two years or so been quite depressed enough as it is, even without extra handicaps. I cannot see many prospective purchasers warming to a grave in the garden. The author of the Consumers' Association book *What to Do When Someone Dies* goes so far as to say unequivocally that the presence of a grave in the garden means the selling price of the house will almost certainly drop by between 25 and 50 per cent. It isn't quite that simple; indeed, such an opinion suggests he has a rather parochial, petit-bourgeois outlook. Moreover, he just happens to be an undertaker himself, so one is just the teeniest bit inclined to question his motives.

Would any multi-millionaire turn down the chance to acquire a prestige riverside property convenient for London and Heathrow Airport (together with an excellent local school over the bridge at Eton) in the shape of Windsor Castle (supposing the present incumbents were forced to sell up, which God forbid), just because of the Frogmore Mausoleum in its grounds? An extreme case, you will protest, but pause to consider: clearly a private chapel attached to one's house, complete with family burial vault, is a *sine qua non* of the old landed dynastic 'lifestyle'.

And while a suburban semi with the remains of one of the previous owners half a metre below the asparagus bed is so far from being in the same league that it partakes of the macabre, there are intermediate cases – a modest manor house, say, seat of one of the lesser gentry – where a few gravestones, if of sufficient antiquity and picturesque appearance, and moreover collected in some discreet corner of the grounds where once a recusant chapel stood, might actually enhance the historic atmosphere, hence market value.

Just to take a handful of the delectable country houses with family mausolea or burial vaults that litter the United Kingdom, there is Blickling Hall, Norfolk, seat of the Hobart-Hampden earls of Buckinghamshire. This has a pyramid designed by Joseph Bonomi, a pupil of Adam, which was erected in 1793 and houses the remains of numerous members of the family, although it was commissioned at the express command of the 2nd Earl, who, corporeally speaking, took up residence there the same year. There are also Calke Abbey, Derbyshire, seat of the Harpur Crewes, a landed-gentry family; Clumber Park, in north Nottinghamshire, a property that once belonged to the dukes of Newcastle, when there were still dukes of Newcastle in existence (the family has now been reduced to possessing a mere earldom, that of Lincoln); Gibside Chapel, near Newcastle, a James Paine creation designed in 1793 to complement the house of the same name (the latter is now just a shell) and commissioned by the Bowes family, to whom the Queen Mother is related through the marriage between a Bowes heiress and the 9th Earl of Strathmore and Kinghorne in the eighteenth century; Castle Howard, formerly seat of the earls of Carlisle, now held by a junior branch of the family and most famous as a location for the shooting of *Brideshead Revisited*, with its Hawksmoor-designed mausoleum; Kedleston Hall, in the same county as Calke, seat of the viscounts Scarsdale; and Staunton Harold, in Leicestershire, built just after the Civil War in 1653 for the Shirley Earls Ferrers.

In Co. Antrim, Northern Ireland, there is a mausoleum designed by Robert Adam to adorn Temple Patrick House, seat of the viscounts Templetown, and specifically commissioned to house General the Hon. Arthur Upton, CB, the 1st

Baron Templetown's third son (it was only in the next generation that the barony was upgraded to a viscountcy). Since Adam died in 1792 and the General not till 1855, this was in every sense a classic example of what the present day funeral touts like to designate 'pre-need planning'.

Would a sane man of taste with a reasonably deep pocket balk at acquiring any of the above houses just because of their commemorative architectural features? If it comes to that, does any student of University College London object to residing there just because the skeleton of the founder, Jeremy Bentham, has a seat of honour on the premises, albeit respectably dressed in early nineteenth-century costume? I certainly have it on the authority of the press office at University College that the Provost, whose private quarters are nearby, sleeps perfectly easily at night.

Any type of land can be developed so try to choose the least likely victim of land deals to bury your relative in. In the country the proximity of a sweet old churchyard often adds to the appeal of a house. On the other hand, a crematorium in the neighbourhood, whether urban, suburban or rural, always depresses property prices.

You never know when what until recently was purely agricultural land may be at risk if it is sufficiently near a town and a change of national government leads to a relaxation of planning restrictions, even in the Green Belt. Deborah Hinton, who is trying to set up an eco-friendly crematorium near Basingstoke, reckons that although lots of people like the idea of burying their relatives in green fields and planting trees over them, they also like to have the graves near where they live. Farmers around the big conurbations are most unlikely to release their land for conversion to cemeteries, however green, because they are always hoping to make huge profits from development.

One objection to burying someone in the garden is that ownership of the grave may pass to total strangers and their successors if you sell the house. 'You can't take it with you,' they say of worldly wealth. But the same is true of human remains under a few feet of earth in your garden when you move on to new accommodation, unless you get a Home Office licence to exhume them. This may only cost from £10 to £20 but the process can be a long-drawn-out one. At least it does not entail compulsory use of a contractor approved by the Home Office (despite an assertion to that very effect by Which's *What to Do When Someone Dies* on page 102 of the text, a proposition recanted in paragraph 3 of its erratum slip).

Nevertheless, digging up corpses without such a licence is a breach of the criminal code. You may decide to let bygones be bygones, abandon the grave and forgo the wearisome business of applying to the Home Office. But who can say what the future may bring in the way of disruption of your present house and its grounds, including the private grave in which you interred your spouse, say for something which is intrinsically disagreeable such as high-density housing, perhaps long after you have left the neighbourhood?

Conventional cemeteries are by no means immune from this sort of thing to be sure, but it has so far been fairly rare and the numbers of other living people whose relatives are buried in a cemetery should give them, together with you, collective clout in staging protests against any authorities who try to pull off a repeat of Westminster City Council's disgraceful trick (they recently sold a cemetery for a peppercorn sum). This is particularly so since under the Disused Burial Grounds (Amendment) Act 1981 and the Pastoral Measure 1983 a personal representative or near relative of anyone buried in the last fifty years before proposed development can object. The trouble is, the authorities are only obliged to give notice of the scheme in one local newspaper for two weeks running and to put up a notice on or near the land. If relatives have moved away from the area they may not hear of the proposed development.

In *Green Burial* J. B. Bradfield suggests that if you want to bury someone in the garden and then have to sell the house, you can retain the necessary small part of the garden without saying why. I don't think this is always very practicable. The spot you chose for burial might well be in the middle of the garden. Indeed, few people will choose a site near a boundary because of the lack of privacy from neighbours or users of the public highway or footpath. It is difficult enough to hang on to a chunk of garden when it is on the periphery of the rest of the property. It is virtually impossible to except from sale to others a plot in the middle of the whole like the space surrounded by a doughnut ring.

If you wish to deal with a dead person on your own (your legal, administrative and other procedural obligations as next of kin or executor are dealt with in the section Regulations Surrounding Bereavement), first lay him out on his back, placing his arms and hands by his side, close his eyes, tie his jaw shut, plug his orifices with cotton wool, wash his body, shave him, brush his hair and dress him in a clean garment such as a nightgown or shirt, in the latter case of the old-fashioned kind for preference, the sort with generous tails. If you are too squeamish to do any or all of these things a nurse would probably step round and perform the task for a few pounds. Make sure you have one to hand, however. If he died peacefully and the end was expected you can also tidy up the bedroom. You should not touch the body if death came suddenly and unexpectedly unless it happened somewhere like the public highway or a domestic thoroughfare such as the stairs. Even then, the police, if summoned, may prefer that everything is left in situ.

Next procure a coffin. It may not be easy to begin with. Jane Spottiswoode (see the Bibliography) tells how she advertised in the *Funeral Service Journal* for someone who would supply coffins direct to the public. She got no answer until two months later, when the proprietor of an undertaker's firm in

Lancashire offered to prepare them for the man in the street for between £40 and £250. Whether you ring the number given for him in the back of Mrs Spottiswoode's book or the alternative one she gives on page 143 of the main text you will get a BT recorded message saying that the number has 'not been recognised'. As of November 1994, Directory Inquiries stated that they could not locate the firm at all. In fact the company, Gibsons of Bolton, is now at 342 St Helens Road, Bolton, Lancashire (tel. 01204 655869), having moved from the address and phone number given in Mrs Spottiswoode's book.

The *Natural Death Handbook* gives a list of undertakers who will supply a coffin, fully fitted, to members of the public without insisting you use any of their other services, for £150 or less. There are one each of these in Avon, Bedfordshire, Buckinghamshire, Dorset, East Sussex, Hampshire, Hertfordshire, Kent, Manchester, Norfolk, Northamptonshire, Nottinghamshire, West Midlands, West Sussex and Wiltshire, and two each in Lancashire, Lincolnshire and Yorkshire (plus a third in the last county who charges slightly more than £150 but is included by the *NDH*'s compilers because he is that rare thing among undertakers, someone who is prepared to furnish a fully itemised price list). There are seven in London (three in east London, one in south London, one in south-west London, one in west London and one in west Greater London).

The Nottingham-based undertaker is cited as preparing coffins painted by artists using water-based pigments which will be entirely consumed by flames, but these start at £500. And there is another Hertfordshire undertaker who, strictly speaking, specialises in coffins for animals but would probably make one for an adult human.

I have already pointed out how much prices quoted for one of the above undertakers have risen since *NDH* went to press. And it is implied in *NDH* that Lear of London is friendly to the go-it-aloner, whereas in my experience the firm is less than cordial even to the impartial inquirer if he ventures on sensitive territory in his questions, a matter to which I shall come presently. *NDH* points out that even the undertakers who sell a single coffin at a time to a member of the public do so at an exorbitant price. No member of the public, it seems, can escape having to pay through the nose where the coffin is concerned, for even if she buys the entire range of services supplied by an undertaker, the latter hides a number of charges under the cost of the single item 'coffin'.

Of course, any jobbing carpenter worth his bag of nails ought to be able to run up a decent coffin, particularly if he makes just a rectangular box (called in America a casket, though usually this has a curved lid) rather than the irregular six-sided receptacle familiar from illustrations of funerary customs. Alternatively, you could construct one yourself if you are sufficiently good with your hands. It should be strong enough to contain the inert weight of a dead person when carried by people who may be family or friends rather than experienced pall-bearers from an under-taker's establishment.

There is no law to say that you must use a coffin, whether for burial or cremation, but most cemeteries (just under nineteen out of every twenty) and crematoria insist on it, and since they are under no legal obligation to bury or burn your dead in the way you want, you just have to knuckle under. This can be particularly distressing for Muslims, who prefer burying their dead in a winding sheet or shroud only, without the use of a coffin. Moreover, if you run up your own home-made coffin and it fails to meet certain cremation-related standards preventing, or at any rate limiting, environmental pollution (for instance, because it is made of materials which will give off toxic fumes when incinerated), the crematorium authorities would be within their rights to forbid the cremation.

These standards are most certainly enshrined in law and

crematoria enforce them by requiring users to sign a declaration saying that the coffin will meet the standards in question. Crematoria regulations on emissions of smoke and other gases or substances have been made much stricter since the Environmental Protection Act of 1990. This is forcing crematoria to spend many thousands of pounds on upgrading their equipment, and it seems likely that the cost will be passed on to customers.

J. B. Bradfield suggests that you could conceivably cremate a body yourself, though no nuisance must be caused (and much bad blood between neighbours has been known to seethe away because of a garden bonfire of autumn leaves, to say nothing of more ambitious projects). The usual certificates must be obtained, however, and *Davies' Law of Burial, Cremation and Exhumation* cites the Cremation Regulations 1930 as amended in 1952, 1965, 1979, the Cremation (Amendment) Regulations 1985 and the Cremation Act 1952, and interprets them as saying that no cremation is allowed unless carried out in a crematorium of whose opening the Home Secretary has been notified.

Moreover, it would be unwise to put up any covered structure in which to cremate a person because this would not only be subject to planning permission in the ordinary way but would have to meet the minimum standards for crematoria laid down in the body of laws culminating in the Environmental Protection Act of 1990. A funeral pyre of the sort that was common in antiquity is little more than a big bonfire in planning terms but there is no apparent getting round the Davies interpretation unless you want to feature as a test case. So seek legal advice.

At least if you have the remains cremated it becomes far easier to dispose of the residue on private property than if you tried to carry out burial there of an intact corpse. The ashes can be buried in your garden or strewn over it. If you bury the ashes within an urn, container and all, you cannot

subsequently dig up the whole thing except by getting a
Home Office licence, as in the tedious process for bodies
described above, but at least it is physically easier to move
ashes in a container from one part of the garden to another.

If the person whose funeral you are arranging died in a
small house, or there are narrow corridors or staircases
between the room where the death occurred and the main
entrance/exit to the house, you should consider getting a body
bag, which is a much more flexible container when negotiating
tight corners during the shifting of a corpse, even though with
rigor mortis setting in from within six to over twenty-four
hours after death (when the body begins to get limp again),
you would have thought it might make little difference. The
deceased can then be taken from the house with the minimum
fuss and awkwardness and put in a coffin later, if desired.
NDH lists a number of crematoria who will accept human
remains in a body bag alone, though it should be laid on a
board to facilitate the moving of the body.

The trouble is that, as with getting hold of a coffin, body
bags are not easily procurable by Joe Public. Jane Spottiswoode in her book *Undertaken with Love* gives the address of
Lear of London as being at Bryson House, Horace Road,
Kingston-upon-Thames, Surrey KT1 2SL, but their telephone
number is 0181-546 2633, not 2663 as printed in the book.
NDH also mentions them. I rang them and spoke to a female
who refused to give her name and was in general highly
evasive about Lear's policy on selling body bags direct to the
general public.

At first this seemed merely ludicrous, but as our conversation continued an almost sinister element began to make itself
felt – at any rate to my mind. First she said they didn't sell
body bags to the public, then that 'we have done, but once or
twice a year only, so it's rare'. This anonymous representative
admitted that the firm were body-bag manufacturers but when
she refused to identify herself she added 'do not quote me by

name as we don't have anything to do with bereavement'.

I asked what the price range was and, after considerable prevarication, with talk of how difficult it was to give an answer owing to the considerable differences in body weight, body size etc. (as if the same considerations don't apply with underwear, sports equipment or children's shoes), she admitted that body bags were sold by size and strength, the latter varying according to not only the weight of the body but also the cause of death. In general it seems they range from £20 to £50.

The coyness and embarrassment of this person at being rung up and asked perfectly straightforward questions were such as I have never encountered. When I mentioned Jane Spottiswoode's name to the Lear spokeswoman, the sound of the Thames freezing over at Kingston was almost audible down the telephone wires: had Lear known Mrs Spottiswoode was a private customer, the spokeswoman said, it would not have had dealings with her. It is only fair to record that my telephone correspondent denied that her employers were in the pocket of the undertaking industry.

I have discussed matters so far as if the only go-it-alone option was to be your own undertaker. But you can still use a standard undertaker for many of the distasteful and tedious chores to do with a recent death and yet choreograph the actual funeral service itself. The writer Tony Walter (see the Bibliography) mentions the case of a dead morris dancer being piped into his grave and a morris dancer's hat being placed on his coffin. Walter claims this was found moving by the bereaved. The trouble is, it might be positively risible to others, including others among the bystanders. It is not just that to many people there is something hugely comic about morris dancing, but that in every gathering of humans with nothing else to bind them together apart from kinship to or friendship with the deceased, emphasis on a person's hobby-horse may strike a distinctly discordant note.

This might be the place to point out that although the state behaves as if the next of kin were the principal sufferers from bereavement and gives them the chief say in how the funeral is to be arranged, it often isn't that simple. The deceased's unmarried lover, whether of the same sex or a different one, may have been far closer to him than any kin, but just because she wasn't married to him or recognised by the family or sometimes even known about by the family, she has to sit through what may be to her a wholly inappropriate funeral – if she is invited at all.

Sometimes a lover of the deceased is excluded from the funeral by his family, but they have no legal right to do this if the ceremony takes place in a church. Moral suasion alone has to do the trick. If the family have hired a crematorium they are on stronger ground, but even then they would probably have to get an injunction to exclude a mourner they found undesirable. That could take some time. The celebrated case in January 1995 where a wife and mistress squabbled over which one had the right to share the dead man's grave appeared to hinge on precisely who had paid for the burial rights. The judge ruled that the mistress was in the right.

Sometimes the deceased might have been loathed by all his family and adored by a paramour, but just because he neglected to make a will or specify how he wanted to be disposed of when gone, the full dead weight of tradition or lip-service to an obsolete ideal comes into play. There are less dramatic non-family relationships than sexual ones between the deceased and a mourner: friends in leisure hours, colleagues at work, business partners, old schoolmates, brother officers. All these people have some claim on the way a person's funeral is celebrated, though it is a moral rather than a legally enforceable one. Orthodox funerals may have their uninspiring aspects, but they are least likely to give offence to, or arouse ridicule among, the widest number of people.

Clearly taste is involved much more than ecclesiastical regulations. It is typical of the modern Church of England that it strains at the gnat of marble monuments or polished granite gravestones or mildly colloquial forms of address in epitaphs (all of which have the most impeccable precedents within long-existing Church of England graveyards), yet swallows the camel of sentimental pop-song lyrics of the utmost banality crooned to tunes of equal banality, while spitting out for the most part the one thing that gave the C of E a vernacular liturgical dignity unique among Christian denominations, Cranmer's prose.

But the truly populist funeral services nowadays are to be found at crematoria or non-Anglican places of worship. Crematoria are commercial establishments, after all. You cannot blame them for trying to please the consumer. One in Southsea in Essex was reported in June of 1994 to be planning to cater for tourists by providing cream teas and pony rides. The Golders Green Crematorium in north London, which is especially popular with showbiz folk, recently hosted a concert of music composed by past subjects of its special service. It is frequently asked by the next of kin to play Whitney Houston's 'I Will Always Love You', a composition that comes across all the better for being played on its state-of-the-art audio systems.

Many crematoria are installing similar technology. Other currently popular recordings are 'Nessun Dorma' sung by Pavarotti and that perennial evergreen 'My Way', more durable, it seems, than any plastic holly wreath. At the City of London Cemetery and Crematorium, Ms Houston is also number one, but here with 'Wind Beneath My Wings'. The City C. & C. claims to be the busiest in the country, perhaps in Europe, with up to forty-six cremations a day and 6,000 disposals a year in 200 acres where there are already 500,000 graves.

Even one of its most conservatively dressed undertaker

users has observed that hymns are much less in demand at its cremations than pop music. The City C. & C. has made provision accordingly. The old Gothic paraphernalia of melancholia is even less popular than hymns: the City C. & C. is soon to install a bar and restaurant facilities. Elsewhere in the UK a staider approach still rules. But in a way the earthy, materialist and irreverent tastes the City C. & C. is catering for are not much different from the old mediaeval japing and jesting over the corpse, with plenty to eat and drink.

The appearance of funerals is changing as fast as the music played at them. The Baptist church at which the thanksgiving service for the life of the entertainer Roy Castle was held in September 1994 allowed balloons on the altar, the painting of themselves with clown faces by many members of the congregation and closed-circuit televisation of the service to the overflow in a hall nearby. It would ill behove me to criticise all this; it is what the deceased had wanted and what his family paid for. I would just mention that amidst all the razzmatazz the deceased's widow was seen to pucker up her face at one point. In the end you cannot keep bereavement at bay.

Eco-Friendly Funerals

I have already mentioned that one of the reasons you might want to organise a funeral is because you are concerned about polluting the atmosphere by cremating the deceased, or cutting down trees unnecessarily to make one of the more expensive types of coffin. If you feel the problems connected with burying a body in the garden are insuperable, you could arrange to have your deceased relation, close friend or spouse laid to rest in one of the local authority burial grounds that are specifically designed not to take on the appearance of the conventional cemetery, but instead to look as natural as possible in the sense of resembling a grove of trees.

Four town councils have started up such places already:

Brighton, Burton-on-Trent, Carlisle and Harrogate. Presumably if demand increases, more and more local authorities will follow suit. These eco-friendly burial grounds are designated as nature reserves. Carlisle City Council led the way, which suggests that few regional variations in the way Britons dispose of their dead survive, for Carlisle is in one of the remoter parts of England yet is a pioneer in eco-friendly inhumement.

As recently as the early 1960s, when Geoffrey Gorer was writing about the subject, such differences were much more pronounced. And historically there would have been a contrast between, say, the West Country, where non-conformists pullulate, and Lancashire, which remained strongly Catholic for centuries after the Reformation. In Wales, for instance, the chapel tradition long militated against cremation, though it was a Welsh doctor cremating his son in Wales in 1884 who helped establish the legality of cremation generally and paved the way for its introduction nationwide.

It is possible that there are still quite substantial differences in attitude and practice between town-dwellers and country-dwellers. Certainly in the big cities and towns 80 per cent of the dead are cremated and only 20 per cent buried, whereas across the nation as a whole the ratio is more like 6:4. And country undertakers tend to be more helpful and sensitive, but then they operate at a more leisurely pace.

Carlisle's Woodland Burial Service operates an annexe to its regular cemetery where oak trees are planted above each grave, the tree drawing sustenance from the corpse as it decomposes. The choice of tree species is appropriate since oak has been used for most coffins since the first half of the nineteenth century, when French polishing them became the fashion. Before that elm had been the standard wood, for being cross-grained it is less liable to split and is also highly resistant to water.

Under the Woodland Burial Service scheme it is held that

conventional coffins slow up the nutritional cycle of body to tree. The oak trees constitute the only visible memorial, for gravestones are forbidden. But a metal plate is buried a few inches below the surface of the earth so that a specific grave can be identified (one hopes these are of corrosion-proof metal so that any engraving on them is not worn away as the years go by). And the authority maintains a plan of the whole grove so that the precise spot in which each corpse is laid is recorded.

There are also three such places in the UK that are independent of local authority control. They are near Manningtree, Essex; Rugby, Warwickshire; and Wolverhampton, West Midlands. At the end of 1994 a Yorkshire farmer, Robert Goodwill, got planning permission to convert three of his 260 acres at Terrington, in the Howardian Hills of North Yorkshire, to a cemetery. He proposes to offer (a) traditional burial at £650; (b) woodland burial (presumably along the lines of the Carlisle scheme) at £450; (c) ash burial (presumably in urns or other containers) at £150; and (d) the scattering of ashes at £50. It is only fair to record that he has not made himself popular with the other 349 villagers there, and most people would not, I think, like to be buried in a place where a head of resentment has built up among locals.

I spoke in late November 1994 to Ken West, the extremely helpful and knowledgeable director of the Carlisle Bereavement Services. He reveals that his city's Woodland Burial Service is open to all, not just locals, and not even just to UK residents – he had recently sold a burial plot to a woman living in France. An option to bury yourself, a friend or a relative which is valid for fifty years costs £169 at time of writing, with an interment fee of £158 for those living within Carlisle city limits and £171 for those living elsewhere.

Brighton's fees are twice as high – again, at time of writing – presumably because in the deep south they have correspondingly deep pockets. The very slight difference in charges for outsiders as opposed to locals in Carlisle's case is at variance with the statement in J. B. Bradfield's *Green Burial* that non-locals can expect to pay two to three times the standard fee. Currently the government doesn't allow the right to use a burial plot to run for more than a century, although it used to be in perpetuity. Carlisle decided to sell fifty-year leases when they set up this scheme, which has been going since July 1993.

It is instructive to compare the growth in popularity of the Woodland Burial Service-type scheme with that of cremation when the latter first started in the late nineteenth century. In the first year after cremation became legal in modern times (1885), only two members of the public availed themselves of the option, according to Ken West (although Professor Ian Morris says that three cremations are known of in Britain in that year). As for eco-friendly funerals, once Carlisle had led the way several other local authority-controlled and private schemes of a similar nature followed within less than a year and a half, and ten more are in the pipeline at time of writing.

The Carlisle system is geared to supplying double graves, typically for husband and wife, with resting places side by side instead of one on top of the other in the way less considerate places operate. Other sites often provide burial spots catering for up to three or four people. Carlisle is thinking of offering half a two-person grave for single people, who, of course, are becoming more and more numerous in modern Britain.

If part of the grave has been used already, say for the husband of a couple, then the renewal fee (that is, the cost of interment, since the right to bury has already been purchased on lease) is less. You might be afraid that if an oak has been planted above one occupant of a twin grave and the surviving partner lives another few years it will be impossible to bury her without damage to the tree when removing it in order to open up the grave again. But I am assured that oak roots can be dug up and then interred again up to ten or fifteen years after the tree has first been planted without irreparable damage, especially if the roots have been sealed in foil to assist healthy resiting.

Obviously, full-blooded eco-enthusiasts tend to have non-denominational or humanist burial services, though quite a few may be pagans, but the majority of people using Carlisle's Woodland Burial Service still employ undertakers and the conventional funeral service appropriate to whatever main-stream religious group they are members of. Nevertheless, one cannot help feeling that as of this moment conventional undertaking has a short life expectancy. Carlisle Bereavement Services offer direct to the public quick-disintegrating coffins, made either of chipboard (as used in conventional funerals) or of cardboard. They also offer woollen shrouds for those who prefer not to use a coffin at all.

Apparently, chipboard coffins break down (the term bio-degradable is, strictly speaking, not appropriate for them) just four weeks after being buried, which is actually more quickly than cardboard ones. But certain elements of which chipboard coffins are made, notably resins and formaldehyde, do not biodegrade. In contrast, cardboard coffins, which are avail-able in three increasingly elaborate models, each looking grander than the last though they are all made of the same material, biodegrade in as ecologically correct a fashion as anyone could wish.

Some modern authors writing from an eco-enthusiastic point of view suggest that the dead could be buried in wickerwork containers, and it is interesting to discover that a similar idea was being put forward by a fellow of the Royal College of Surgeons as long ago as 1875. Mind you, the coffin, unless it is made of some very unusual material such as iron, is not invariably the most resistant feature of a burial to corro-sion by the soil. There is an example of a shroud that survived from an ancient Greek burial around 1000 BC. And dead children and old people biodegrade more quickly than adults who have been cut down in the prime of their youth.

Cautionary Tales

That the bereaved are vulnerable emotionally is a truism. It is often forgotten that they are vulnerable in other ways, too. News of a death will bring the chief bereaved person not just the usual swarm of official forms and doctor's certificates to fill in, taxes to pay up, bank accounts and club memberships to close down and library tickets to hand in. It will also summon forth self-styled friends of the deceased.

So many people lead their social lives in several compartments that it is quite possible that someone very close to you, even a husband or wife, could have had several acquaintances, professional or semi-professional, whom you never met. You may never even have heard their names mentioned. Enter the 'knocker', who calls on the widow with effusive condolences a day or two after her husband has died, inquires discreetly whether she is 'in difficulties' and offers to lend her money to tide her over till probate is granted on the security of a stick or two of furniture. The 'stick or two' he will have assessed with an expert eye, and the upshot will be that the widow has parted with a Chippendale commode worth £50,000 for £500 in cash and some honeyed expressions of sympathy.

A cruder version of the knocker is the professional housebreaker who scans the death columns in the press and notes the precise date and time of day a funeral or memorial service is due to take place. He then simply cleans out the house of the bereaved, assuming, usually rightly, that nobody else will be at home. He may not even wait till then. Rear-Admiral Sir John Fleming, the fleet meteorologist to Admiral Sir Bertram Ramsay who commanded the landing force on D-Day in 1944, died in early November fifty years later. His obituary appeared in various national newspapers, mentioning among other things that his wife had predeceased him. As a result he had lived alone. The night before his funeral burglars removed from his house in Surrey antiques, a tapestry his wife had made and memorabilia connected with his naval exploits.

So by all means advertise to your friends and relatives just when and where the obsequies are to take place, but leave a brace of Rottweilers at home and alert the police to your absence. Some undertakers offer a house-sitting service for the duration of the funeral. Even after the funeral is over a single person on her own in a house is more vulnerable than the married couple who occupied it up till a few weeks ago. Even burglars are human, and would have been more likely to be inhibited from breaking into a property when the man of the house was in residence, even if he was elderly. So if you don't wish to acquire some fierce guard dogs in the aftermath of your bereavement, think about getting a friend or relative to stay with you for long periods until you have made a more permanent arrangement. Since loneliness and consequent brooding are two of the pitfalls of bereavement anyway, this might also help alleviate them.

The better sort of undertaker would be the first to agree that you should not rush into a decision on how elaborate a funeral to have. Not all undertakers are the better sort, though. Most insist on visiting the bereaved person at home. That is very thoughtful of them. But some will use it as a reconnaissance expedition to assess how well-off you are and pitch their proposals accordingly. Bereavement is the last moment when most of us wish to 'shop around' for the best quote. If you can't bear to do so yourself, delegate the task to a trusted family friend or relative.

An acquaintance of mine whose wife was instantly killed when the car he was driving was hit from behind, catapulting her from the back seat through the windscreen, went straight home and by the end of the day had bundled up not just every single item in her wardrobe but every item in the house that reminded him of her and taken them all round to the nearest Oxfam shop in black plastic bags. My father, on the other hand, left every piece of my mother's clothing and every piece of her footwear in the house exactly as it had been on the day she went into hospital; he never even redecorated the house in thirty-two years. His wife's twin bed remained made up next to his in perpetuity.

These two extremes might be called respectively the Teddy Roosevelt and the Miss Havisham approach. Neither would, I suppose, be regarded as entirely 'healthy' according to fashionable notions of what constitutes a 'proper' sense of bereavement. But my purpose is not to discuss which of them may be the more deplorable, or for that matter how deplorable either approach is – that would be a purely speculative exercise. It is, rather, to point out that once you have given your dearest one's clothes, shoes, jewellery and other chattels away they are gone for good. Try to arrange a staggered distribution if you can, leaving yourself plenty of time in which to have second thoughts.

You may wish to keep things in the family and hand out selected gifts to relatives. You should ascertain first whether they think dead men's shoes are ghoulish things to wear; some do, some don't. Jewellery tends to be more acceptable, however many dead women's throats a necklace has encircled, or wrists a bracelet has clasped, or fingers a ring has been entwined about. Opticians periodically collect old sets of spectacles for the Third World, so you could present the deceased's pair or pairs to them.

Somebody must go through all the dead man's effects: his handkerchief drawers, his stud box, his bureau, his escritoire.

253

You as the widow might find some disconcerting surprises: old love letters, and not ones from or to you; still worse, recent love letters. Dr Charles Bovary only finds out about the affairs of the most famous adulteress in fiction, his wife Emma, after she has taken poison and he sorts through her possessions. So again, you may want to delegate the task to a close friend or relative, giving him editorial carte blanche to destroy anything distressing and only to come to you with queries about which tie to give to which nephew now, or which pair of gold and carnelian cufflinks to put aside till a great-nephew comes of age in fifteen years' time.

A lot of nonsense is talked about everyone feeling anger at some stage of a bereavement. I for one have never experienced it in either of my two major bereavements, let alone the dozen or so others. But I do not say that anger is never felt by anyone. Here, however, I wish to speak of anger directed at the professionals who had charge of the deceased. If your husband or wife or mother or father or brother or sister was diagnosed as having their fatal illness too late, or seemed to spend their last days in considerable pain, or underwent a series of operations that proved not only distressing at the time but futile ultimately, it is natural to resent the doctors and surgeons involved.

Sherwin Nuland, the author of *How We Die* (see the Bibliography), is at his best when he tells us of the guilt he suffered after advising a dearly loved brother to undergo an operation which prolonged his life but at great cost in pain and degradation. The saddest thing I came across in sorting through my father's effects was a correspondence with a lawyer in the months after my mother's death thirty years before in which he had discussed suing the doctors for not diagnosing her breast cancer in time.

Doctors do make mistakes, of course. A recent proposal to list which ones had the worst record of keeping their patients alive, along the lines of the good-and-bad-schools tables for exam passes, was shot down. But a moment's thought will tell you that some must always be worse than others. Do not clutch at straws, however. Because in the first few weeks of a bereavement you are spending a lot of time in negotiations with tax authorities, lawyers, probate officials, the district valuer and perhaps even the police and a coroner, it may seem natural to extend your operations into the field of suing people at the drop of a hat. Don't. Or don't without excellent reason.

Finances

Tax

In 1694 the Marriages Duties Tax was passed. This levied 4s (or 25p in decimal currency) to be paid as a tax for burying people. It was repealed in 1706. Today undertakers' services, together with clergymen's, cemeteries' and crematoria's, can be paid for without your having to add VAT where the funeral itself is concerned. But the services of anyone providing flowers or printed service sheets for the funeral or baked meats after it (as a caterer), together with the cost of memorials and inscriptions, are subject to VAT.

In the ancient world, as I have shown, a greater burden of coping with bereavement was often placed on women than on men. Our present civilisation, at least that part of it to do with income tax, operates the other way round. A widow (but not a widower) is granted by the Inland Revenue a widow's bereavement allowance worth £1,720 for the tax year 1994–5. In other respects the modern state, like the Ottoman sultanate, discourages widows from remarrying.

True, it does not strangle them with bow strings or throw them into the Bosphorus in sacks. Instead it extends the allowance to the following year, too, provided the widow has not taken another husband in the tax year in which she is bereaved. If the dead husband claimed the married couple's allowance his widow can take up the slack in it, that is to say the unused part, if there is any, at the time of her husband's

257

death. In addition the Department of Social Security, like the benevolent eunuch of a seraglio spared by the new Sultan, presents a recent widow with a £1,000 lump sum if she is under sixty or if her late husband was under sixty-five or over sixty-five but not getting a pension from the state.

It is just conceivable there are still a few widows around who can claim Category C pensions. These are available to widows of men who had reached pensionable age by 5 July 1948 and met certain other conditions. There are also widowed mothers' allowances, age-related widow's pension, widow's basic pension, invalidity pension under special rules for widows, war widow's pension and industrial injuries widow's pension. Widowers get some similar state payments but not as many. There are some pensions available to children of someone who has died as a result of war service. The whole subject in all its huge, Byzantine complexity is covered in *A Guide to Widows' Benefits* (NP 45), *A Guide to Retirement Pensions* (NP 46) and *What to Do After a Death* (D49), available from your benefits agency.

There is even a National Association of Widows, at 54–7 Allison Street, Digbeth, Birmingham B5 5TH (tel. 0121-643 8348), which runs an information service for bereaved wives and will put them in touch with groups of similarly placed people near where they live. There is no widowers' association that I know of, though men tend to be much worse than women at picking up the threads of their social lives after a bereavement.

If the deceased's house is not occupied it is exempt from council tax up to grant of probate and after that for six months or until the house is either occupied or sold, whichever occurs sooner. Probate, from the Latin for 'approve', is the state's method of confirming that the executor or executors have the authority given them in the deceased person's will to distribute his assets to the beneficiaries. There is a fee to be paid to the probate office which is related to the size of the deceased's estate but which is quite separate from inheritance tax (IHT).

It may take some months before you will get a grant of probate. After the actor Peter Sellers died it took ten years for his executors to get probate, one of the lengthiest ever. The time from the death to the final distribution of assets to the persons mentioned in the will is called the administration period. Income accruing to the estate during this period (for example, national savings interest) is taxable at the basic rate.

IHT is the chief disbursement to which you are likely to be subject if you were left any substantial legacy. It is the descendant of the old death duties. A fatuous little rubric in the Inland Revenue pamphlet *Inheritance Tax – An Introduction* boasts about it being good news that over 96 per cent of estates don't have to pay any. (Only some 25,000 estates paid IHT in the last year for which figures are available.) I don't think one is being unduly self-centred if, on being subject to a revenue bill in six figures, one responds with 'What is that to me?'

Indeed, on a wider view it is a scandal that after all these years so little wealth is owned by such a high percentage of the population of these islands, once the most affluent in the world. Moreover, we have been subject to so much inflation this last half-century that a handful of sovereigns which would once have bought a night at the Ritz and a crate of champagne will scarcely nowadays cover the price of a dozen boxes of matches. And it is not as if child mortality is high any more – if it were, a high percentage of estates would be those of very young persons with few or no assets. Yet despite all this, only 4 per cent of estates are worth more than a measly £154,000 (from 6 April 1995 the IHT exemption ceiling), taking into account the value of the deceased's house, car, bank account(s), building society ditto, pension, unit trusts, stocks and shares.

IHT3, the more bureaucratic version of the title *Inheritance Tax – An Introduction*, is available from the Capital Taxes

Office, Minford House, Rockley Road, London W14 0DF, tel. 0171-603 4622; or Huntingdon Court, Mansfield Road, Nottingham NG1 4HJ, tel. 0115 9859111; or 16 Picardy Place, Edinburgh EH1 3NB, tel. 0131-556 8511; or Dorchester House, 52–8 Great Victoria Street, Belfast BT2 7BB, tel. 01232 236633. It is only fair to state that once past the rubric, IHT3 is a model of clarity. Presumably a new version is planned following the hike in the IHT exemption ceiling from £150,000 to £154,000 in the November 1994 budget. Also models of clarity are IHT8, *Alterations to an Inheritance Following a Death*, and IHT2, *Inheritance Tax on Lifetime Gifts*, which are available from the same sources.

There exists another booklet, IHT1, a much more elaborate affair running to ninety-five pages of relatively complex information printed on A4-sized high-quality paper. As recently as autumn 1994 it was only available in the 1991 edition, though the Inland Revenue stated that a revised version incorporating changes in legislation would be available towards the end of 1994 from the Customer Service Manager, Urquhart House, 3–5 High Pavement, Nottingham NG1 1HF.

All the above booklets are free – at the point of issue. (It is surely unfair that the majority of the population who leave that 96 per cent of estates which pay no IHT subsidise the publication of an expensive brochure for the tiny minority represented by the 4 per cent who do.) The corrigendum sheet issued with the 1991 edition of IHT1 itself contains at least one error: Amendment 3 talks of the second sentence of the statement of facts in Example 9 on page 15, whereas the sentence to be amended is in fact the third.

This is not the place to whinge in detail about IHT. Writers only marginally less able than I have pointed out for many years how little revenue it raises for the exchequer and at what cost in time for executors, to say nothing of anguish for the bereaved forced to part with a family home to meet the demands of the Inland Revenue. Moreover, it bites particularly savagely at the middle classes.

A middle-class head of the family is likely to have only one house, the principal family home, which, even now, with the property market in the doldrums, is likely to be worth a substantial percentage of his total estate. True, our man could give it away to his chief heir provided he lives another seven years. That way his heir will avoid incurring a liability on the part of the family estate represented by the house. But for Papa it is at the cost of having nowhere pleasant to pass his last years, unless he has sufficient income to pay his son a fair market rent for the property as the tax laws insist, and by doing so can stay on there. Even then it presupposes that there is sufficient trust between father and son for the older man not to fear that his son might kick him out and take over the place himself.

Those members of the upper classes who are still landed are better placed. Squire Allworthy or Lord Loamshire can hand over the big house to his heir seven years or more before he himself dies and slope off to the dower house, which in many cases is sunnier, warmer and cheaper to maintain. But if two or more deaths of major holders of the family property occur within a shorter period than seven years, an ancient estate can be wiped out in no time. Something like that appears to have happened recently with the Frasers, the lords Lovat.

The muddle among the tax authorities adds insult to injury. After my father's death I as executor had to deal with no fewer than six branches.

The Probate Problem

I don't suppose my experience is any different from that of many other executors so far, but all books on bereavement tend to lean heavily towards the anecdotal. That is how they supposedly bring comfort to others in the same, or a similar, boat. In one aspect of finance I was unusually fortunate, however. My father planned his suicide some time in advance (I stress that I was fortunate only in a financial sense, not in an emotional one). Being a methodical man, he had arranged that the bulk of his personal estate was in the form of life assurance policies written in trust for myself and my sister, the sole co-beneficiaries of his will. It was therefore possible for these to be released to us by the companies concerned on receipt only of the death certificate, which, as with all death certificates, we were able to obtain from the registrar in a matter of days.

The problem came in paying quite large sums into a joint account. My sister and I were living some sixty miles apart at the time, so any joint account we opened was going to have to be usable with only one signature. We each had ordinary bank accounts but wished to continue to use these separately for day-to-day individual transactions. I tried to convert an old building society account of mine which I had kept in a state of dormancy for some years with £0.89p in it to a joint one. It took ages. When you receive cheques for largeish sums of money you want them to start earning interest as quickly as possible. I mention all this to joint executors so that they can consider setting up a joint account well before they need to start using it.

Had my father's personal estate been in any other form – bank or building society accounts, say, or stocks and shares – it would have been necessary for us to wait for grant of probate before the sums could be released to us. We did in fact have to wait for probate before we could use his building society account. Grant of probate can take several months to obtain, since before that the executor must sort out what if any inheritance tax liability there is, and that can take its own time. But all the dead person's other assets are frozen from the moment of his death, so this can lead to considerable problems. The bank may lend money to pay the first tranche of IHT, rather like bridging loans for house purchase, if the deceased's assets remain frozen. As with bridging finance, the interest can be horrendous.

Alternatively, if a bank or building society account has been a joint one, either between a now deceased husband and his surviving wife, or former elderly widow (now deceased) and flourishing daughter, or again widower in poor health (subsequently grown so much poorer that he dies) and young, hale niece, the loss of one of the partners will not lead to its being frozen. If you agree to act as someone's executor you might try to persuade him to open a joint account with you for just such an eventuality. Many banks (including the TSB) and building societies, also National Savings, will often in practice allow up to £1,500 to be withdrawn from the account of a recently deceased person by an executor if they are presented with a copy of the death certificate. Others have been known to bounce cheques written on that account by the executor over and over again, even when they have undertaken not to do so.

Other things you should have done already if you are an executor are: (a) got the testator to tell you where the will is; (b) got him to let a minimum of two other people into this piece of information; (c) monitored the activities of the solicitor who drew the will up in case he moves elsewhere or retires.

If the deceased died without having made a will, letters of administration will be granted to the next of kin (surviving spouse, children, children's children, parents, siblings, nephews/nieces in that order). If there is a will but no named executor the chief beneficiary can apply for a grant of representation. If there is no will the administrator is bound by the law of intestacy as to what he can distribute to whom among the deceased's other relations. In effect, the government writes the will for you.

Funeral Expenses

The cost of the funeral is deductible from the deceased's estate for the purposes of calculating any inheritance tax liability, and it is a long-established principle that the estate should bear the cost of the funeral, even if the person dies without having made a will. (If that happened her personal representatives would hold her estate on trust for sale and be obliged to pay funeral expenses, as well as other administrative costs, out of the sale proceeds.)

But technically it is the executor who is liable to pay the funeral costs and he then recovers them from the estate of the deceased. (If a man's wife dies and leaves little or no estate it seems that her husband would be liable for the cost of the funeral.) This means that if the deceased fails to leave enough money to cover the costs, or if the executor is deemed to have overspent on the funeral, the latter must pay the difference out of his own pocket. An executor could still be liable even if it was not he who had ordered the funeral, for instance if he neglected to order it and someone else had to.

The amount you can spend on a funeral and then recover from the deceased's estate varies. It is supposed to be a 'reasonable' sum, which is defined as one commensurate with the deceased's circumstances and position in life. This is the only instance I know of where social status as opposed to mere wealth has a bearing in law on the relations between a creditor and debtor and hence on the amount of tax the beneficiaries of a dead person's will must pay. (Peers have certain legal privileges and immunities but they do not constitute the entire membership of a social class.)

In three deliciously Thackerayan early nineteenth-century cases cited in the current edition of *Davies' Law of Burial, Cremation and Exhumation* (see the Bibliography for further details) the amount the court reckoned it was reasonable to spend on the funeral was influenced by the fact that in one case the deceased was a half-pay army captain, in the second an earl, and in the third a tradesman in a small way of business. The half-pay army captain, for instance, was deemed to be entitled to twice as expensive a funeral as the petit-bourgeois tradesman.

The case of the last Mordaunt Earl of Peterborough (of the

1628 creation) is slightly more complex. He died in 1814 and was thought at the time to be worth around £40,000 in personal wealth (perhaps £2,000,000 in today's money), though it turned out to be nowhere near that owing to some unfortunate speculation in canal shares. Indeed, his estate ultimately proved insolvent. By personal wealth is meant cash, chattels etc. as opposed to landed estates and so on.

His executors planned what they called a 'respectable' funeral but with an eye to economising approached a Bath undertaker rather than a London one, the Earl having died near Bath. When the executors got to where the funeral was to take place they found it was to be a very elaborate affair indeed. The undertaker whipped out his estimate and claimed his directions had been given to him with the agreement of Lord Peterborough's brother-in-law, whose daughter's son was heir to the bulk of Lord Peterborough's property, though not of course his titles. Despite some misgivings, the executors decided they would attend the funeral all the same. When they got the undertaker's final bill they refused to pay it on the grounds that it was exorbitant. The undertaker took them to court and on the advice of their lawyer they paid £2,100 into court. The 'appropriate' cost of the funeral was assessed by the court at less than the sum the undertaker demanded but greater than the £2,100 by several hundreds of pounds.

Even if the estate is solvent, the executor or personal representative must take care not to overspend on the funeral. The case of Stacpoole versus Stacpoole is even more complex than the Peterborough one. To look it up is to be plunged into a maelstrom of family feuds among the landed gentry in late eighteenth-century Ireland that reads like a cross between *Castle Rackrent* and Jarndyce versus Jarndyce in *Bleak House*. To cut a long story short, the funeral of John Stacpoole of Craigbrien cost £1,200 but was assessed by the court as being 'worthy' (for a man of his station) of an expenditure of £200, even though he left over £31,000 in personal estate. That, then, was how much the obsequies of a country squire in John Bull's other island 'deserved' to have spent on them compared with an earl's on the 'right' side of the Irish Sea – that is, about an eleventh.

Quite what the court would have assessed as the appropriate cost of a Stacpoole funeral a few years later, when John Stacpoole's nephew George was created a count by Louis XVIII of France, or in the next generation, when George's son was created a marquis by Pope Leo XII, or a few years later still, when the Marquis de Stacpoole was advanced to the dignity of a papal dukedom by Gregory XVI, is anybody's guess. The marquessate was conferred before Catholic emancipation, the dukedom afterwards, which might have complicated matters even further. A nice touch was that the initial hearing came before the 1st Earl of Clare (father of Byron's bosom friend), whose own funeral procession in Dublin was hounded by a mob screeching curses because he had engineered the 1800 Union of Irish and British parliaments.

Commentators on the above cases always stress that they took place a long time ago. Nevertheless, the principle on which they rest is still valid. So today if you wished to give a friend or relative a good send-off by having Mozart's 'Requiem' or Beethoven's 'Missa Solemnis' performed at his funeral, it would rather depend on whether you could get the cost of it all deducted from the estate for IHT purposes. (Sir Edward Heath, for instance, a well-to-do Knight of the Garter, musical man of some note and even a former Prime Minister, would be an ideal subject.)

The cost of elaborate musical obsequies would depend on what score you chose, how professional an orchestra and singers you chose to perform it, and where you had the funeral or memorial service at which it was performed. The Mozart 'Requiem', for instance, being fairly lightly orchestrated, might cost as little as £15,000; Beethoven, a more luxuriant-toned composer, nearer £20,000. You should seek professional musical advice on where to have the requiem performed as some churches are better acoustically for a given sound than others.

Damages for Severe Mental Shock and Other Legal Action

It is perhaps more materially comforting to know that if your relative's coffin is upset when the hearse carrying it to the funeral is hit by another vehicle you may be entitled to damages for emotional upset. In a 1939 case in Liverpool a court awarded £75 to the deceased's mother, £100 to a female cousin, £15 to an uncle and £11 to the cousin's husband. These sums would be worth about £2,250, £3,000, £450 and £330 respectively in today's money.

Currently a family is reported to be demanding compensation from a firm of undertakers and a council in Yorkshire. The council runs a cemetery where the grave dug for a septuagenarian lady proved too small. The pall-bearers initially tried to lower the coffin in sideways and gravediggers had to be called in to enlarge the hole. Workmen continued smoking after arrival at the graveside.

A Surrey pall-bearer who smoked during a funeral was given the sack, sued for wrongful dismissal and had his claim allowed but received no compensation as the dismissal was held to be entirely his own fault.

Press Notices

Obituaries

Usually the national press prepares obituaries of distinguished people many years in advance and updates them from time to time as and when the distinguished person is awarded new honours or advanced to new posts. But some newspapers find themselves behindhand with their stock of subject matter, and in any case not every person deserving an obituary is brought to their attention. Hugo Vickers, who writes a number of obituaries for the national press every year, says that when he goes to discuss with the family how best to obituarise the deceased, the very discussion seems to bring comfort to them.

If you feel your relative was worth a mention in the obituary columns of the press, whether national or local, by all means phone them up and give a short account of her achievements. You may offer to write the obituary yourself or you could nominate a friend or relative who has some knowledge of the person and/or writing ability. If it is a very busy time the paper may not be able to slot in an obituary straightaway. Aldous Huxley and Randolph Churchill, who died respectively at the same time as Jack and Bobby Kennedy were assassinated, suffered this fate. Indeed, it is often said that nobody outside their immediate families noticed they had left us until some weeks had passed.

If you write the obituary yourself and are not familiar with the genre, you should bear in mind that certain statements, innocent enough in themselves, have become loaded with innuendo. 'He never married' or 'He was unmarried' is often taken by the knowing to mean he was homosexual. 'He remained a bachelor' can be interpreted by unkind people as meaning he was a promiscuous homosexual. I do not defend this inference, merely report it.

The leading national newspapers have in recent years started to be a bit less purely laudatory and euphemistic, but even now seldom reveal unpleasant truths. Nonetheless, there is a risk that enterprising newshounds will follow up hints in an obituary and make life uncomfortable for the next of kin. So you may care to keep your head down rather than pester the press into giving your aunt an obituary, however much her pioneering work as an aviatrix or dog-breeder may have deserved one.

The most backhanded compliment in an obituary I know of was used about the grandfather of a friend of mine. And this was back in the early 1920s, long before they had dropped the principle of *nil nisi bonum*. He was a Protestant detective inspector in the Royal Irish Constabulary married to a Catholic (hence disowned by his family; at one point she threw their engagement ring in the Liffey, though that is not germane to the story) and living in Kilkenny – at that time neither the healthiest post nor the healthiest posting. He was shot by the (old) IRA, but before being taken from the morgue to the place of interment began twitching and was found to be alive. He recovered completely and was able to read his own obituary in the local press. It concluded with the words: 'He was as well liked as any man in his position could be.'

The authorities of the school, university, club or regiment of which your dead relative was a pupil, graduate or member may ask you for details of his life and write the obituary themselves. At this fairly depressed level of distinction they will probably know relatively little about the deceased and it may therefore be better for you or a friend with good powers of self-expression to do it.

All obituaries are the better for giving a portrait of the subject 'in the round' rather than a laundry list of achievements and positions held. Even the obscurest alumni bulletin is likely to have limited space, so if writing the piece yourself lean towards the 'portrait' rather than the 'curriculum vitae', as it were. You can always list the positions held in a staccato paragraph at the end, after the article proper, and some newspapers do this as a regular practice. You can reasonably expect a small fee for an obituary published in the national press. Elsewhere it will probably be a labour of love on your part.

Death Announcements

Death announcements in the press have to be paid for. If you cannot persuade a newspaper to publish an obituary you can write a brief biography of the deceased and put it in the deaths column as an extended version of the usual announcement. Unless you are very sure of your literary powers it would be wise to get help. Some announcements of this sort, mostly I am sorry to say by Americans, read absurdly. There is a touching variation on the death announcement. It is for a surviving member of the family, usually a spouse, to put a notice in the papers thanking the staff of the hospital or hospice for everything they did for the deceased.

At the time of writing there are really only two newspapers with a national readership as far as general death announcements are concerned: *The Times* and the *Daily Telegraph*. If your relative or friend was of progressive temperament a notice in the *Guardian* might be appropriate. If he had regional connections one in the *Western Mail*, the *Scotsman* or the *Belfast Telegraph*, as appropriate, might be a good idea. If he had connections in the Irish Republic the *Irish Times* is the place to put the announcement. If he died in Ireland (whether in the

North or the Republic), Scotland or Wales, an announcement in *The Times* or the *Telegraph* is often made as well as one of the smaller-circulation papers mentioned above.

Rates for *The Times* at the time of writing are £11.50 a line plus VAT and for the *Daily Telegraph* £12.34 a line including VAT. The latter stipulates a minimum of two lines, the former no minimum. If sending in an announcement by post you must include a daytime telephone number and home telephone number if different. You must also authenticate the announcement by including your name, with a signature, and permanent address. Announcements will not be published unless they have been confirmed. *The Times* needs announcements two working days before publication. Despite the newspapers' precautions I have come across at least two announcements of titled personages in the last year which on the face of it appeared to be bogus, so jokers do slip through the net erected by vigilant staff on the court circular pages.

The average announcement runs to about ten lines and includes the full names of the deceased, the forename of a spouse and children, sometimes even grandchildren, sometimes also of a 'partner' (increasingly these days whether of the same or opposite sex), a place, date and time of the funeral and directions about where to send flowers, if any, or donations to charity in lieu of flowers.

Recent guidelines for Catholics issued by the Church authorities stipulate that the wording should read so as to include the phrase 'reception of the body at the church' and the time and date of the 'vigil', if there is one. The term 'funeral mass' should be used rather than 'requiem mass'; alternatively the term 'funeral liturgy' should be used if no mass is to be said. If the term 'committal' is used in the announcement of a Catholic's death, it means the service is to be at a cemetery or crematorium.

The Times is still slightly 'grander' than the *Daily Telegraph* as a forum for announcing a death. Many people who put an announcement in the former also put one in the latter, but not nearly so often the other way round. On the other hand, the *Telegraph* has many more death notices, often extending to a whole page, whereas *The Times* seldom fills more than half a page at most. The latter's circulation is still less than half the former's, so this is not surprising.

If you are going to pay over £100 for an announcement of someone's death in the papers, it is worth getting the form right, as well as more respectful to the deceased. I will list some of the grosser solecisms that have cropped up in the press over the last year and a half. (For a comprehensive guide see *Debrett's Correct Form*.) When I once gave a lecture on the history of Debrett's, the more knowledgeable questions came from a member of the audience who worked on the court circular page of *The Times*. From that I conclude that the errors listed below were probably made by careless members of the public sending or phoning in garbled announcements rather than by the newspaper staff. The actual names in the following examples have been changed to spare the blushes of the family.

'lieutenant Colonel Sir Harry Firebrace BTTDDL, aged 91.' This should have read 'Lieutenant-Colonel Sir Harry Fire-brace, Bt, TD, DL, aged 91' or 'Bart' instead of 'Bt' (referring to his baronetcy).

'LOAMSHIRE – The Right Hon. Mark Andrew Achilles Baron.' This was a peer, but 'Baron' was printed in such a way as to sound like a forename. 'The Right Hon.' was redundant since all peers below the rank of marquess are entitled to this honorary prefix, and the peer in question was not a true member of the privy council, which was the only circumstance in which mention of it might have been justifiable. Moreover, if you abbreviate 'Honourable' it is absurd not to do so with

'Right'. The notice should therefore have read: '**LOAMSHIRE** –
Mark Andrew Achilles, 6th Baron.'

'**POLE** – On June 12, 1994, peacefully in St Robert's Hospital,
Anne, aged 83 years. Much loved wife of Tim and only
daughter of the late C. P. Johnson Esq. and Mrs L. M.
Johnson, of Horsham . . .' Here the 'Esq.' strikes a discordant
and pompous note. For some decades now every non-titled
gentleman has usually been addressed formally on an envelope as 'John Smith, Esq.' but it is absurd to put it in a death
notice.

'**BELLWAY** – On 2nd May, tragically at home, William Christo-
pher George, GC, MA(Cantab), PhD, aged 82 years . . .' If
the doctorate (the PhD) was a Cambridge one it is always
taken to include an MA, so the latter should not be listed as
well. If it was not a Cambridge one, the MA should have been
listed after the PhD as it is a more junior degree, even if it was
earned earlier in time. The '(Cantab)' should have had a point
at the end – '(Cantab.)' – and have been separated from the
'MA' by a space. Lastly, what were the tragic circumstances in
the case of an eighty-two-year-old? The reader is inflamed
with vulgar curiosity, which was surely not what was intended.

'**INVERTAY** – There will be two services of thanksgiving for the
life of 'Richard' Alexander Walkinshaw, the 13th Earl of
Invertay. The first will be held at Summerlake, Ballacolla, Isle
of Mull, overlooking Richard's Coombe on Sunday 29th May
at 2 p.m. (in the event of inclement weather Calow Parish
Church will be used). The second will be at Holy Trinity
Church, Prince Consort Road (behind the Royal Albert Hall)
on Sunday 5th June at 2 p.m.' Not much wrong here, but the
'the' before '13th Earl' was redundant. And the lack of a
comma between 'Coombe' and 'on' suggests that on that day
and that day only the spot known as Summerlake would be

overlooking the Coombe. The 'Albert Hall' is sufficient, without the 'Royal', and it would be nice for readers to be told that this place is in London.

'CANLAKE – On Dec. 23, peacefully, Dora, aged 95 years. Daughter of Sir Henry Canlake (deceased), mother of John (deceased), in-law to Jasmine, granny to Lily and Derek and great granny to Simon, Bess, Clara and Billy. Service at Croydon Crematorium on Tuesday, Jan. 4 at 2.15 p.m. No flowers please, but donations, if desired, for Multiple Sclerosis, may be sent to . . .' It is so extremely unlikely that a ninety-five-year-old woman would have a father still living that a note of levity is struck by including the first '(deceased)'. Was Dora a mother-in-law to Jasmine, a sister-in-law or what? And surely she was a great-granny to Simon and the others, though she may well have been a great granny, in the sense of a splendid one, to Lily and Derek. There should be a comma after 'Jan. 4'. The 'please' and 'if desired' also strike a false note.

'CADWALLADER – Lady Cassandra Margharita, wife of Lord Cadwallader of Pimlico, died peacefully in The Royal Morden Hospital on Sunday January 31st. On Monday next February 7th there will be: At 2 p.m. a Service at St Gregory's Greek Orthodox Church at Kingsbridge upon Thames for family and older friends. At 3 p.m. Interment at Pimlico Cemetery. At 4 p.m. a gathering at Palaeologue House Hotel, East Approach, Wembley Vale. All friends are warmly welcome but please telephone (081) 123 4567 and leave a message for Philip Williams if you intend to come so we may have some idea of numbers. Cassandra loved flowers and these may be sent c/o the Funeral Directors . . .' Much of this is quite attractively worded. But the use of the forename after the title 'Lady' is one of the commonest solecisms. It implies she was a duke's, marquess's or earl's daughter. Although I have changed the names, I can assert utterly unequivocally that the original person was no such thing. And in the actual case the 'of Pimlico' is part of the full title since there is another Lord Cadwallader, Lord Cadwallader of Peckham to give him his full title, who is not 'of Pimlico'. The announcement should therefore have read '**CADWALLADER OF PIMLICO** – Cassandra Margharita, wife of Lord Cadwallader of Pimlico' or '**CADWALLADER OF PIMLICO** – Lady (Cassandra Margharita), wife of Lord Cadwallader of Pimlico . . .' The illiterate use of the upper-case initial letter after the colon detracted from the charm of the rest. And one is left wondering how old 'older' friends have to be before they will be considered suitable to attend the 2 p.m. service. Avoid comparatives like these.

'**HILDING** – On November 1st 1994, peacefully in Torquay, Lady Bonnie Dinah Hilding, daughter of the late Lord and Lady E.I. Hilding of Goldsbury, Loamshire . . .' Clearly what had happened here was that somebody on a nursing home or residential hotel staff had inserted the notice in the papers and was deplorably ignorant of the correct form in these matters. There had indeed been a Lord Hilding, whose barony was created in 1908 (it became extinct in 1951). Bonnie was the 2nd Baron's only daughter by his second wife. She should have been referred to as 'The Hon. Bonnie Dinah Hilding' and her father and mother as simply 'the 2nd Baron Hilding [no 'E.I.'] and his second wife Alice'. Ten minutes spent by matron with *Burke's Peerage & Baronetage* and *Debrett's Correct Form* would have preserved the reputation of a certain Torquay nursing home as a fit place for gentlefolk.

Another very common mistake people make when drafting death announcements is to say of a knight bachelor '**BLOGGS** – Sir John Rupert Bloggs, KT, on Wednesday 7 June, dearly loved husband of . . .' If Sir John was a knight bachelor any letters after the name to do with his knighthood, for example

'Kt' or 'KT', are redundant. You can tell he is a knight bachelor simply by the form 'Sir' then a forename then a surname. In particular the letters KT (note the upper case 'T') should only be used of a Knight of the Thistle (roughly the Scottish equivalent of a Knight of the Garter, and therefore a very high honour indeed). Other knighthoods, for example of the Bath or St Michael and St George, have the appropriate letters after the surname (see *Debrett's Correct Form* or the appendix on Precedence in my *Debrett's Guide to Entertaining* for further details).

The ways of stating that someone has died are many and various. Here are some:

'peacefully into the presence of the Lord'.

'after a miserable year's illness'. How refreshing to meet with such honesty instead of the hackneyed 'after a brave struggle', though I hasten to say that I am not implying that nobody puts up a brave struggle. Obviously some people do.

'in tragic circumstances'. Perhaps too intriguing to be strictly advisable. One does not want to arouse mere idle curiosity, after all. But at least no age was given here, which would render the reader's curiosity insatiable.

'after a long and turbulent flight a gentle landing by a brave professional'. The deceased had been an aviator. Rather nice, I think.

'Edwina's many friends will be sorry to hear that she lost her battle to restrict the onset of her illness on the evening of the 14th July 1994.' This is too convoluted, combining the hackneyed with an attempt to be original.

'He died as he lived with dignity and gentility'. The archaic 'with . . . gentility', which was presumably intended to mean 'with . . . good manners', might easily be interpreted as 'in a genteel fashion', that is, in a mincing, 'refained' fashion. Beware of words such as 'gentility' which have changed their meaning in the last 150 years. A comma after 'lived' would have improved the rhythm of the sentence.

'I have only slipped away into the next room. I am I, and you are you . . . I am waiting for you, for an interval. Somewhere very near, just around the corner.' This sounds like a Christian Science sentiment, but was actually by Canon Henry Scott Holland, an Anglican. There is much more than this in the original announcement in the deaths column of *The Times* of 2 November 1993.

'Contrary to what was implied in yesterday's death notice of Sgt Major B. K. Rush, the funeral service on Friday 16th December is private.' There followed details of a memorial service at a later date, to which all who wanted to give thanks for the deceased's life were welcome.

'FRANKENBERRY – Marigold, Setter Lady of Eastcombe . . .' I take this lady to have been a woman admirer of the breed of dog known as a setter; the upper-case initial letters make it hard to be sure, though she was certainly not titled, at least not genuinely.

'HEWIT – On May 2nd at Kiel, Germany, Benedict Hewit of Liverpool died of burns after heroically saving his family from their burning yacht.' The notice went on to mention his 'desolate partner, Charlotte', although the distinction between his 'many grieving relatives' and 'many, many grief-stricken friends' was an example of what Fowler stigmatises as the elegant variation. Mention was made of a reception at a London restaurant after the sung requiem mass, to continue till 7 p.m.

'**MICHAELS** – On July 1, suddenly but peacefully after a stroke, JOANNA. She wished her body to be used for medical research, so instead of a funeral, there will be a celebration of her life with refreshments and music on Saturday, July 16 at 3 p.m. in St John's Church, Ladbroke Grove, Notting Hill, London W11.' Those wishing to attend were asked to ring a telephone number, presumably so that the organisers could get some idea of how many were coming.

In drafting the announcement of a memorial service there are some sonorous ways of describing the officiating clergy: 'Father Gervase Tresham and the Rev. Brian Jones were robed and in the sanctuary' for an ecumenical function.

Clothes, Rendezvous and Deportment

In the autumn of 1994 the widow of Roy Castle wore a blue polka-dot dress at the service of thanksgiving for the life of her husband, the entertainer and self-styled victim of 'passive smoking'. That was her privilege as chief mourner. But you as a guest would do better to follow the example of Sir Harry Secombe, who gave an address at the same function, and wear a black tie and sombre dark suit if a man, or for a woman dark colours such as navy blue or maroon if you cannot abide black. Dress warmly, even if it is summer, as churches are usually cold places. Wear dark clothes under a dark coat so that at the graveside, where it may be quite warm if the funeral is in summer, you can take the outer layer of clothing off.

A woman should wear a hat for preference, again dark in colour and sober in style. Camilla Parker-Bowles favoured a pill-box affair for the memorial service for her mother, Mrs Bruce Shand, in October 1994, but then she was married to an officer in the armed services at the time, and one, moreover, who had done a tour of duty in Northern Ireland, so the pill-box was unusually appropriate.

If you have the slightest suspicion that the funeral may be a 'fun' one and fear that turning up in black would depress the others, you could wear a reversible coat and tie, black or charcoal on the outside, cheerful colours on the inside. That way you can suit your clothes to the prevailing mood, reverential or keeping a brave face, as the case may be.

In the past there were fairly elaborate invitation cards for funerals. They have all but disappeared today. Instead the time and place of the funeral is announced in the press along with the notice of death itself. This usually gives would-be mourners very little time in which to prepare for the occasion. A typical timing of a funeral will be as little as three or four days after the death has been reported in the papers. The hectic pace of modern living often means that only a few friends and relatives can turn up, though employers are usually sympathetic to requests by members of their staff at short notice for time off to attend a funeral. Nevertheless, it is probable that there will be a relatively small turn-out at the funeral, perhaps just the immediate family.

The big affair is increasingly the memorial service, which may take place several weeks or even months after the death. A big church in a major city is booked, readings from favourite texts are given by celebrated connections of the family and leading members of the family itself, and a favourite piece of music may be performed. The reading need not be from a sacred scripture, and often is not. The delay gives more time to organise the function, book in busy personages and rehearse the musicians and choristers. Some musicians of my acquaintance earn the bulk of their income from this sort of thing.

The cortège used to set out from the family home, for that was where the deceased had been laid out. Nowadays he is likely to have been taken into the custody of the undertaker at a chapel of rest and the mourners simply gather at the church or other place of worship, cemetery or crematorium. Many undertakers provide a limousine in which their clients can follow the hearse, and this may of course pick up the immediate family from their residence.

The congregation normally turns up at the place of worship where the funeral is to take place and seats itself before the arrival of the coffin. This is then brought into the building by pall-bearers and the congregation rises. If the funeral is at a crematorium people may gather outside the chapel and follow the chief mourners in. The latter follow the coffin in, it having been delivered by the undertakers.

It is customary for the front pews of a chapel or church to be occupied by the immediate family and friends, conventionally to the right of the aisle, the widow or widower in the seat immediately next to the aisle. If friends or relatives are to carry the coffin out of the church after the service they should seat themselves as near the front of the place of worship as possible, and in aisle seats. Apart from these, the immediate family and close friends leave the building before everyone else, as at a wedding.

Flowers

Nobody who reads the death notices in the newspapers can have failed to observe that the trend today is more and more against the sending of flowers to a funeral. In many cases the death announcement itself says that there should be no flowers and requests that any contributions be sent to charity. Another beneficiary might be the hospital where the deceased spent her last days, though the family who insert the notice in the papers are usually too delicate to say this. You may have to set in train discreet inquiries therefore, though if you lived nearby or were a close friend or relative of the deceased you would presumably have visited her in hospital during her last illness.

Moyses Stevens, of Sloane Street in London, are the leading florists in the UK. They also run Interflora, which will deliver flowers for you anywhere in the civilised world. In Moyses Stevens' experience there has been a radical change in the popularity of sending flowers to funerals. Only fifteen years ago they did 'tons' of funeral work, as their spokeswoman puts it. Nowadays it is only one or two cases a week. Speaking purely personally, the spokeswoman said she'd send flowers only to the funeral of someone close; otherwise she'd send money to a hospital. Of course you could also send flowers to the hospital to cheer up the surviving patients. It is sad when flowers are sent to a crematorium for a funeral and then thrown away after just a day, the Moyses Stevens' spokeswoman thinks. But some enlightened crematorium managements do send them on to the local hospital.

Even when friends and family do still send flowers to someone's funeral the trend is now away from the old arrangements in the form of crosses and wreaths unless the deceased is a victim of crime, mob violence or terrorist action. After an acrobat at the Blackpool Tower Circus fell to his death on Boxing Day in 1994 the floral tributes at the funeral were predominantly made up to resemble characters from the Big Top. In fact the custom of sending flowers to a funeral is not that old. It first became popular in this country after the American Civil War. It is therefore odd that the DSS will indirectly subsidise florists by sometimes giving the poor a grant to cover the cost of funeral flowers.

Even in some of the above cases flowers placed in later years after the tragedy near a commemorative plaque or memorial have often been simple offerings of a few blooms only, or bunches tied together with no further attempt at arrangement. Anyone who passes through St James's Square in London can observe this at the place outside the Libyan Embassy where the policewoman Yvonne Fletcher was gunned down in 1984. At the John F. Kennedy Memorial on the slopes of the hill above Runnymede just south-west of London, where people leave a few flowers all the seasons round, year in year out, the arrangements are similarly informal.

But annual remembrance services for the fallen of both world wars at cenotaphs, particularly at the main British Cenotaph in Whitehall, are still marked by elaborately shaped collections of flowers. And in a brief survey I carried out of churchyards in the Thames Valley I found that about 60 per cent of recent graves with any commemorative offerings at all had wreaths, mostly of holly, sometimes real, sometimes plastic. Holly has the great advantage of being long-lasting but it also has faintly pagan connotations.

Anyone who wants to justify the placing of wreaths of artificial vegetation on a grave can take heart from the royal mausoleum at Frogmore. Inside that there are three wreaths of bronze, tributes to Queen Victoria presented by the Emperor Menelik of Ethiopia, the officers of the Brazilian warship *Floriano* and the inhabitants of Butterworth District in South Africa, or at any rate such of them as were Her late Majesty's 'native subjects' there.

For the actual funerals themselves, however, it is the fashion nowadays to arrange flowers in the loose formation known in the trade as a 'spray on oasis', the oasis being that green-coloured block fashioned out of a spongy-looking material that resembles volcanic rock in texture. The oasis itself is usually long and low so that the flowers appear almost as if they were growing naturally in a flower bed.

The overwhelming majority of the flowers Moyses Stevens are asked to supply for funerals are white, or at the most in pastel shades. These are probably for the most part sent to Christian funerals. It is customary among many Americans to commemorate the dead with poinsettias, usually red, but also the creamy, very pale green variety. I have seen fake red poinsettias in some kind of light cloth material, possibly a man-made fibre, on recent English graves, too.

Clearly, whether you commemorate your dead relations or friends with artificial flowers rather than fresh ones is a matter of taste rather than etiquette. If you live near the churchyard or cemetery it is possible to replace fresh flowers frequently, though this can be expensive. If you live far away you will want something more long-lasting, such as holly. If the churchyard is frequently attacked by vandals, then again something tough and cheaply replaced such as holly is preferable to something easily stolen or torn apart such as a bunch of fresh flowers.

A typical floral arrangement at a funeral in the mid-1990s would cost between £35 and £155 depending on the season. Prices reach their highest point around St Valentine's Day, in the depths of winter. Elderly people do not seem to differ much from their juniors when it comes to preferring one sort of floral arrangement to another, or flowers at all as opposed to charitable donations, but they do seem to be slightly behind the times when it comes to anticipating what the flowers will cost.

I might just add that although it is perfectly understandable that a busy executive should get his secretary to order the flowers for a funeral, he ought to write the note expressing sorrow and condolences in his own hand. The logistics of getting the card to its destination are complex when the funeral is far away, but if time is short and distances long he could always fax a message to the local florist in his own writing which could then be reduced in size on a photocopier and incorporated in a laminated visiting card-size tag attached to the flowers themselves. The sight to next of kin of a card with a personal note from an absent but dear friend or relative of the deceased, but written out in the semi-educated round-hand of the average florists' employee, can be oddly distressing. Good florists should be thinking of ways to get round this problem.

Meanwhile, a thoughtful person will make a note of any particularly strong preferences in the flower line of her closest elderly friends and relatives so that if it ever comes to attending their funerals she can break away from the more hidebound selection of flowers and contribute a more personal selection.

Condolences

If you live under the same roof as a dying relative or friend, or are the person who most often goes to see her in hospital, it can be helpful when dealing with relatives and other friends who live far away, particularly abroad, if you write what one might call a pre-condolence letter, gently but unambiguously warning of the approaching end.

Similarly, after the death itself, you as executor or personal representative may have to write to a number of people all over the world announcing the news, particularly if they don't see the newspapers in which you have announced the death. A telephone call will do for people in the UK who may not have seen the papers or in cases where the deceased has left instructions that his death is not to be announced in the press. A brief factual statement is sufficient here, though not so bald as to be without some kind of opening emollient along the lines of: 'You will be sorry to hear that . . .' They can then write back a lengthier reply expressing their feelings.

The message of condolence proper, from you as friend of the family to the next of kin, need not be a letter. Some people these days send cassettes or even videos of condolence instead. Clearly the immediacy is greater; the warmth too, if the sender is 'good' on screen. If he isn't, it is better to write the old-fashioned letter. A letter of condolence is the most difficult literary exercise there is. But a good one can be carried around on her daily circuit by the bereaved, pulled out and read and re-read and re-read again, over and over, on a bus or while queuing for one – anywhere.

It is said that everyone in a state of bereavement likes to be sent a letter of condolence. That is simply not true. The sort who likes to nurse his grief in solitary fashion often does not. And adolescents can be very embarrassed by them. If the letter of condolence is very banal it can be plain irritating. Cards – one can hardly call them greeting cards – are obtainable in shops, but they are mostly very insipid affairs. One I came across recently said 'With sincere sympathy', as if sympathy could ever be anything but sincere. And the design tends to be disappointing: pallid lilies, kitsch arrangements of silver-coloured raised lettering – like the trashier sort of wedding cards only with less glitter.

Letter-writers who cannot express themselves other than tritely sometimes give up and send no letter at all. If you are no good at composing English spontaneously you should be prepared for considerable mental labour to achieve a more comforting effect. Some authorities (for example, the author of the Chosen Heritage pamphlet on condolence – see the Bibliography) declare that you should send the letter off quickly inasmuch as it is distressing for the principal bereaved person to receive a letter of condolence some weeks after the death. With great respect, I think that is nonsense. Some friends and relatives of the family don't even hear about the death till many months afterwards, particularly in these times of widely scattered families who seldom get together and may well not even phone each other except at Christmas, if then. Besides, the most intense bout of anguish for the principal victim of bereavement lasts anything up to a year, sometimes longer. So take your time in drafting the letter of condolence if an extra week's concentration will make it more expressive.

This is an occasion on which you should contemplate getting in an expert to help you write better. He need not be a Nobel literature prize-winner. A journalist, schoolmaster or don would do at a pinch, though Eng. Lit. dons are some of the worst at using English. Scientists, who have to write lucidly and unaffectedly, otherwise the results of their experiments are unintelligible, make much better prose-writers. In our present age of so-called universal literacy we rather look down our noses at societies where people employ a professional letter-writer. But the recipient of your condolences is not to know that you have called in an expert in self-expression to hone your epistolary skills – provided you do not let him use flowery phrases or colloquialisms which are uncharacteristic of your personality.

As a very rough rule of thumb, the older the bereaved person, the more he will appreciate a letter of condolence. Such letters are not an exclusively Western custom either: they are very much in use among Hindus, for instance. If you were the deceased's colleague, particularly if you were his boss, you must write to his widow. If you employ a nanny, au pair, cleaning woman, gardener or other casual worker, whether part-time or full-time, again you simply must send some kind of letter if they are bereaved.

The Chosen Heritage pamphlet on condolence has an unfortunate misprint in its section on letters to a dead work-mate's family, repeating the word 'friends' so as to make nonsense of the syntax. I regret to say that it is not a satisfactory model letter anyway. It ascribes qualities to the notional deceased, such as 'excellent worker', 'always good-humoured' and 'considerate', which may be true of some people but will never be true of everyone. If the deceased was lazy, bad-tempered and selfish and you cannot come up with anything more truthful than the above, forget it.

In practice you should always be able to avoid outright lies. If you are writing to a widow, concentrate on *her*, telling her how much the people at the office grieve for her. There are a number of epithets or phrases – 'He will live in our memories',

'She leaves the office a much duller place', 'His agile
mind . . .', 'Her great gift of repartee . . .' – which will
describe a misfit, a troublemaker, a backbiter and an hysteric
without you perjuring yourself. But don't try for irony. It is
completely out of place on such occasions. Be a bit of a Jesuit
or a Lord Armstrong of Ilminster:

   ' "Bear not false witness . . ." (Deuteronomy);
   But do with truth practise economy.'

The death of a friend's or relative's child is the most difficult of
all in this regard. By all means write about the small boy's
sunny nature or the little girl's winning ways if these were
genuine features of their personalities, but if he was morose,
or she was a Down's syndrome victim, this simply will not do.
Again, concentrate on the parents' sense of loss and the very
natural shock of their offspring dying before they do.
    Unless you are intimately acquainted with the couple, do not
hint at their having another child or children ('Robin will always
live on in your hearts as your first-born, I know, but others will
arrive in the years to come and although they can never replace
him . . .'). Robin may have been adopted because the parents
were unable themselves to conceive, or Robin's mother may
have had a hysterectomy after giving birth to him.
    If you are writing to a child or adolescent who has lost one
or both of her parents, offer some concrete prospect – a
treat such as a trip to the zoo, say. If you are the child's
godparent you should take your responsibility very seriously
and devote a lot of time to the child over the next few years,
taking her on holidays, having her to stay, introducing her
to new friends.
    Where you can let rip in the cliché department is in offers of
help: 'Do let me know if there's anything I can do.' But you'd
better mean it. In fact, a cliché regains something of its
original force if you back it up with a rider such as: 'I really

mean this. I'm going to ring you regularly to see what errands I can run.' Likewise, if you offer to listen to the bereaved person's reminiscences of the deceased – you don't put it like that of course; you say, 'If you'd like to talk about Anthony, I'm always here' – mean it.

Be prepared for something like a stream of consciousness. You should be a good listener already. If you're the type who fidgets it's a mistaken kindness to offer this sort of service. Tailor your assistance to the sort of things you are good at. If you're practical, you can offer to help the widow with mending her lawn-mower. If you're good at accounts you could help with sorting out her finances, though great tact is needed before offering to pry into someone else's monetary affairs, and professional detachment tends to suffer when you help old friends.

Be chary of saying, 'I know how you feel,' but be equally chary of never saying it. Some writers on this subject baldly state that you can never know how others feel in such circumstances. I wonder. That line of argument comes close to the sceptical position in philosophy which maintains that you cannot be sure a dog is pleased to see you just because he wags his tail, or that a baby is distressed just because it howls, or that you have caused pain in an old gentleman by kicking him in the groin just because he doubles up with a grimace.

You should not set yourself up as 'melancholier than thou' just because you have suffered more numerous or more hurtful bereavements than the person you are com-forting. But if you have ever gone through the same kind of experience, there is no reason on earth why you shouldn't say so. Sympathy simply means that you feel similarly, so it is absurd for arbitrary agony aunts to decree that you should express sympathy yet deny you the most succinct way of expressing it, which is and always will be, 'I know how you feel.' If you want to inject some humility or diffidence into the statement you might amend it to: 'I can imagine how you feel.'

Another commonplace item in a condolence letter is 'Please don't bother to answer this.' If you are writing from far away and have good reason for believing that the bereaved person is snowed under by similar letters, this is perfectly acceptable. But it may be read by the recipient as an attempt to choke off further communication. If he has been left a lonely old widower he may want to take up the threads of ancient friendship. You could propose a visit to him in the course of the letter, even if it's several months away. He may want to host a meeting entirely at home or agree to your proposal for an outing to the theatre, cinema or restaurant. Try out both plans. And keep trying. By and large, with bereaved people you should only take no for an answer after rather more rebuffs than in the case of ordinary human relationships.

These days there is such a variety of religious beliefs, and even a variety of disbelief, that it is probably more advisable than ever to avoid expressing your own in a letter of condolence. At any rate, go easy on specific statements about what happens to the soul or body after death. The letter by Joyce Grenfell on page 174 of *A Book of Condolences* (see the Bibliography) is a different matter. Joyce Grenfell was a Christian Scientist and ordinarily the Christian Science belief in there being no death can be intensely irritating to other people. In this letter she does not spell it out too overtly but the belief infuses her language with a great feeling of hope. It is a good example of its kind, I think.

If you deploy words for your living, whether you are the seediest of hacks, most shamelessly commercial of advertising copywriters or just a typically overpraised prize-winning novelist, do not write 'What can one say?' It is like a bishop questioning the virgin birth – unprofessional. For others it is a useful way of catching breath. Letters of condolence are perhaps all the better for a bit of incoherence. To that end, it does not pay to make them too well-constructed, though that should not preclude passages of uplift, even beauty. Try to achieve this through simplicity. If it is any consolation, many of the letters in *A Book of Condolences* from the most famous writers are either not very convincing or somewhat lamely expressed. In that sense, a bereavement truly diminishes us all.

Pets

No more cogent justification for feeling a sense of bereavement at the loss of an animal has been delivered than the one by Dennis Barlow's employer in *The Loved One*. I swore I was not going to mention this classic, if only because everyone else does when the subject of bereavement comes up; I should have known that you can't keep a good book down. Copyright laws prevent me quoting it verbatim, but here is the gist. Pets stand by you in bad times as well as good, sickness as well as health, poverty as well as riches, failure as well as success. Humans don't. Yet humans get the lion's share of the funerary rites. Animals are lucky to avoid getting hauled away by the trashman.

In fact some animals do very well when their human companions die – at least materially. But it is one of the most touching things about a dog, for instance, that even though he may have been left £1 million he will pine for his master. Many die quite soon after the human does, rather as widows or widowers frequently follow their dead spouses to the grave within months. Sometimes the owner dies of grief for his pet. In the late nineteenth century, the Lord Petre of the day is said to have done so after his dog passed away, dying before the animal could be buried. In the spring of 1994 a Buckinghamshire parish councillor drowned himself in the Grand Union Canal because his cat had disappeared. He left a note to his wife saying so.

A true love of animals strives to accord them the same dignity in death as is enjoyed by humans. A tribe in the Jachie region of Ghana has had such reverence for a troup of sacred monkeys that they have buried them with the identical rites they use for each other. A Gloucestershire woman who was widowed in 1968 succeeded in getting the words 'Also of "Eddy" his poodle' put on her husband's gravestone, the dog having died not long after his master. She hoped Eddy could be buried with her husband but the cemetery authorities forbade this, though they did at least allow the inscription to stay. Their grounds for objecting to the burial followed the specious reasoning of the repressive schoolmaster down the ages: 'A line has to be drawn somewhere in case somebody might wish to bury a pet elephant.' In the event Eddy was cremated and his ashes strewn over the grave.

Cemetery managements are more accommodating than the Church in these matters, but if you wish to bury a pet with his late master or mistress the answer so far has been to go the whole hog and arrange a green burial in your own garden (see the Go-It-Alone section). Although the Environmental Protection Act of 1990 states that any clinical waste must be burned, a pet undergoing treatment from a vet would only count as such if it died or was put down after suffering from a highly contagious disease such as rabies or anthrax. So whether or not you bury a human in the garden you can certainly do so with a dog, cat, gerbil or budgerigar which has died in the ordinary way. The freedom to do this is reinforced by the Waste Management Licensing Regulations of 1994.

In December 1994 the Rossendale Pet Crematorium in Lancashire sought a permit from the council to allow owners to be buried with their pets. Some thirty humans had already had their ashes buried there but so far no intact bodies had been interred at the crematorium. A decision was still pending at time of this book going to press. And since midsummer 1994 the Society for Companion Animal Studies has been operating a telephone service to comfort owners of pets who have passed on. Their phone number is 01891 615285. Clearly the portents for a merging of human and pet burial practices are good.

Other burial grounds include the Hyde Park Pet Cemetery, which has been closed since 1903 because it is full up and is therefore of antiquarian interest only. It was in any case as exclusive as any 'restricted' area in Forest Lawn, being confined to dogs, and mostly dogs belonging to upper-class owners at that. Other dog burial grounds include one at Max Gate, Thomas Hardy's old home in Dorset, and Stanway House in Gloucestershire.

Cemeteries which still have room for pets and which don't confine themselves to dogs seem to be mostly in the south of England: Chestnut Lodge in East Grinstead, West Sussex (tel. 01342 712976); Claver Hambury Pet Cemetery and Crematorium, east London (tel. 0181–529 0979); Pets Meadow and Willow Haven, both in Hertfordshire (tel. 01923 852470 and 263536 respectively); and Silvermere Haven in Surrey (tel. 0181–546 7591). Prices range between £45 and £95 for coffins, £70 and £300 for burial and £41 and £120 for cremation, though some of the higher prices include maintenance and a container for the body, or a marble headstone and surround. Urns for the ashes, if any, and lettering on a headstone are usually extra.

Clearly Hertfordshire is to animals what the territory of the ancient Etruscans was to humans in terms of reverence for the dead. I have already mentioned Pets Meadow and Willow Haven. There is also the Cambridge Pet Crematorium, near Royston in Hertfordshire (tel. 01763 208295). It is said to be Europe's biggest, cremating 35 tons of cats and dogs a week. It claims to base its prices – £25 to £30 for a cremation as reported in mid-1994 – on what elderly people can manage. You might also care to contact the Association of Private Pet Cemeteries and Crematoria at 200 Westerleigh Road, Pucklechurch, Bristol, Avon BS17 3PY, and/or The Pet Bereavement Counselling

Service, 25 Townsend Street, Dublin 2, Republic of Ireland (tel. 01-677 5097 if in Ireland; if from the UK 00 353 1 677 5097).

Pet-lovers of high rank who have marked their dogs' graves with some kind of memorial include the Queen with her corgis; Her Majesty's great-great-grandmother, Queen Victoria; and Lord Byron, who typically composed an elegy for his Newfoundland that might equally be heroic or mock-heroic. The great Duke of Wellington, less prone to irony, commemorated his horse Copenhagen with a grave and marker. I often used to visit it, as did other trippers, when I lived near His Grace's country seat of Stratfield Saye on the Berkshire–Hampshire border. More recently I visited Powerscourt, former seat of the viscounts of that name in the Wicklow Mountains above Dublin. There is a pet cemetery there which is thought to be the biggest in any private garden anywhere. The graves are neatly arranged in rows, one for dogs, then one for horses and a third for dogs again. Among the epitaphs is one to:

Eugenie
Jersey Cow
Died 1967 aged 17 years
She had 17 calves and produced
Over 100,000 gallons of milk

also to:

Princess
Aberdeen Angus Cow
Died 1972 aged 11 years
Three times Dublin Champion

Factual epitaphs like the above carry the most emotional force in the long run. If you compose your own epitaph try to avoid clichés like 'gentle giant' when commemorating a wolfhound, however languid he was.

300

People can be embarrassed when you have lost a human. When it is an animal they can be very insensitive indeed. Try to behave to your dog-deprived neighbour as if she were Queen Victoria. Try to treat your friend's little girl whose horse has had its neck slashed with the same courtesy you would have extended to the great Duke of Wellington.

Scotland and Abroad

Scotland

Although Scotland is still an integral part of the United Kingdom at the time of writing, the country has its own legal system, which in many ways is different from that of England and Wales. This is because the legislatures of the two countries were not amalgamated until 1707 and little has been done since to impose a unified framework in which to administer the output of that amalgamated legislature, even if the laws it passes are valid for both sides of the border. Before that there was an even wider contrast. In 1681, for instance, the Scots Parliament passed a law limiting guests at funerals to a hundred at most. Signs of that famous Scottish parsimony here, perhaps. In fact Scottish law is as generous as English law in that even the most curmudgeonly old screw cannot disinherit his wife or progeny completely, *mutatis mutandis* a female miser with her husband and offspring.

There are still differences in nomenclature between Scotland and England. The Scots refer to a grave as a 'lair' and to a 'lair certificate' when speaking of the purchasable right to burial in a particular place. The term 'confirmation' is used of an estate instead of probate. The differences extend to custom as well as the law. A coffin is sometimes fitted with 'courtesy cords' and close family friends or members of the immediate family are asked to hold one of the cords while the coffin is lowered into the grave.

The cords are not utilitarian, that is, load-bearing, in the way the straps are which the undertaker's men use to steady the coffin, but symbolic of contact between the mourner and the deceased. Sometimes too a mattress or other piece of soft material is placed on the coffin lid to soften the clatter of earth being shovelled on to the wood as the grave is filled in.

Back to law: the executor who collects monies due to the estate following confirmation is said to 'in-gather' them. If the deceased died intestate, the person who applies to become the executor sometimes has to get an instrument called a 'bond of caution'. This is a device for insuring against loss in winding up the estate. In this context the word 'caution' is pronounced to rhyme with 'station' not 'portion'. There are executors nominate, who are the ones appointed by the will, and executors dative, who are appointed by a court when the deceased made no will, but they in-gather and administer the estate in exactly the same way.

The Scottish Office uses 'lair' in its pamphlet *What to Do After a Death in Scotland*, obtainable from the Central Inquiry Unit, New St Andrew's House, Edinburgh EH1 3TG (tel. 0131–244 5151, fax 0131–244 4785). To the student of national differences there are other fascinating aspects to this Scottish Office publication, even where it is giving essentially the same information as its English counterparts. It refers more often to the need for caution in expenditure. It also goes out of its way to reassure its readers that a public authority-funded funeral is quite different from the old paupers' burials. The English pamphlets lack these homely little touches.

In Scotland any doctor can make out a certificate of death. Usually it is the one who attended on the deceased in her last illness, but if she died suddenly and apparently in the best of health, a doctor totally unconnected with the family can do so, though further investigation might be necessary. The registrar can register the death even if no medical certificate is forthcoming, for example because the deceased had no doctor in regular medical attendance before she died and the cause of death is open to question, conjecture or investigation.

In that case the registrar will report the matter to the Procurator Fiscal, who in a case which is under investigation takes possession of the body in the legal sense and has the ultimate say in its disposal, whatever the next of kin's wishes. The Procurator Fiscal is a full-time law officer of the crown. He has no precise counterpart in England but is more like the examining magistrate in France. He can in other words both investigate a case (though interviewing the deceased's relations or other relevant witnesses is usually done by the police, acting for him) and institute judicial proceedings.

He also fulfils the role of coroner, though the equivalent of an inquest is called a fatal accident inquiry. In this capacity he broadly has the same duties and powers as his English counterpart, though if he decides on a post-mortem the sheriff (chief local law officer) must give prior permission. It is in the sheriff court that a fatal accident inquiry would be held, with the sheriff presiding and the Procurator Fiscal questioning witnesses.

Deaths must be registered within eight days, either in the registrar's office covering the area where the deceased died or the one for where he lived, unless he was a visitor to Scotland, in which case it is the former. Scotland does not use disposal certificates. Instead the registrar's certificate of death registration authorises burial or cremation. Other than a certification of registry of death for National Insurance, which is free and can be used only for National Insurance claims, death certificates cost £6 each if requested up to a month from registering and £8.50 thereafter, though there is a special one for Department of Social Security claims which costs £5.50.

Even after the executor has got his confirmation, he must not distribute the estate until six months from the date of death are up. This lets anybody with a claim on the estate apply for settlement of debts. Surviving spouses and children have legal rights to a certain amount of the deceased's personal estate – not real estate such as a house or land, but chattels, cash and shares – whether there is a will or not.

If there is no will the surviving spouse and any children have what are called 'prior rights', which are slightly different to the equivalent for close relatives in the case of a person dying intestate in England and Wales. Widows, in their relations with the DSS and tax authorities, do better than widowers. If a woman was judicially separated from her husband and he dies intestate she may have certain claims on his property. A man in the same situation cannot inherit anything from his separated wife. The publication *Rights of Succession*, obtainable from The Scottish Office Home and Health Department, Division 1A, St Andrew's House, Edinburgh EH1 3DG, gives further details.

To remove a body from Scotland you need a certified extract from an entry in the Scottish death register. The death must be registered in Scotland beforehand. Once that is done, you will then need in addition a letter from the Procurator Fiscal to say that removal is permitted; it should state the place and cause of death.

Abroad

If someone dies while overseas or aboard a foreign-owned ship or aeroplane you must follow the foreign country's rules when registering the death. In particular you should procure a death certificate and register the death independently with the local British consul. A burial or cremation on the spot is cheaper than bringing the body home. If you do bring it back to Britain you must get permission from the country where the death took place and get a properly translated version of the foreign death certificate before having the funeral in Britain, also a certificate of no liability to register from the local registrar in England or Wales, though this latter is not necessary if a coroner has made out an authorisation for burial or cremation himself. A coroner can hold an inquest in Britain even if death took place abroad, though he would only do so in the same circumstances as if the death had occurred in Britain.

If you wish to remove the deceased's body from England or Wales for a funeral elsewhere you must apply to the coroner, even if the coroner would not normally have been called in.

Bereavement in High Life

So many current writers on death and bereavement exaggerate our age's break with past attitudes. By going back to the ancient world and pointing to several recurrent patterns, I hope I have already shown that in regard to this subject almost everything in twentieth-century behaviour (hence almost certainly feeling as well) has a precursor. There are only a finite number of ways we can mark the passing of a companion. Even if in every era we favour a different tone or accent to reflect our preoccupations – now burial, now cremation, now high ceremonial, now a descent into informality – we always come full circle back to one of the other variables within a generation or two.

Even the most solemn and elaborate types of obsequy may be brought out of the storage cupboard and dusted down for reuse today if the situation seems to warrant it. As recently as 1965, when Sir Winston Churchill died, a state funeral with ample use of heraldic devices was mounted, as if he had been a great man from a much earlier age (which in a way he was). The great man as a national phenomenon has rather gone out of fashion since, though doubtless not permanently.

In any case there are still families who celebrate bereavement with all the attention to sumptuous detail of their forebears, notably the Cecil marquesses of Salisbury, who are also staunch upholders of the Anglican faith in general. (Their cousins the Cecil marquesses of Exeter, however, are the exact opposite. The 7th Marquess, who died in 1988, started up a branch in Canada of the Emissaries of Divine Light, founded in the USA during the 1930s by one Lloyd Meeker, and on Lord Exeter's death his son assumed both the marquessate and the local spiritual leadership.)

The Salisbury Cecils staged a notably elaborate funeral for the 5th Marquess ('Bobbety', the Conservative Party king-maker of the 1950s and early 1960s) when he died in 1972. Among other accoutrements some members of the family, in particular the 5th Marquess's widow, Elizabeth (known to family friends as 'Betty'), wore full mourning attire of the Tudor period. This was, appropriately, the age in which both the Cecils and the church they support first rose to greatness.

The most noticeable feature of Tudor mourning dress is the widow's-peak cap for women, where a white fitting which juts forward over the top of the forehead in a point is surmounted by a black headdress with a veil. Some of the most celebrated portraits of Mary Queen of Scots in the sixteenth century show her wearing this headgear and there is a grimly awesome photograph of Queen Mary at the funeral of her son George VI in 1952 draped in a similar device. Queen Victoria had worn it, too, when in mourning for Prince Albert and had set something of a vogue for it among other European queens.

As recently as 1990, just after the 15th Earl of Huntingdon died, his body lay in state the night before the funeral proper in his coffin in the church in Leicestershire where many of his ancestors had been buried. (The family seat there, long since sold I am sorry to say, had served as one of Mary Queen of Scots' residences in the sixteenth century.) Members of the local clergy watched over it in a vigil. His coronation robes, surmounted by an earl's coronet, were draped over the coffin and heraldic hatchments were displayed.

A fine colour photograph of a similar nobleman's lying in state is shown in plate 24 of Julian Litten's *The English Way of Death* (see the Bibliography). Not all earls are so traditionally minded. The 18th Earl of Derby, who died in 1994 and whose title is even older (1485) than Huntingdon's (1529), was borne in his coffin to the local church in Lancashire on a trailer pulled by a red tractor. He did not care for hearses.

The word hatchment is a corruption of 'achievement', meaning in this case a heraldic achievement or full display of armorial bearings, and it depicts the coat of arms of the deceased person, who must of course have a legitimate right to bear arms, though he need not be a peer. A hatchment is always shown in the shape of a lozenge or diamond in a black frame.

The hatchment itself began life in the Low Countries as a two-dimensional representation on canvas or wood of the full array of three-dimensional, indeed highly solid, armorial accoutrements which were borne in the procession accompanying a dead man of noble or knightly rank during the Middle Ages. These comprised chiefly the shield and helm (or helmet) with its crest on top (the armorial crest, a minor decorative identifying sign, is often confused by ignorant journalists with the full coat of arms). Originally they would have been the actual objects the deceased had used in battle, though in later ages replicas were knocked up for funerary purposes by jobbing carpenters and blacksmiths and later hung in the local church.

In a hatchment the coat of arms usually appears on a black background or badger-pied background of both black and white. The background is important as it shows what the marital status of the deceased was. An unmarried man's arms are supposed to be in true shield form surmounted by his crest although the background, which is black, is diamond- or lozenge-shaped. An unmarried woman's arms would be lozenge-shaped themselves as well as being displayed against a lozenge-shaped background of black. They would have no crest but instead be adorned on the topmost point of the lozenge by a bow called a lover's knot, however little our hypothetical spinster was actually the object of anybody's amorous attentions in life – one of heraldry's more touching chivalric conventions.

If the deceased was a married man survived by his wife, his arms would take up the left hand of a shield, as you look at it, divided down the middle between his own arms and those of his wife. His side would be on a black background, while his wife's arms would occupy the right-hand side of the divided shield on a white background. (This assumes his wife had the right to bear her own arms, of course.) The whole coat of arms would be in true shield shape although the background would be lozenge-shaped. In addition the shield would be sur-mounted by the man's crest on top of the whole, though occasionally you will come across a cherub or cherubs instead and sometimes a skull, which is supposed to mean that the deceased was the last of the family.

If the deceased was a woman whose husband had survived her, her arms would be shown on the right-hand side against a black background and his on the left on a white background, again both in shield form against a lozenge-shaped background. There would be no crest on top, nor even a lover's knot. If the deceased was a widower, his and his wife's arms would be on the left and right respectively of a shield divided down the middle between them but on a wholly black background. As is usual when a man's arms are depicted, the crest would sit on top of the shield. If the deceased was a widow her husband's and her own arms would be divided left and right respectively, as before, but on a lozenge-shaped depiction against a lozenge-shaped back-ground and with no crest or lover's knot on top.

There are further refinements involving smaller parts of the lozenge background being white if a man has died leaving a second or other subsequent wife behind him, or if a second or other subsequent wife has died leaving her husband still alive. If a man had divorced his wife before dying her arms did not appear at all. And whereas ordinary coats of arms have a specific motto peculiar to the family, hatchments often have the single word '*Resurgam*' (Latin for 'I will arise') inscribed on the bottom.

When all armigerous persons were orthodox Christians this implicit belief in the resurrection of the body was a standard feature. Nowadays it might not always be suitable. And in the case of Sir Currimbhoy Ebrahim, Bart., whose arms are 'Argent in base on waves of the sea a Chinese junk sailing to the sinister, in chief also on waves two dhows sailing to the dexter all proper; a chief per pale gules and or thereon a pale azure between a rose of the first and a lotus flower also proper, and charged with a mullet issuant from a crescent, above five mullets in crescent also of the first', with for crest 'above an Indian lily on water proper, a mullet radiated or', a hatchment might be a breach of the Muslim prohibition on idolatry, for the Ebrahim baronets have always been true to Islam. On the other hand, neither Sir Currimbhoy nor Sir Hirji Jehangir, 3rd Bart., nor Sir Jamsetjee Jejeebhoy, 7th Bart., would ever have to drop the '*Resurgam*' as belief in the resurrection is as much a part of the Zoroastrian faith of the last two as of the Islamic faith of the Ebrahims.

From the seventeenth century it became the fashion for hatchments to be put up over the door of the house in which the dead person had recently passed away. There is a reference to several of them (complete, in one case, with cherubs) in Thackeray's *Vanity Fair*, though in the first instance they are described as having been placed over the middle drawing-room window. Later in the book, in Chapter xiv, a hatchment is mentioned as having been put up on the front of the Crawley house in Great Gaunt Street in Mayfair after the death of Sir Pitt Crawley, Bart.'s second wife Rose. (Thackeray gets in a bit of a muddle about her, first calling her Rosa, daughter of G. Grafton, then later Rose, daughter of John Thomas Dawson, an ironmonger.)

In this case, however, the woman has not died in the

family's town house but in the country. And with his usual cynicism Thackeray observes that the same hatchment had done duty for Sir Pitt's mother, the Dowager Lady Crawley, a few years before. Yet Rosa or Rose has not been granted arms (she is a mere ironmonger's daughter in an intensely snobbish age), and the arms 'quartered' with Sir Pitt's (that is, divided on the lozenge in the way described above) are therefore not hers. Probably a great many other families used to recycle their hatchments in just such a careless fashion, contrary to the laws and usage of heraldry.

After the mourning period (conventionally a year) was over the hatchment was then often lodged in the local place of worship, which is why you usually come across them in country churches, though examples have been found in other places. The armorial achievement is occasionally accompanied by inscriptions or a date. Lord Huntingdon is not the only person this century to have had his death commemorated in a hatchment: nearly a hundred other examples are known.

There is no reason why the custom should not be revived generally, at any rate among the families of those who have coats of arms. Moreover there is nothing to prevent other, as yet non-armigerous, readers applying for a grant of arms. Consider: a gravestone is cumbersome and any inscription on it, being out of doors in a churchyard (where there may not be room for your remains anyway), is liable to defacement by vandals or obliteration by the weather. You can only have a text inscribed on a gravestone. The amount of space available limits the message. (Indeed, the word lapidary refers specifically to the brevity dictated by having to carve letters on stone.)

Even the wording is subject to the linguistic bigotry of some little jack-in-office of a vicar prohibiting 'Mum' or 'Dad' as too vernacular. In contrast everybody knows that a picture is worth a thousand words. A hatchment is therefore a much better memorial. It allows you to be commemorated after

314

your death in a colourful yet dignified, decorative yet matri-
monially allusive, long-lasting and decipherable yet portable
sheet of wood or canvas.

It is one of the paradoxes of social history that heraldic
devices became most popular as decoration and identifying
marks after the age of chivalry was over. That is also true of
the bereavement phenomenon known as the heraldic funeral.
This was a hugely elaborate and extremely expensive commemorative gesture by the bereaved towards a recently
deceased personage, who had, of course, to be of some social
distinction. The heraldic funeral flourished most gloriously in
the sixteenth and seventeenth centuries.

It is called heraldic because coats of arms and other heraldic
devices overshadowed all other decorative features almost to
the point of obliterating them. One might hazard a guess that
the parvenus of the time (who, I regret to say, included the
Cecils) found it an effective way of enhancing their very
recently minted prestige. Mind you, there were plenty of
people who were commemorated heraldically after death
whose status was beyond cavil. Edward I's Queen, Eleanor of
Castile, died at Harby, in Nottinghamshire, in 1290. Her
corpse was transported to Westminster Abbey for burial in
great style. The journey took twelve days and at each overnight stop Edward set up stone crosses with heraldic embel-
lishments showing the arms of Castile and England.

And one of the most magnificent examples of a heraldic
funeral took place on the eve of the Reformation. In 1524 the
2nd Duke of Norfolk of the 1483 creation died and what
followed has been called the last great funeral of the Middle
Ages, though it would be equally legitimate to call it the first
great funeral of the Renaissance. The body lay in state at
Framlingham Castle in Suffolk for a month. It was then
transported twenty-four miles to Thetford Priory in Norfolk,
where his ancestors were buried. Nine hundred people
stepped out in attendance on the funeral car, including Garter

King of Arms and Clarenceux King of Arms, also Carlisle Herald and Windsor Herald.

Each of the four heralds carried either the Duke's helm and crest or hatchments. They were accompanied, among others, by torch-carriers in black hoods. At the priory the Duke's coffin rested on a catafalque illuminated by 700 tapers and surrounded by wax effigies dressed in black holding eight small banners. The climax of the funeral – from a military ceremonial point of view – was when a man wearing His Grace's armour and holding His Grace's battleaxe upside down (the equivalent of the reversed arms position in military funerals today) rode a charger into the church.

I trust there are still some vicars left in the Church of England today who would allow a similarly stirring ceremony to take place. The funeral would have to be that of a suitably distinguished military man, I suppose, though arguably any equestrian could be commemorated in such a way. For instance, a hunt servant could ride the favourite hunter of a deceased master of fox hounds into the nave holding the whip in the reversed position, similarly with a deceased showjumper or three-day eventer.

But what was really going on at the priory, apart from any genuine mourning? One might make several observations. First, the College of Arms had only recently been instituted (by Richard III in 1484), although heralds as such had been in existence in some cases for several centuries and in the person of the chief heralds (Garter King of Arms and the two provincial kings of arms, Norroy and Clarenceux) are generally reckoned to have had the right to license the organisation of funerals by lesser heralds since perhaps as early as 1417, in Henry V's reign. I say 'generally reckoned', because in discussing the ordinance that records this right Sir Anthony Wagner, himself currently Clarenceux King of Arms, adds the proviso 'if genuine' when assigning it a date in his book *Heralds and Heraldry*.

After initial downgrading by Richard's successor and rival dynastic representative Henry VII, heralds began to be rehabilitated and by 1524 stood on the threshold of the most important era in their existence, not just as regards superintending heraldic funerals but in their visitations, where they recorded the histories and rights to bear arms of the leading families around the country. They would surely have been keen to make a great show. The 2nd Duke of Norfolk's father had been the disgraced Richard III's principal supporter and owed the dukedom to him. The dukes of Norfolk were then not nearly as grand a family in the male line as they subsequently became through the process of time, being originally from a relatively obscure provincial gentry background until their advantageous marriage with a Mowbray heiress in the early fifteenth century. Like Henry VII himself, their claims to greatness were through a maternal line, therefore. And in heraldry you can display your mother's family's arms provided she was a heraldic heiress. Sumptuous heraldic display would have helped here.

On the other hand, the 2nd Duke of Norfolk was a genuinely distinguished military commander, having routed the Scots at the Battle of Flodden in 1513 while his master Henry VIII had brought off relatively footling successes on the southern front in simultaneous hostilities against the French. It is arguably just this combination, reminding onlookers of a man's authentic battle honours together with histrionic but somewhat shaky claims to consistently distinguished ancestry, for which the heraldic funeral was ideally suited.

Among the subsequent heraldic funerals that are best recorded are those of Oliver Cromwell in 1658 (taken to the grave with crown and all, even though he was a mere Protector), General Monk, architect of the Restoration of 1660, in 1670, he having been created Duke of Albemarle shortly after the Restoration, and the great general John Churchill, 1st Duke of Marlborough, in 1722. These fit the

317

pattern. Like the Duke of Norfolk in 1524, the last two were from old but not terribly distinguished gentry families in the male line yet had personally achieved great prowess on the battlefield. (Oliver Cromwell was of newer stock, but still gentry.)

In the expense to which the family of the deceased were put over heraldic funerals, together with the increasingly close supervision by the heralds of the College of Arms, an institution which had been set up by the crown and which is still part of the royal household, we may perhaps see a specifically funerary version of the fines the Tudor monarchs imposed on heirs when they came into their patrimony. It was, after all, the living who had ultimately to pay for all this display, just as it is now and always has been. Bereavement can bring you a sudden accession of riches but there are always people lurking around, whether the state or the heralds or the undertakers or the clergy, who want and get their cut.

And the heralds didn't try to superintend funerals for just the heavy swells among the nobility, but for classes as humble as lesser gentry and well-to-do urban merchants. They laid down rules as to how many mourners there should be in the principal body of those attending: 15 for an emperor, 13 for a king, 11 for a duke, 9 for a marquess or an earl, 7 for a viscount or a baron, 5 for a knight and 3 for an untitled esquire or gentleman. Clare Gittings, in *Death, Burial and the Individual in Early Modern England* (see the Bibliography), misunderstands this as meaning that there had to be eleven other live dukes to attend on a dead one. That is absurd: there were never more than three other dukes at a time in the English peerage apart from Norfolk throughout the sixteenth century (and from 1546 to 1553 and after 1572 not even Norfolk, as the holders of that dukedom were attainted), let alone fifteen other emperors to attend on Charles V, say. No, these principal mourners would have been of very high rank, but not precisely of the same rank as the deceased.

Until the rise of the undertaker the heralds made a pretty good thing out of funerals, charging fees for attendance and fees for certification of the genealogies of the families concerned. In the early seventeenth century the tariff for certification by the heralds of upper-class funerals was: archbishops, dukes and duchesses £45; marquesses and marchionesses £40; earls and countesses £35; viscounts and viscountesses £30; barons, baronesses and bishops £25; baronets £13 6s 8d (£13.33 in decimal currency); knights £10; esquires £6 13s 6d (£6.65); and gentlemen £2. Multiply by not less than fifty to get some idea of mid-1990s equivalent sums.

Heralds also got professional perks such as the cloth after it had been used on the hearse (at this time a sort of baldaquin, like the canopy over a four-poster bed, rather than the vehicle we now know it as). The cost of the cloth was a major part of the funeral expenses so this was worth having. And the heralds restricted the kinds of armorial accoutrements that could be displayed. The number, size of depiction and variety had to match the rank of the deceased.

This sort of thing was going too far. The heralds overreached themselves, their once-captive clients dug in their heels and refused to acquiesce in a network of regulations made the more irksome because they were costly to observe, and the heraldic funeral declined from the late seventeenth century onwards. In the same way there are signs today that the undertakers may have similarly overreached themselves through foisting unnecessarily expensive funerals on the bereaved, being secretive about the extent to which they operate a near monopoly and refusing to itemise bills sufficiently, to say nothing of being slow off the mark to capitalise on the growing enthusiasm for eco-friendly funerals.

Yet the heraldic funeral did not entirely fade away just because members of the College of Arms found themselves being ousted as funeral organisers by undertakers. Indeed, it has been asserted that certain features of funerals for quite ordinary people in the nineteenth century, such as the staves swathed in sheets of black cloth, the tray of black plumes carried on the head of a funeral attendant and the batons and wands held by the pall-bearers and still other attendants, were dim shadows of former heraldic devices and customs.

The full heraldic funeral proper certainly became rarer, but in a few cases a variant on it grew to be even more magnificent than the most notable examples from the past. From the eighteenth century to the present day there have been a number of state funerals for national heroes: Pitt the Elder in 1778, Nelson in 1806, Pitt the Younger later the same year, Wellington in 1852, Gladstone in 1898, Lord Roberts (the Boer War general) in 1914 and Sir Winston Churchill in 1965. For a funeral to count as a state one it has to be ordered by the monarch and funded by the public purse following a Parliamentary resolution to that effect.

Given the necessity for a royal command, the case of Gladstone is interesting. Queen Victoria was not fond of him and you would have thought that if she had ordered a state funeral for any of her prime ministers it would have been Disraeli, not Disraeli's Liberal rival. Perhaps the Queen sought to make atonement after Gladstone's life was over for her detestation of him during it. On the great Duke of Wellington's death she had gone still further and had decreed both that the court should go into mourning (an unheard of honour for a mere subject) and that the army should undergo the same mourning protocol for him as if he had been royalty.

In the case not only of the national hero who had thwarted the Corsican tyrant by land but of that brother hero who had dished him at sea – I mean of course Nelson – the funeral cars were of particularly extravagant design. The canopy over Nelson's was supported by reproduction palm trees, commemorating his victory of the Nile, and the chassis itself protruded fore and aft with likenesses of the figurehead and stern of HMS *Victory*. Being essentially a land vehicle, however, it was provided with wheels as well, to the number of four. The Iron Duke's had six, weighed 11 tons (the same figure in thousands of pounds as it had cost to make, though Lady Longford in her biography of Wellington says it weighed 18 tons) and required a dozen horses to pull it. It was until recently to be seen in the crypt of St Paul's Cathedral but is now at Stratfield Saye.

Where Lady Longford is definitely wrong is in saying that Wellington's was the last heraldic state funeral. Whether a funeral counted as heraldic or otherwise was not at this stage a question of absolutes as much as of degrees. A strong heraldic element in a state funeral was inevitable where the person honoured had been a distinguished military commander, in the way Lord Roberts was, for instance, as well as the Duke of Wellington.

It was fortunate from the antiquarian point of view that Churchill's ancestry was so distinguished. Because that was the case it was possible for the heralds at the College of Arms to devise an even more impressive send-off than if he had been an entirely self-made man, though the honours he had earned, such as his Garter, Order of Merit and Companionship of Honour, as opposed to the armorial bearings he had inherited, constituted the bulk of the decorative features.

Sir Winston's coffin lay in state at Westminster Hall for three days and was viewed by huge crowds. The banners carried in the procession to St Paul's for the funeral service included one that displayed his coat of arms – no modern grant this, but rich in references to his illustrious ancestor the great Duke of Marlborough of Anne's reign, not to mention the house of Spencer. The Dukes of Marlborough bear what is called an honourable augmentation on their arms which includes fleurs de lys and alludes to the royal arms of France; this commemorates the great Duke's victories over the French. Sir Winston's arms included this allusion too, though a more appropriate honourable augmentation for him would have incorporated a swastika, or at the very least a lump of coal commemorating his victory at Tonypandy.

Sir Winston Churchill's crest, shield, spurs and sword also featured. They were displayed at St Paul's Cathedral, being carried by four heralds. John Brooke-Little, the present Norroy and Ulster King of Arms (and coincidentally grandson of James Brooke-Little, the leading authority on the law of burial in the late nineteenth century), points out in his book *Royal Ceremonies of State* that these essentially mediaeval accoutrements were unusual in being the dead man's own and very real tools of war, apart from the shield, which had to be specially made for the occasion.

It might at first seem strange that the sword and spurs were working implements when Sir Winston Churchill is remembered chiefly as a national leader in a time of intensely mechanised conflict. But of course he had once been a cavalry officer and had taken part in 1898 in the mounted charge by the 4th Hussars at the Battle of Omdurman, the last major cavalry engagement by the British Army in its entire history.

Even for slightly less distinguished figures, heraldry still influences mourning. Military funerals for the topmost officers in the armed services, that is to say of a field marshal, admiral-of-the-fleet or marshal of the RAF rank, incorporate heraldic features, for such people are always members of one of the orders such as the Garter or the Bath. At a funeral of, or memorial service for, a member of the Order of the Garter in St George's Chapel at Windsor his banner is marched up to the altar and a procession of military knights of Windsor is in attendance. Burial in St Paul's or Westminster Abbey is by invitation only, and a royal one at that. As so many previous distinguished figures have already been laid to rest there, space is limited to cremated remains.

Royal funerals have tended to become more public occasions over the last two and a half centuries, though in this century that was going to be inevitable once radio and television existed which could diffuse immediate details of an event to virtually everyone in the country, if not the world. When Queen Victoria was dying the machinery of government began to seize up even before she breathed her last. Since the old lady was unable in her last days to sign commissions, judges could not travel round the country to preside over assizes. Dispatch boxes accumulated at Osborne House, on the Isle of Wight, where she had spent most of her time for years. The conduct of foreign affairs was particularly hard hit. It was as if the state was suffering from arteriosclerosis in a kind of bureaucratic sympathy.

After the Queen's end had come and news of it reached London, the theatres shut their doors and the great bell of St Paul's Cathedral was tolled every minute on the minute for two hours. Six torpedo-destroyers escorted the yacht bearing the coffin from Cowes to Portsmouth through endless ranks of battleships, each ship's band playing Chopin's *Funeral March* as it passed by. Bystanders along the railway line from Portsmouth to Waterloo knelt as the train transporting the coffin swept past. In one jail in the home counties female prisoners were seen to have tied black bows made from shoelaces to their uniforms.

Jailbirds might favour black; not so the late Queen. She had ordered a white funeral. A number of authors have interpreted this as a desire for a minimum of mourning. Certainly she had instructed her executrix, Princess Beatrice, to see that her body was transported on a gun carriage rather than a hearse at the funeral and for the pall to be only partly draped with the royal standard. But Victoria personally had indulged in a cult of the dead for decades after losing Prince Albert. She had used up all the available stocks of black cloth in the period immediately following his death, despite the aversion to that colour he had expressed in life. As we have seen, use of the colour white had a long tradition where mourning for and by females was concerned. So the white pall on the dead Queen's coffin and the white dress, cap and veil she was buried in were all in accordance with convention.

The white tradition came in useful as recently as 1938 and even helped cement Franco-British relations. On the eve of the state visit to France by George VI and Queen Elizabeth, the Queen's mother, the Countess of Strathmore and Kinghorne, died. Initially it looked as if the projected wardrobe to be worn by the Queen would have to be jettisoned. Worse, if she was going to have to wear black all the time it was likely to cast considerable gloom over the visit, particularly in Paris, the shrine of haute couture.

Luckily, there was not just the general precedent of white as a mourning colour for women but a specific custom for queens of France to wear white when newly bereaved. This had survived till as late as the seventeenth century, and Mary Queen of Scots, for instance, who was briefly married to King Henry II of France before his early death, had worn what the French called 'deuil blanc' at the French court before she returned to Scotland in 1560. So Norman Hartnell spent fourteen busy days refashioning the Queen's dresses in white. It was apt that the visit, which proved a great success, took place in summer.

In some respects Queen Victoria had been an innovator where bereavement was concerned. Sovereigns of England before her had been buried in churches, in particular the vault beneath St George's Chapel at Windsor Castle. Victoria constructed a mausoleum at Frogmore, where her mother, the Duchess of Kent, lived out her last years and which, although in the grounds of the castle, stands well away from St George's. Victoria attended the funerals of her cousin the Duke of Cumberland in 1878 and her youngest son Prince Leopold, Duke of Albany, in 1884, although the sovereign usually does not go to other people's funerals. (It would seem that a queen dowager can, however, once she ceases to be a queen consort: the Queen Mother attended the funeral of her old lady-in-waiting Lady Victoria Wemyss, the 6th Duke of

Portland's daughter, in May 1994.)

Leopold's was the first full military funeral in modern times. At Queen Victoria's own funeral the horses who would normally have pulled the gun carriage grew fractious and were replaced by seamen at the suggestion of Prince Louis of Battenberg (the late Lord Mountbatten's father, evidently as fertile in ideas for shaping royal tradition as was his son). This has become such a well-developed tradition that most people think it dates back centuries.

The death of a sovereign is one of only three occasions on which the curfew bell of Windsor Castle is tolled, the others being for the birth of a prince or a royal marriage. On the death of the sovereign the court goes into mourning for six months, with those who generally wear uniform putting on a black armband and those who do not donning a dark suit and black tie if male or a black dress if female. Queen Victoria was greatly agitated about what the correct mourning drill was for a foreign sovereign with whom One was at war on hearing of the death of Tsar Nicholas I in 1855, during the Crimean War.

Readers of Anthony Powell's novel sequence *A Dance to the Music of Time* may recall Lady Frederica remarking that she ought to buy a new black dress in the sales as so many royals were getting into their eighties that she was bound to be needing one frequently. Convention dictates that those who are in mourning of this sort should not be seen in public places such as restaurants, theatres or dances till the full mourning period has come to an end, which usually means after the funeral. The Earl Marshal, one of the hereditary great officers of state (the post is always held by the current Duke of Norfolk), sets the date of the funeral and is in attendance at it. Heraldic devices feature at a royal funeral too.

Mourning for a member of the royal family other than the sovereign is regulated by the sovereign herself and tends to be observed only by the royal family and members of their households. It has usually been thought unsuitable to dispose of a royal corpse locally, whether it is a major or minor member of the reigning house, if the death took place abroad. In the days before refrigerated mortuaries and swift air transport, that could pose problems.

Queen Victoria's son-in-law, Prince Henry of Battenberg, (known as 'Liko' to the family) died unexpectedly in 1896. He was at sea at the time off the coast of west Africa, and since the body had to be repatriated to the UK, not buried at sea as with commoners, he was pickled in naval rum in a container fashioned from biscuit tins before the ship headed back to Portsmouth. The custom is an old one. In ancient Greece the Spartans brought their dead King Agesipolis home from Chalcidice on the northern shore of the Aegean Sea preserved in honey, and another dead king, Agesilaus (444–360 BC), from north Africa covered in wax.

When a sovereign dies and is buried, the great officers of state such as the Lord Chamberlain and the Earl Marshal break their staves or wands of office and cast the pieces down on to the dead king or queen's coffin. When heraldic funerals were all the rage in the sixteenth and seventeenth centuries, the dead nobleman's senior functionaries, such as his steward, would do likewise. This custom, too, is very old. There are examples from late Bronze Age and Iron Age tombs of deliberately broken or bent swords and sceptres, so the notion that an emblem of power should be rendered unusable on the death of a person who wielded power is found in all sorts of societies. Saxon and Viking tombs have been found with mutilated weapons or regalia as well. Some ancient Roman burials have been discovered with bent sceptres in them and the Pope's signet ring (otherwise known as the Fisherman's Ring), which dates from at least 1265, has since at least 1521 been ceremonially broken on the death of each pope. When the king or queen of Sweden dies his or her coat of arms is ritually destroyed.

It would be going a bit far to agree with Auberon Waugh,

who, when the 16th Duke of Norfolk died, wrote that the death of a great nobleman diminishes us all. But people do feel a genuine sense of bereavement when a popular sovereign or revered statesman dies. These days pop stars (Elvis Presley), divas (Maria Callas) or actors (James Dean) can produce a feeling of loss among people who have never known them personally. Many entertainers know no national boundaries.

Politicians seldom generate a sense of bereavement outside their own countries and perhaps not that often inside them, though Jack Kennedy in 1963 is a notable exception. The officers of the Chilean navy are said to wear black ties in mourning for Nelson on the anniversary of the Battle of Trafalgar. In Britain, sad to say, at any rate outside naval circles, Trafalgar Day is little regarded, though from time to time elderly patriots write to *The Times* suggesting it be made a public holiday instead of May Day. Most people couldn't even say exactly when it falls (it is 21 October).

There are few other people alive today who would elicit the sort of emotion Kennedy called forth; possibly the Pope, had he been assassinated in 1981 instead of just wounded, and possibly Nelson Mandela, had he been gunned down at his inauguration as President of South Africa in early 1994. The human capacity for developing a sense of bereavement is so great that no amount of debunking will eradicate it from some idiots. On Christmas Day 1994, a group of Romanians held a vigil by the grave of Nicolae Ceausescu, the dictator-monster executed by his own guards five years before.

The other sense of mass bereavement develops on Remembrance Sunday, which is usually celebrated on the closest Sunday to 11 November each year. Doubtless many of the people who observe it most reverently are mourning a specific friend or relative who gave his life in one of the two world wars. But it is nevertheless also a genuine expression of national bereavement for a collective loss. True, as fewer and fewer people survive from the Second World War, let alone from the First, Remembrance Sunday has become less solemnly commemorated.

In the first few decades after 1918 the entire country came to a halt during the two minutes' silence at 11 a.m. on 11 November itself. The change that has come over the country since is neatly encapsulated in the advice promulgated in November 1994 by the chairman of the north-west Hampshire bench. This buffoon suggested that magistrates should not wear their poppies in court lest it upset the accused person in the dock. The latter might suspect the poppy-clad JP of bias in giving a verdict or sentencing, it was explained. Despite the inevitable tendency of newer generations to forget precisely the events of 11 November 1918 and 1939–45, I doubt if Tony Blair would ever make the mistake one of his predecessors as Labour leader, Michael Foot, did of turning up to the White-hall Cenotaph ceremony in a donkey jacket. It might be going a bit far to claim that if any single act of folly by Foot lost Labour the 1983 general election it was probably that, but it is certainly the only memorable event of his leadership.

The ceremony at the Cenotaph in Whitehall in London is the high point of Remembrance Sunday. Cenotaphs – the word derives from the Greek for 'empty' and 'tomb', meaning a monument to someone who is buried elsewhere – were known in ancient Greece, when just a large stone might commemorate the missing body of the deceased. In Roman times cenotaphs were erected to those who had been lost at sea or in battle overseas. Mourners invited the soul of the deceased to enter the cenotaph by calling on it three times.

Burial at Sea

While Nelson and 'Liko' might have been brought back to land for disposal after death, others like to be taken out to sea and buried there, even when they have died on land. The state recognises that people who have strong connections with the sea have a claim to be buried under it, although it mildly discourages the practice generally.

You cannot bury an embalmed body at sea since the delay in decomposition means that the body is more likely to get entangled in fishing nets or washed ashore. In fact, there are very few places around the coasts of the United Kingdom where you are allowed to bury people at sea at all. Around the south coast, for instance, there are only Plymouth, the Needles off the westernmost tip of the Isle of Wight and the stretch between Hastings and Newhaven along the Sussex shore. You need to get a letter from the local district inspector of fisheries at the time of the disposal of the body. This will specify a place and time, but if bad weather makes it difficult an amendment to the licence must be obtained.

If you wish to bury cremated remains at sea the position is simpler. The authorities prefer this method, and provided the ashes are to be scattered over the surface of the sea rather than sunk in it inside a container, there is no obligation to advise the fisheries officer. It is a good idea to do so nevertheless, as he can give guidance as to precisely where to perform the ceremony.

If a body is buried intact at sea it should be placed in a coffin of a material other than a wood such as oak, which has a long life in water. Nor should it be made of any non-corrosive metal, particularly copper, lead or zinc. But since any coffin must have weights placed in it to ensure that it sinks, whatever metal is used should be iron or steel, with added weight in a light concrete mixture, if desired, of around 2cwt (just under 102kg). The entire coffin should be weighted with 4cwt (200kg), whether of metal or concrete.

The coffin should be drilled with a minimum of twelve holes to let the water in, each ¾in (1.905cm) wide (elsewhere the Ministry of Agriculture, Fisheries and Food documents say 2in – 50mm – wide, though they stress that this is a draft document). If a shroud is used it should not be made of canvas, since this can survive under water for a long time, but something less durable such as cotton or paper. The body should have a neck tag in plastic or some other non-biodegradable material, marked with a phone number and reference number. This is so that the remains can be identified if at some later date (as was being proposed with Sir Francis Drake in early 1995) he is dredged up from the sea bed.

The cost of sea burial is high. A boat must be hired or borrowed. You must sail to exactly the right spot, which will necessitate the use of navigational aids. In late November 1994 it was reckoned that all this would set you back about £3,000.

If a body is lost at sea, a shore-based coroner can hold an inquest if it is likely that the death took place either within a coroner's area of jurisdiction or near it. The Home Secretary has to order the inquest.

Children

Which of the dead are most tenderly and passionately deplored? Those who love the survivors the least, I believe. The death of a child occasions a passion of grief and frantic tears, such as your end, brother reader, will never inspire. The death of an infant which scarce knew you, which a week's absence from you would have caused to forget you, will strike you down more than the loss of your closest friend, or your first-born son – a man grown like yourself, with children of his own.

William Thackerary, Vanity Fair

One may quarrel with the above. A child has an intimate animal relationship with its mother, certainly, and sometimes with its father too. That may not quite amount to love as adults know it among each other, but only if you insist that love needs to be based on knowledge of character to be worthy of the name. Thackeray, however, was writing in an age when upper-, upper-middle- and middle-class children saw more of servants than parents. And his own children had to be sent abroad to be brought up away from him after his wife went mad. Indeed, he rather gives the game away about his own attitude to children by writing 'which' instead of 'who'.

The passage is still a useful reminder that the Victorians too could find the loss of a child afflicting, even though they usually had many more of them to lose than we do. The orgy of grief among Dickens' readers when he killed off Little Nell in *The Old Curiosity Shop* is another example. Still other harrowing literary descriptions of parents losing a child include that in Dickens' *Dombey and Son*, where the death of his son Paul makes Dombey even stiffer and prouder than before, to say nothing of inducing him to enter into a disastrous second marriage.

In the twentieth century there are Aldous Huxley's *Point Counterpoint*, in which the death of the Quarles' son from meningitis is particularly affecting, and Evelyn Waugh's *A Handful of Dust*, in which Tony and Lady Brenda Last's son's fatal blow on the skull from a fractious horse's hoof also smashes up a tottering marriage. Further, it induces the father to travel in places so far-flung that he becomes lost to civilisation altogether. As a result an extensive landed estate goes to a cadet branch of the family, even though the head of it is still alive. One sometimes feels that in Waugh's eyes this is the gravest part of the tragedy.

In general, because of the high rate of child mortality before the twentieth century, most human societies tended to be a bit callous in their treatment of child death, perhaps because that was the only way they could school themselves into fending off the bitterest grief. In the early part of the first millennium BC in Greece children seem to have been buried in so casual a manner that archaeologists have found very few of their graves. Some historians have gone so far as to suggest that children were regarded as expendable, not full people, in fact.

Another point is that early child graves in Greece are often found near dwelling places, even though burial away from the residential quarter was supposed to be obligatory, certainly for adults. It is true that later, in the classical period, children were often buried with their families away from the home. And some seem to have been buried with their mothers. But the remains of many child corpses have been found stuffed into the mouths of jars or in holes cut in the sides, the jars then

332

being buried on their sides and the mouths closed up with a slab of stone or a tile.

Children were usually buried even when the rest of the population was cremated. The Elder Pliny (AD 23–79), a Roman writer, tells us that children were not cremated unless their second teeth had come through, but he is an uncritical author and took much of his material from other sources, not direct observation. Plutarch, writing around the end of the first century AD, says that dead children are not subject to the usual funerary customs as they have no part in the world: no offerings of drink are made to them, nor do their parents honour their graves. Even their newly dead bodies are not laid out, nor does anyone watch by the body. Indeed, to mourn the very young is against the law.

There may have been a more sinister side to it. Some historians have suggested that both the Greeks and the Romans went in for mass female infanticide to keep the population down, rather as the modern Chinese have done. This would certainly explain the much greater number of male skeletons as opposed to female ones in certain known grave sites, as regards both adult and child dead. Some unwanted newly born children were certainly exposed to the elements, particularly in the case of the Spartans with girl babies.

As late as the Reformation there were subtle differences in the way dead children and dead adults were treated. An object called a chrysom cloth or chrism-robe was used as a headband when anointing a child at its baptism (*chrism* – cognate with Christ – is simply the Greek-derived word for anointing). Children who died under the age of one (other sources say within a month of baptism) were buried in their chrysom cloth and swaddling clothes. Thus the expression 'chrysom child' came about. The Book of Common Prayer of 1549 orders the 'whyte vesture, commonly called the Chrysome' to be used, but before the anointing with oil, not afterwards as in pre-Reformation times. It was then to be given back to the priest at the rite known as the churching of women, which is the thanksgiving ceremony for their having given birth successfully. The use of the chrysom cloth was officially dispensed with in the more avowedly Protestant prayer book of 1552. The women of the family sometimes made a set of garments for a child to be buried in when getting the rest of her baby clothes together.

The bringing up of a child by servants instead of parents may have made it hard for the two generations of parents and offspring to get to know each other. It had other even more deleterious consequences. A child farmed out to a wet nurse for nourishment in its early life may have been twice as likely to die young as a child suckled at home by its mother. The decline of the wet-nurse custom from the late seventeenth century onwards almost certainly contributed to improved life expectancy in the eighteenth century.

Unfortunately, children suffered during the Industrial Revolution even more than their elders. In Glasgow between 1820 and 1840 – a mere couple of decades – the death rate for children went up by more than one and a half times, from 1.3 per cent to over 2.08 per cent, while in the latter year in Manchester over 57 per cent of working-class children never reached the age of five.

Catholics have special liturgical texts for children. If the child dies before being baptised, which she would need to do at a very early age since Catholics baptise their young as soon as possible after birth, the Church still tries to comfort parents, even though doctrine states that the child goes to limbo. For stillbirths or deaths soon after birth there is a straightforward service of commendation which can be celebrated at home, in hospital, at church or at the graveside, whether in a churchyard or cemetery.

In Islam the prayer for a dead boy differs slightly from that for a man. After the third 'God is most great' (see the section on Islamic funeral rites in Part II), one adds 'O God, make him a precursor to lead the way for his parents, and make him a recompense and a treasure laid up for them,' instead of the usual prayer for God to forgive the deceased.

Methodists have two funeral services for children, one for an initially successful birth, the other for a stillbirth. Both are entirely distinct from the services for adults. In the first, the congregation gather, there are brief readings from John ii, 25–6; Matthew v, 4; Psalm xlvi, 1; Mark x, 14; John xiv, 1; Romans viii, 39; and Revelation xxi, 5; then a hymn, then prayers interspersed with a short silence. The ministry of the word follows.

Next there are further readings from the Bible: Psalm xxiii; Mark x, 13–16; John xiv, 1–6, 27; and Revelation xxi, 1–5. There may be a short address by the minister afterwards. The service continues with a commendation and committal (2 Corinthians i, 3–4; Psalm ciii, 13; and Isaiah xl, 11 are recited), then come prayers in which a hymn is sung and short prayers recited with silences in between.

For a stillbirth the child's name is used if he has been given one. Otherwise the minister refers simply to 'this child'. The service follows the same essential pattern as the other but is much shorter. There are readings from Matthew xviii, 1–5; Matthew xi, 27–30; and 2 Corinthians i, 3–7. There may also be a short sermon.

Traditionally in England, stillborn children were supposed to be buried, not thrown away, though the very existence of laws to enforce this suggests that the remains often were thrown away, particularly if the child was illegitimate. A stillborn child is not regarded as a person, although in the last ten years the point at which a birth is defined as stillborn has been moved back from twenty-eight weeks after conception to twenty-four weeks, and the mother may be able to claim statutory maternity pay or maternity allowance.

In Spain at the end of 1994 a touching tale emerged of a

supposedly stillborn baby, born on Christmas Day and appropriately named Jesús, who was seen to move when his father asked to see him one last time as he lay in a refrigerated chamber in the Virgen de Rocio Hospital in Seville. The poor little mite weighed only 24–5oz (682–711g) and had been pronounced dead ninety minutes earlier. You would have thought that the refrigeration could not have done him any good, but actually it may have saved him by putting him into a sort of hibernation.

Registrars have four categories of death for very small babies. These are used for compiling statistics. There is perinatal, where death occurs twenty-four weeks or more after conception (including all stillbirths) but earlier than seven days after being born. There is neonatal, where a baby is born but dies before it is twenty-eight days old. There is postnatal, where a baby dies between the ages of twenty-eight days and one year, and infant death, which comprises any baby dying between birth and age one year.

All the foregoing deaths need a registrar's or coroner's certificate before the body can be disposed of. Anyone whose child has died of what is called a 'cot death' may like to get in touch with The Cot Death Society, of 7 Friars Walk, Thornby, Merseyside L37 4EU (tel. 01704 870005), or The Foundation for the Study of Infant Deaths, of 35 Belgrave Square, London SW1X 8QB (tel. 0171–235 0965). Parents whose child has been born dead or died before it is twenty-eight days old may like to contact The Still Birth and Neonatal Death Society (SANDS), of 28 Portland Place, London W1N 4DE (tel. 0171–436 5881).

Any product of conception that is less than twenty-four weeks old is called a non-viable foetus, or in plain English a miscarriage. It does not need a registrar's or coroner's certificate of disposal and is either buried or cremated. Nearly all miscarriages occur in the first half of this twenty-four-week period, sometimes even before the woman knows she is pregnant, which, of course, comes as an extra shock. If the woman was in hospital at the time the hospital authorities will probably offer to dispose of the foetus, the more sensitive ones doing so with the involvement of a hospital chaplain at a simple ceremony. But if the parents wish they can arrange for burial or cremation, with any amount of ceremony. Most women who have been given the chance to view the foetus and who have been interviewed on the subject say they are glad to have done so, though this probably depends on how well-formed the foetus was. There is a Miscarriage Association, at 18 Stoneybrook Close, West Bretton, Wakefield WF4 4TP. It has a twenty-four-hour ansaphone on 01924 200 799.

Undertakers often give their services free on such occasions as stillbirth burials or cremations, though items such as crematoria fees must still be paid. Stillborn children are so small that if they are cremated there may be no remains at all and parents are usually asked beforehand to sign a statement to the effect that they appreciate this. As with bereavement generally, it may take some time before full realisation of what has happened hits you. That is particularly the case for a woman who has been in physical pain during the process of miscarrying.

It has been suggested that there are as many as 100,000 miscarriages a year in the UK, or one in four pregnancies. A woman who has had only one or two miscarriages is just as likely to give birth successfully the next time she gets pregnant as if she had never had a miscarriage at all. Only after the third miscarriage can one speak of a woman as suffering from habitual or recurrent miscarriages. Even then the chance of having a successful birth after the next pregnancy is evens and after that two in three. On the other hand, if a couple has difficulty in conceiving in the first place then there is a slightly greater risk that when the woman does become pregnant it will end in a miscarriage.

The Compassionate Friends, whose address and telephone

number are given in the Acknowledgements at the front of this book, was set up just over twenty-five years ago to comfort bereaved parents. And by parents it means men and women of any age with offspring of any age. Countess Mountbatten of Burma is a patron, for instance, having lost one of her grown-up sons in the terrorist incident in 1979 that also killed her father, the Earl. The Compassionate Friends is run by a national committee which consists entirely of bereaved parents and is also made up of representatives from its regional bodies. This meets roughly once every two months.

It publishes a newsletter four times a year which for the most part contains contributions from bereaved parents writing in with their difficulties, together with articles describing an individual parent's experience of her particular bereavement. I especially wrote 'her' in that last sentence because Denise Watson, the spokeswoman for the Compassionate Friends, says that women tend to seek her organisation's help more than do men – British men, at any rate. When delegations from affiliated organisations in the United States get together with people in this country from the Compassionate Friends and like-minded organisations, Denise Watson notices that American men and women are far more prone to mourn together. Most of the women who come to the Compassionate Friends are middle-aged.

The Compassionate Friends has a network of contacts and helpers in most counties and regions of Britain. When a person loses a child – whether through a road accident, meningitis, suicide or, most horribly of all, murder – she often gets in touch with the Friends, who have two particularly important sub-groups called Parents of Murdered Children and Shadow of Suicide (for those whose children have killed themselves).

The Friends try to put the bereaved parent in touch with someone else reasonably nearby who is in the same boat, even to the extent of having lost a child to the same disease or type of violent end. Prior to that, however, a Friend may go and see the bereaved parent, talk to her (or let her talk, which can be just as comforting) and generally get to know something of her. The Compassionate Friends stress that they are trying to help people through friendship itself, which they identify as more informal, rather than counselling, though they say that friendship complements counselling. They are in touch with affiliated organisations in twenty to thirty other countries round the world.

From time to time other organisations with similar aims to those of the Compassionate Friends have been set up in Britain. Some years ago there was, for instance, the Bereaved Parents Helpline, with an address in Harlow in Essex. It seems no longer to exist. And about two years ago an organisation connected with the Great Ormond Street Children's Hospital was started up.

In the autumn of 1994 a new charity was set up called the Child Bereavement Trust. It aims to train doctors, midwives and nurses specifically to help in paediatrics. Even nowadays, when public health is so much better than in the past, there are over 7,000 deaths of newborn babies in the UK a year and a further 15,000 of children up to the age of fourteen. The very saddest of such deaths are those of babies given paupers' burials in places such as the East End of London. By a pauper's burial is meant the most basic of ceremonies and interment in a mass grave holding up to around twenty in all. Even that costs the DSS £180 a time, which seems an awful lot.

The London *Standard* of 9 January 1995, which drew public attention to the phenomenon in rather hysterical fashion, claimed that about one baby a week was being buried in this way. The single case it reported from direct observation had no mother in attendance, and the paper's editor, who was the author of the article, added, 'why we do not know but are

339

permitted to guess'. He gave his readers no hint of what the reason was. One can only suppose it was because the baby had been abandoned.

The other great involvement of children with bereavement is when a surviving parent or other relative has to break the news of a death to them. The Royal College of Psychiatrists puts out a pamphlet on bereavement which suggests that children do not usually comprehend what death means before the age of three or four. After that they can mourn the loss of someone close to them just as much as adults, although it seems they pass through the various stages of grief more quickly, having a swifter pace of growth generally.

The RCP suggests that when you arrange the funeral of a close relative you let the children attend it. Some parents put off telling children that a grandparent or sibling has died, and some who have just lost their spouses take the perilous step of postponing the moment when they break the news of the death of the other parent. My father did this to me and my sister in the case of our mother and was much criticised by his relatives for it. I cannot speak for how it affects others, but I bore him no ill will and believe it did no harm, or rather that it didn't make matters any worse. The period involved was only a week or two anyway.

Lily Pincus (see the Bibliography) gives a truly macabre example of a parent failing to break the bad news to a child, one which clearly did matter a great deal. A boy of three and his sister of four were packed off to the country, where their father visited them every week and told them that their mother was ill. He always brought presents for them. After about a year he turned up with a female companion who he called their 'mother' and who he encouraged the children to address as Mother. The four of them then returned home. Remember that by this time neither child had seen their real mother for a year, which is an enormous length of time to a child at their ages.

The boy seems never to have voiced his doubts as to the new 'mother's' identity, although both he and his sister were aware that their grandparents on their mother's side of the family, to whom they were very close, were not the new woman's parents. The boy's grandfather took him to synagogue once a year to pray for the dead but never specified any particular dead. The reason for the cover-up became clear later in life, when he learned that his beautiful and talented mother had drowned herself in a fit of insanity.

Suicide

Although it is callous, invidious and a gross over-simplification to draw up a pecking order of painfulness when it comes to bereavement, the sort that arises from another's suicide would probably feature high up on most people's list. Somewhere just below the death of a child, perhaps, and easily top if it is one's child who has committed suicide. A close second would be suicide by a parent, particularly if at a very delicate stage in the growth of any children. I once had a friend who hanged herself in her bathroom and was found by her children. They were about five and six at the time.

Emile Durkheim, the founding father of what for want of a better word is called sociology (see the Bibliography), reckoned that suicide in the modern age was more common among those who were not snugly absorbed by a human society. An example in a very broad sense were Protestants, whose creed laid emphasis on the individual, as opposed to Catholics, whose creed laid stress on obedience to a traditional hierarchy and body of doctrine. Another suicidal 'type' was the person who was outside family life, what we would call the 'loner' or in extreme cases the misfit. Again Catholic countries seemed to have fewer people of this sort, placing as they did great importance on the family.

On the other hand, Durkheim reckoned that even in strongly collectivist societies there could be tendencies to suicide among those whose individuality was so submerged in the community that they would obey commands to sacrifice themselves, either in a religious sense or out of unswerving loyalty to a political programme. We continue to recognise this sort of personality in suicide bombers, such as some fundamentalist Muslims, for example in the Middle East. Again, some cases of terrorist action in Europe over the last twenty-five years would qualify as suicide or suicidally inclined.

From the bereavement point of view even fundamentalist Muslims and terrorists have families and friends who may be devastated by their deaths. The families and friends of their victims are likely to feel extra hard-hit because of the sense of futility of purpose when a random victim is killed. For the bereaved, as for the terrorist, in theory, every victim of a terrorist atrocity is a random one, though a distinction might be made between members of police forces or the volunteer armed services killed during attempts to arrest or frustrate terrorists and civilian bystanders caught in street crossfire, a bombing or an aeroplane hijacking.

Durkheim also observed that sudden wealth could lead to suicide, as when the 'victim' found he couldn't cope. Divorce is famously a precipitator nowadays but in Durkheim's day divorce itself was a good deal rarer, so his linking of it with suicide was less obvious than it would be today.

There seems also to be a family predisposition to suicide in some cases. Durkheim cited the case of a landed proprietor in France who bequeathed his seven sons a substantial legacy. Six continued to live in Paris, where they had already made their homes before inheriting the fortune, and made sensible use of their wealth, not squandering it but investing wisely and even increasing their capital. All seven were in good health, too. Nevertheless, the entire brood killed themselves within a space of forty years. In another case, four children of the total of six of an upper-middle-class businessman killed themselves. A fifth made repeated attempts to do so. Sometimes the same implement was used by an entire family who committed suicide, though they did so over a number of years.

In the days when suicides used to be buried by the side of the public highway with a stake through them it was not just to prevent subsequent hauntings but to act as a terrifying warning to others. Thomas Hardy recalled a girl suicide in his youth who was buried where two roads met, with earth heaped all around the stake driven through her body, along the lines of an ancient tumulus.

It was not till 1821 that an act permitted suicides to be given a Christian burial, and even then it had to take place between 9 p.m. and midnight. Usually the north side of the churchyard was chosen. Indeed, that area was used exclusively to bury suicides in. Within living memory some clerics have refused to officiate at a funeral service of a suicide. I know of one Methodist minister who did. I also know of at least one non-conformist minister who has conducted a funeral service for a young man who committed suicide and who was not even a Christian, let alone of his denomination, though his mother, who had been an Anglican in earlier life, was a member of the minister's congregation.

It was not till the Suicide Act of 1961 that killing oneself ceased to be a crime. The act also had the effect of allowing any religious funeral service, providing that this was celebrated in an orderly fashion. It is not against the law to take no action if someone talks of committing suicide. Indeed, short of keeping a person so inclined under twenty-four-hour observation there is very little you can do. A cousin of mine who is a Jungian psychotherapist informs me that people over the age of fifty should be taken much more seriously than younger people when they talk of suicide.

If a person informs you or you discover by some other

means that he has taken steps to kill himself, for example by swallowing poison or sleeping pills, then you have a duty to let the police know instantly. This was the point which the former head of Corpus Christi College at Oxford, Sir Kenneth Dover, had to clarify when debating with himself how most expeditiously to rid the college of a troublesome don back in 1985. The account in his autobiography, *Marginal Comment*, of this ultimate act of marginalisation aroused a good deal of comment itself, by no means marginal, when it was published in the autumn of 1994.

If you discover an apparent suicide you follow the procedure described elsewhere in this book for dealing with dead bodies generally and specifically the procedure for informing the police and coroner. If a note is found you may be asked by the police to identify the handwriting on it. You will be asked to identify the body too, but if a householder is found in his own home you need not look on the face of the deceased. At any rate I was not obliged to do so when I found my father with an opaque black plastic bag over his head and a bottle of sleeping pills washed down with a pint of whisky inside him (allegedly the most foolproof method of committing suicide). In such circumstances the doctor and police will take away any drugs or other accessories which may have to do with the means of bringing about death.

Even humanists recommend that one tries to be 'positive' when referring to the death of a person who has committed suicide. This suggests that humanists are no happier with suicide as a way of exiting from life than are people who believe in a deity. But humanists ought to salute a person who has chosen to end it all in a spirit of calmness and for a number of good solid reasons. These may include any or all of the following: declining mental powers; ditto physical agility; impairment of sight, hearing and sense of taste; loss of mobility stemming from withdrawal of a driving licence, itself consequent upon the foregoing impairment of faculties; the demise of old friends such that our would-be suicide's social life is impoverished (particularly if the old friend was finished off by means of a stroke or other debilitating final illness that serves to remind the would-be suicide how undignified it can be to linger on as a cabbage); dwindling financial resources; and the possibility of forced removal to sheltered accommodation or a nursing home, with concomitant loss of independence and financial ruin for the would-be suicide's children.

The wonder is that more elderly people don't commit suicide. As it is, the rate for the over-eighties, at around 1 per cent, is already the highest of any age group. Prosperous types such as Hampstead residents do it more than the impoverished in places like Tower Hamlets, perhaps because the latter have few financial resources and little mobility, while removal to an institution wouldn't make much difference compared to life on a council estate.

The British Humanist Association goes some of the way down the path of reason. They suggest in their literature that the celebrant at a non-religious funeral service for an old or terminally ill person who took his own life might refer to the deceased's bravery and lack of selfishness in doing what he did. When the suicide is a young person even the BHA booklet admits that it's more difficult to confront the problem. It rather lamely suggests stressing that it was the deceased's sensitivity that made it impossible to deal with existence in today's world while reminding the assembled company of all the worthwhile things he accomplished in a brief life. Blaming today's world is always a bit of a cop-out, whatever piece of social deviance someone has perpetrated, but at a time like a non-religious funeral for a young suicide a little copping out is forgivable as long as it's therapeutic for the parents and other close friends and relations.

A more full-blooded humanist position would surely be to

remind family and friends that a person's life is her own to do what she likes with, and that it is no more acceptable for others, however close through ties of blood or companionship, to dictate what that person does with her life than it is to insist she chooses a particular profession or a particular spouse. Humanism in such circumstances ought to be as close to liberalism as it is in practice in most other circumstances. It is the weakness of some humanists' position that they cannot bring themselves to recognise and accept this.

It has been suggested that there may be as many as three times more actual suicides than those that are recorded. In some cultures the suicide's family, friends and professional attendants such as clergy turn a blind eye to evidence of suicide in order to give the deceased a conventional funeral. It used to be said that this happened in Ireland, an intensely Catholic country where Christian burial in consecrated ground was long denied, not just to suicides but to stillborn and other unbaptised children.

Sometimes the next of kin of anyone committing suicide is ineligible to benefit from insurance policies and a cover-up on financial grounds occurs. This is tantamount to fraud. Sometimes with old people it is convenient from an administrative point of view for a doctor to put down heart attack rather than drug overdose as the cause of death – after all, you can always find some evidence of arterial disease in the elderly.

There is no one correct path for coping emotionally with the suicide of your close relative or friend. My own practice is to talk about it incessantly, but others may wish to cover up what has happened. Alternatively you could talk to a discreet friend, cleric or counsellor. Read accounts of the ancient world, where suicide was regarded as less reprehensible; this may help to put the event in perspective. In order to cleanse suicide of its association with guilt, remorse and despair you could try to read up about heroes who nobly sacrificed their lives for a cause, which in many circumstances is virtual suicide. This brings us full circle back to Durkheim's observation.

The bereaved generally are sometimes advised to keep a diary. Doing so in circumstances you particularly don't wish to discuss with others, for example suicide, could be soothing. I did something along those lines after my father's suicide. I wrote this book.

Bibliography

Anon: *The Royal Mausoleum Frogmore* (©HM Queen Elizabeth II, 3rd edition 1991). A useful little pamphlet on that important testament to Queen Victoria's revolution in bereavement practices.

Bland, Olivia: *The Royal Way of Death* (Constable, 1986). A brisk anecdotal account of the way deaths in the royal family have been handled, from the Tudors to the present century. Some contemporary accounts are quoted.

Boston, Sarah and Trezise, Rachael: *Merely Mortal, Coping With Dying, Death and Bereavement* (Methuen, in association with Channel 4 Television Co. Ltd, 1987). Not a joint writing effort so much as two completely separate works, each by completely different authors, stitched together to make a single volume. Sarah Boston's discursive essay on death is full of generalisations – by no means valid ones, unfortunately – interspersed with unacknowledged references to excerpts from many of the distinguished writers anthologised in D. J. Enright's *The Oxford Book of Death* (*qv*) and autobiographical passages about the death of her son in childhood.

The latter experience is always a hugely devastating one, and no critic with any sense of decency is going to attack with gusto writings by someone who has suffered such a disaster. Nevertheless, I am sorry to have to say that she is a trite, derivative and careless author. At one point she

351

manages through an inattentive reading of W. E. Henley's famous poem 'To W. R.' to claim that the poet describes death as both male and female, whereas the first stanza actually reads as follows:

> Madame Life's apiece in bloom
> Death goes dogging everywhere:
> She's the tenant of the room,
> He's the ruffian on the stair.

Nonetheless I am grateful to her for the information that Yoko Ono, like Queen Victoria, for many years kept a room in the household she had shared with her dead husband exactly as it had been when he was alive, though Ms Boston lacks the wit to make the comparison herself. Rachael Trezise is better value, giving short accounts of what the legal position is regarding dead bodies, who to contact for bereavement counselling, etc. But inevitably some of the information is out of date.

Bowlby, John: 'Pathological mourning and Childhood Mourning' in *Journal of the American Psychoanalytical Association* (1963, II, 500). A specialist publication.

Boyce, Mary: *Zoroastrians – Their Religious Beliefs and Practices* (Routledge & Kegan Paul, 1979; reprinted with corrections in paperback, 1986). One of the titles in the Library of Religious Beliefs and Practices series published by RKP. A scholarly but readable account of the development of one of the world's oldest religions, originating possibly as much as 3500 years ago.

Bradfield, J. B.: *Green Burial: the d-i-y guide to law and practice* (2nd edition, 1994). This is a greatly expanded version of the first or draft edition of 1993, and it is essential that you study this one rather than the other as it is much more thorough and up-to-date. It was compiled for the Natural Death Centre (NDC), which, however, states that it does not necessarily endorse every view expressed by the author, although it is sympathetic towards the idea of 'green' burial. J. B. Bradfield is one of the NDC's consultants. He is very good on the legal position as to what you can and cannot do with human remains; in particular he cites a scandalous number of incidents in which officialdom have given out the wrong guidance on what is legal or illegal. The case histories highlight what an extremely grey area this is, in the sense of uncertain as opposed to dull. But the book is perhaps a little too impassioned at times and the author's fondness for exclamation marks, while not quite on Queen Victoria's scale, lends a touch of undergraduate naivety which ultimately diminishes rather than increases one's confidence in the wisdom of what is being said. The NDC asks reviewers to mention that *Green Burial* is available from them at a cost of £9.85, or £10.26 if paying by credit card; postage and packing are included. The NDC's address is in the Acknowledgements.

Brook, Stephen: *The Club: The Jews of Modern Britain* (Constable, 1989). Not much to do with bereavement, but a well-written guide to the complexities of Jewry in this country, not least the many, many degrees of religious opinion, observance and attitude towards non-Jews.

Catholic Truth Society publications:

Bernardin, Cardinal Joseph: *Euthanasia – Ethical & Legal Challenge* (Incorporated Catholic Truth Society, 1989). A pamphlet based on an address delivered by the Cardinal to the Center for Clinical Medical Ethics at the University of Chicago Hospital in 1988.

Dove, Anthea: *When My Brother Died* (Incorporated Catholic Truth Society, 1987). A pamphlet written for children, presumably valid also for those who have lost a sister.

Knott, Peter, SJ: *Safe in God's Hands* (Incorporated Catholic

Truth Society, 1989). A pamphlet written for parents (and other close relatives, e.g., the baby's brothers and sisters) who have lost a baby; very simple in style.

Monk, Matthew: *Comfort for the Bereaved* (Incorporated Catholic Truth Society, 1980). A pamphlet written in a very simple and warm style; recommended.

McNicholas, Neil: *Death – A Friendly Companion* (Incorporated Catholic Truth Society, 1992). A relatively sophisticated booklet by a Jesuit who during his period of training worked with social workers at an American cancer research centre.

Chosen Heritage Limited publications (see also the Introduction and my comments there on the following):

Coping with the Shock of an Accidental Death

Cremation – some questions answered

Grief – A Time to Heal

'I'm Sorry to Hear . . .' – a brief guide to writing letters of condolence

'Should I Wear Black?' A guide to funeral etiquette

Taxation When Someone Dies

What Can I Do To Help – some questions answered

What You Will Need to Do When Someone Dies

When Someone Chooses to Die – some words of help for those bereaved by suicide

No date to any of them but judging from the code on the back flaps all were printed in 1993 or 1994.

Cohn-Sherbok, Dan: *The Jewish Faith* (Society for Promoting Christian Knowledge [SPCK], 1993). A first-rate introduction to Judaism, comprising developments in the USA and Israel as well as in the UK, by a lecturer in theology at the University of Kent, Canterbury.

Consumer Association: *What to Do When Someone Dies* (*Which* Books). This latest revised edition was published in April 1994, but subsequent editions will presumably be regularly issued as and when changes in legislation regarding burial, death certificates, inheritance tax and so on require it. Over the last few years several earlier revised editions have appeared already. A practical, but by no means a severely practical, guide. As with all *Which* publications, it is written with the greatest clarity and intelligibility. However, its author is an undertaker and tends to approach practical matters to do with disposing of the dead rather too much from the restricted point of view of the trade. And J. B. Bradfield (*qv*) asserts that the number of mistakes in stating what the law is on death, burial, cremation, etc. has actually increased in this edition.

The Cremation Society of Great Britain: *What You Should Know About Cremations*, n.d., available from the CSGB at Brecon House, 2nd Floor, 16–16a Albion Place, Maidstone, Kent ME14 5DZ (tel. 01622 688292). An explanatory pamphlet.

Crichton, Ian: *The Art of Dying* (Peter Owen, 1976). A fairly short book, and much of its subject matter is obsolescent, for instance the information given on mortality rates, the legal position with regard to death and even the medical side. But it is better written than Nuland (see below) and much more palatable to British sensibilities.

Cunnington, Phyllis and Lucas, Catherine: *Costume for Births, Marriages and Death* (A & C Black, 1972). Almost two-thirds of the book is devoted to death, although the subject is only one part of a tripartite title. A historical survey, very thoroughly researched (the bibliography takes up ten pages and each chapter cites many references). There are plentiful illustrations from old prints and pictures, but almost entirely in black and white, which in a work on costume must be reckoned a defect, particularly as they are not terribly well reproduced.

de Lange, Nicholas: *Judaism* (Oxford University Press, 1986). A short but competent introduction to the subject by a lecturer in rabbinics at Cambridge University who is also a rabbi himself.

Duggan, Margaret and Bennett, Robin (eds.): *Funerals* (CIO Publishing, no date). Pamphlet number 7 in the series *Explaining the Church of England*.

Durkheim, Emile: *Suicide*. First published in English in 1951 by the Free Press, an American publisher, using a translation of the 1930 edition in French. The latter had appeared thirteen years after Durkheim's own death and thirty-three years after the first edition. But Durkheim (1858–1917) is still so central a figure in sociology (he was one of what one might for the sake of brevity call its inventors) that, whatever one may think of sociology as it has been twisted for dubious ends in our own time, he is still very much worth reading.

Gittings, Clare: *Death, Burial and the Individual in Early Modern England* (Croom Helm, 1984). A great deal of research clearly went into the preparation of this book but I regret to say that the author's intellectual equipment is not up to the task of discussing changes in attitude. They are enormously difficult to measure at the best of times where such a subject is concerned. Specifically, she begs the question of whether a shift came about from a more collective attitude to death in pre-Reformation times to a more individualistic one later (her repeated assertions to that effect do not constitute proof). She does not define what the 'Early Modern' period is. Her sampling of evidence from the four counties of Berkshire, Kent, Lincolnshire and Somerset is inadequate for England as a whole anyway, but particularly so because she speaks of a north-south divide in religious and death-related cultural patterns whereas Lincolnshire, her northernmost sample county, is not truly of the north, let alone typical. Reductionist anthropologising and numerous errors of fact or style related to the nobility throw further doubt on any claim of this book to be a serious work of history. At the same time the stodginess of the prose style renders it inadequate as entertainment. Where it is useful is in gathering together a large number of small facts, such as an indication of how frequently white rather than black was used as a mourning colour.

Gorer, Geoffrey: *Death, Grief, and Mourning in Contemporary Britain* (The Cresset Press, 1965). The subtitle is a bit of a misnomer given how long ago in terms of social change the book was published. Nevertheless, nobody since seems to have attempted such a wide-ranging survey of mourning and funerary customs across the various regions and classes of Britain.

Grinsell, Leslie V.: *Barrow, Pyramid and Tomb – ancient burial customs in Egypt, the Mediterranean and the British Isles* (Thames & Hudson, 1975). Extremely dry but very informative, the book includes instructions on how to get to the sites discussed (now rather out of date as regards roads, bus and train services, etc.). The 'British Isles' of the subtitle includes Ireland and there is a very full description of the celebrated tomb complex of New Grange in Co. Meath.

Harding, Rachel and Dyson, Mary (eds.): *A Book of Condolences, from the private letters of illustrious people* (Continuum, New York, 1981). An anthology which could come in very useful for discreet cribbing when you are faced with having to write a letter to a bereaved friend or relative and cannot think of what to say. Much of the material is inevitably expressed in old-fashioned language, however, so paraphrasing is necessary. Alternatively, you could give the original letter full attribution and preface your quotation from it with the words: 'As John Donne [or whoever] so nobly puts it . . .'

Help the Aged: *Bereavement* (no date). A short pamphlet of sixteen pages drafted in consultation with CRUSE–Bereavement Care and sponsored by Dignity in Destiny Ltd (a pre-paid funeral plan company) together with Oaktree Funeral Services, a chain of undertakers. A good short guide on practical aspects. Its psychological assertions are more open to cavil (see the Introduction to this book). The sales pitch by Dignity in Destiny and Oaktree on the back cover comes across as rather unctuous and its assertion that the 'funeral director is an integral part of a traditional funeral' only holds good if you believe traditional funerals started two centuries ago.

Ironside, Virginia: *Goodbye, Dear Friend – coming to terms with the death of a pet* (Robson Books, 1994). A fairly slight work by one of the country's most famous agony aunts. It quotes numerous letters written to the author; indeed, these constitute the bulk of the book. People's attitudes are subjected to little or no independent critical analysis and the indifference of non-pet-owners seems to me to have been exaggerated in order to justify the writing of the book in the first place. This is a pity because the idea is a good one and a more thorough study would be well worth writing. The historical sophistication of this book can be judged from the statement that Martin Luther was the 'founder of the Protestant Church'.

Jones, Mary: *Secret Flowers; mourning and the adaptation to loss* (The Women's Press, 1988). The author, currently a counsellor with CRUSE, writes simply and affectingly of her personal experience following her husband's death from cancer. Recommended.

Kübler-Ross, Elizabeth: *On Death and Dying* (Tavistock Publications, 1970). Perhaps the most celebrated author to deal with the subject in modern times. Some of her purely medical definitions of death as set out in some of her other writings have recently been challenged, but her reputation as an expert on the psychology of death and dying is still solid. I almost hesitate to say 'surprisingly' solid, but I feel I must, all the same. From my admittedly rather restricted point of view – that is to say, an interest in bereavement, or the attitudes of those left behind, as opposed to the attitudes of those who are dying – she has in this book little to offer that is germane. Only from pages 156 to 159 (in the section 'The Family After Death Has Occurred') does the book deal with bereavement. And here the author rather egotistically assumes that the reactions to bereavement experienced by her editorial 'we' are valid for all mankind. They most certainly are not. Nor do I think that it is particularly insightful to say, as she does, that it would be cruel to ridicule those who make it harder for themselves to face the reality of someone's death. It is, rather, a mere truism. Her psycho-analytical passages in this section likewise are both sweepingly generalising and depressingly unsubtle. Only one author is ever cited in epigraphs above each chapter heading: Rabindranath Tagore, a windy and restricted choice of guru.

Kupfermann, Jeanette: *When the Crying's Done, a journey through widowhood* (Robson Books, 1992). A highly personal account, rather woman's mag-ish.

Kurtz, Donna C. and Boardman, John: *Greek Burial Customs* (Thames and Hudson, 1971). Highly academic, as well as a bit repetitious. It also does not make any concessions to what may be the reader's ignorance about everyday life in ancient Greece.

Leroy, Margaret: *Miscarriage* (Macdonald Optima, 1988). This was published in cooperation with the Miscarriage Association. About half the book explains what happens medically in good plain English which could serve as an ideal model for others trying to explain technically complicated matters. The last part is concerned with women's feelings, which inevitably take centre stage, though men's are not overlooked. Rather good, and refreshingly free of any anti-male bile.

Lewis, C. S.: *A Grief Observed* (Faber & Faber, 1961). An Oxford Eng. Lit. don's account of how cancer struck down an American woman who admired his imaginative writings and whom he married, partly it would seem out of pity, when the disease had already asserted its grip. It is now the basis of a major motion picture – *Shadowlands* – with Sir Anthony Hopkins as C. S. Lewis and Debra Winger as Lewis's wife.

Litten, Julian: *The English Way of Death: the common funeral since 1450* (Robert Hale, 1991). A first-rate piece of research and writing by the author, plus presentation by the publishers, being beautifully illustrated. It is, however, shockingly proof-read. Julian Litten knocks his competitors such as Clare Gittings into a cocked hat when it comes to English prose and seems to me to be every bit as erudite. (He is funerary historian and curator in public affairs at the Victoria and Albert Museum in South Kensington, as well as an honorary consultant to the National Death Centre.) He deals in great detail not just with mainstream subjects such as burial but with cases of embalming in English history, also funeral trappings such as palls, clothing, coffin casing and metal fixtures and fittings.

Morley, John: *Death, Heaven and the Victorians* (Studio Vista, 1971). The famous account of high Victorian funerary practices, complete with almost orgiastic detail, that caused such a stir when it came out. A contemporaneous exhibition of pictures and artefacts to do with death in nineteenth-century England complemented its publication, bringing the extravagance of the previous century's thanatomania home to the public in a way no mere book could.

Morris, Ian: *Death-Ritual and Social Structure in Classical Antiquity* (Cambridge University Press, 1992). One of a series of books called Key Themes in Ancient History, this is by an associate professor in the departments of history and classics at the University of Chicago. It is useful for reminding us how many variations there are in ancient methods of disposing of the dead and it repeatedly makes a strong plea for historians and archaeologists to view 'finds' and literary evidence such as epitaphs in context. The book lists an impressive forty-six pages of bibliography.

Morris, Sarah: *Grief and How to Live With It* (Allen & Unwin, 1971).

Nuland, Dr Sherwin B.: *How We Die* (Chatto & Windus, 1994). Not, as they say, for the squeamish. It is chillingly free with clinical detail, though this is explained well for the layman. On the other hand, at any rate as I interpret it, the garbled judgements of the more inattentive reviewers, to wit that whatever form death takes it is highly unpleasant, are not quite accurate. Indeed, the only reviewer I came across who had read the book with sufficient care to realise that some deaths are not too bad was himself a doctor. (As he put it, '*For the most part* dying is a beastly business, best avoided . . .' – my italics.) Accordingly that aspect of *How We Die* may arouse mild optimism. Unfortunately, Dr Nuland's literary gifts do not match his medical ones and the style is somewhat trite, or where not actually trite over-striving for effect, in the way of so many American practitioners of 'fine writing'; the philosophical musings are jejune too.

Orbell, Joy: *Wiccan Rites for the Dead and Dying* (Pagan Hospice & Funeral Trust Information leaflet number 4, 1993). A very brief introductory work, only four pages long.

Padma Sambhava (discovered by Karma Lingpa, trans. Robert A. Thurman, with a foreword by His Holiness the Dalai Lama): *The Tibetan Book of the Dead* (Harper-Collins, 1994; original text between AD 700 and 900 but 1994 translation). The English version, long vulgarised under this title, of the *Bardo thos grol* or *Bardo thos grol chen mo*, to give its fuller title (more literally 'the great book of natural liberation through understanding in the between' – that is, 'between state'). This version adds an extremely lucid account of Tibetan history and the growth of Tibetan religious sensibility. The translation of the original work is thus set in context, though some readers will find an invocation that starts 'Hey, noble one!' a bit too American.

Some of Thurman's commentary will be found tendentious, for example a passage in which he urges the bereaved to canalise grief so that it becomes cheerful and advises against crying and lamenting just because the bereaved feel like it on the grounds that such emotions are culturally determined and conventional behaviour. That surely begs a very large question. On the other hand I rather like his assertion that the deceased is the principal guest at a funeral.

The Pagan Federation: *Information Pack* (3rd edition, 1994) and *Witchcraft Information Pack* (2nd edition, 1993). For further details of the PF see Acknowledgements under Tony Gardiner.

Pincus, Lily: *Death and the Family, the importance of mourning* (Faber & Faber, 1976). An intelligent and sympathetic work by a former practitioner with the Tavistock Clinic. (She is now, sadly, dead, but is an inspiration to late developers everywhere as she only started writing in her seventies.) See also 'Loss throughout the life-cycle', a chapter in *The Challenge of a Long Life* (Faber & Faber, 1981) by the same author, which I defy the stoniest-hearted reader to follow without a lump in the throat. I was reminded of Flaubert's *Un coeur simple*, and in my eyes there is no higher praise than a comparison with Flaubert.

Lampen, Diana: *Facing Death* (Quaker Home Service, 1979). A round-up of how death is viewed by the Friends, whether it is their own or others'. Unusually well written by today's standards, but then literary skills seem to come naturally to Quakers.

Slaughter, Joanna: *Caring and Coping* (Pearl Assurance, 1994). Rather a good booklet (sixty pages long) which covers the emotional and basic financial problems of bereavement about as well as anything can do in the space available. It is, of course, skewed towards persuading the reader to take out insurance, but that is a perfectly reasonable aim. One case history tells of a widow who collected only £4,500 from her husband's life assurance but who spent £2,000 on his funeral. She was obviously traumatised by her husband's death and it is a great shame that nobody dissuaded her from incurring such an unnecessarily expensive undertakers' bill.

Smale, David A.: *Davies' Law of Burial, Cremation and Exhumation* (Shaw & Sons, 6th edition, 1993). The standard legal work on the subject, updated by a past president and current fellow of the Institute of Burial and Cremation Administration. He is also a former superintendent and registrar of ceremonies for the Brighton Crematorium and Mortuary Services. When reading the publications by the Natural Death Centre and J. B. Bradfield (*qqv*), this work should be consulted simultaneously.

Spottiswoode, Jane: *Undertaken with Love* (Robert Hale, 1991). The author's account of how she and friends, without undertakers, arranged the disposal of her husband's body by cremation. The pettiness, unhelpfulness, humourlessness and meanness of spirit exhibited by many of the people she negotiated with in trying to cut out the undertakers are staggering though not perhaps surprising. But a representative of the local authority, to his credit, comes out of it very well. She and her husband had lived a life of eco-enthusiastic self-sufficiency in north Wales, and her account of how they found and restored an ancient water mill takes up the first third of the book. Although the how-we-fell-in-love-with-a-ruin-and-converted-it-to-*House-and-Garden*-standard theme is an almost tediously well-worn one, this particular instance actually makes the onset of her husband's last illness more poignant. The fact that she lived in the open spaces of north Wales made her disposal of her husband's body in unorthodox fashion more practicable than if she had lived in a big city – a point one of the undertakers has made when discussing this work.

The last part offers advice on how to manage a similar disposal yourself, but although the book was published only three years ago, many of the telephone numbers or postal codes in the addresses she lists at the back are out of date or so badly proof-read that they are just plain wrong. I was particularly saddened to see the author of the *Devil's Dictionary* cited as Andrew Bierce rather than Ambrose Bierce. (Bierce has not been seen since about 1913; in fact, like Lord Lucan, he just disappeared, so it is particularly important to get his name right when discussing bereavement.)

Stott, Mary: *Forgetting's No Excuse* (Faber & Faber, 1973).

Summers, Peter (general ed.): *Hatchments in Britain* (10 vols., Phillimore, 1974). A survey of all known hatchments. A work of antiquarianism rather than historical analysis, but very thorough as far as it goes.

Toynbee, Jocelyn M. C.: *Death and Burial in the Roman World* (Thames & Hudson, 1971). Highly academic, with excellent plates, though unfortunately in black and white.

Walter, Dr Tony: *Funerals and How to Improve Them* (Hodder & Stoughton, 1990). A disappointingly unintelligent book, diffuse, repetitive, unthinking and surprisingly ignorant of Church history considering that the author claims to be a practising Christian. (I am told he has a couple of much better books due out in 1995.) But the book listed above may be useful to those who wish to get away from orthodox attitudes to bereavement: the author does at least take a constantly upbeat line. I only hope its information on the law is more accurate than its author's garbled account of the sixteenth-century Reformation and seventeenth-century Civil War period. (J. B. Bradfield, *op. cit.*, mentions one or two instances where Walter is wrong even on the legal position.) Of it the present Archbishop of Canterbury is quoted on the cover as having said: 'I regard this book as being of fundemental [*sic*] importance.'

Whitman, G.: *The Funeral Guide and Information Handbook* (apparently self-published, 1991). Not well written and tends to over-simplification. I have found his information about certain attitudes and practices by non-Christian religions to be inaccurate. The author is an undertaker.

Woods, Reginald: *Only One Intention, the Salvationists' attitude toward life and death* (Salvationist Publishing and Supplies Ltd, 1963). The Salvation Army view. Rather stirring.

Willson, Jane Wynne: *Funerals Without God, A Practical Guide to Non-Religious Funerals* (British Humanist Association, 1989; 3rd edition 1992). I have already delivered a critique of this in the section on humanism. I would only add that the edition of *What to Do When Someone Dies* cited in Jane Wynne Willson's bibliography has been superseded by the edition mentioned in this bibliography.

Lastly, it should not be thought that the bibliography of bereavement is confined to books in the material sense. There is a lay-by on the information superhighway where computer enthusiasts can stop off and contemplate the hereafter. The Uniform Resource Locator (computer-speak for address) is: gopher.//

gopher.rivendell.org.9004

This is Griefnet, which gives information on the Internet about coping with bereavement, chiefly a bibliography and other 'resources'. Most of the material is North America-oriented at present, though information from the rest of the world is constantly being added. The people who run Griefnet are Rivendell Resources, a non-profit-making organisation. They also publish a periodical called *Bereavement & Loss Resources*. For further information you can also access Cendra Lynn, who is to be found on griefnet@rivendell.org

Index